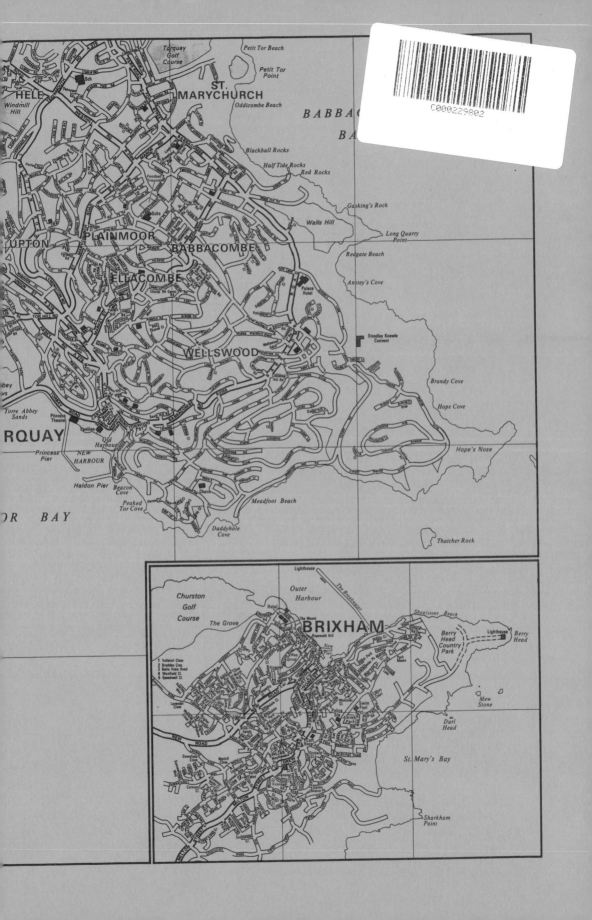

TORQUAY & PAIGNTON

The Making of a Modern Resort

TORQUAY & PAIGNTON

The Making of a Modern Resort

HENRY JAMES LETHBRIDGE

PHILLIMORE

2003

Published by
PHILLIMORE & CO. LTD
Shopwyke Manor Barn, Chichester, West Sussex, England

ISBN 1 86077 260 9

Printed and bound in Great Britain by
MPG BOOKS LTD
Bodmin, Cornwall

CONTENTS

ACKNOWLEDGEMENTS

Grateful thanks to Bob Brewis, Sir Rivers Carew, Bt, Brenda Cox, Judy Diss, Michael Dowdell, Ian Handford, Roxanne and Trevor Heathcott-Drury, Chris Pancheri, Jen Reynolds, Ron Thomson and Avril Vincent née Narracott.

Thanks are extended also to the following for permission to reproduce illustrations: Christies Images Limited 2003, 8; English Riviera Tourist Board, 3, 61, 87, 92, 95; The Francis Frith Collection SP35QP, 52; Herald Express Publications Ltd, Torquay, 49, 79, 88 (upper illustration), 89-91; Hulton Archive/ Getty Images, 62; The Paignton Masonic Hall, 56-58; Sotheby's Picture Library, 17; Jim Stanes (from Robin Stanes, *A History of Devon*), 72; Tele-pages Directories Ltd (Michaela Lawrance), endpapers; Torbay Library Services, 70, 73; Torquay Museum, 28, 32, 51, 68, 85, 88 (lower illustration); Torre Abbey, Torquay and Henry and Wendy Cary, 12; Mr Hamish Turner, 24; Mr J.R.A. Wilson, 33, 40, 66. Nos. 37, 39, 64 and 65 are reproduced courtesy of the National Portrait Gallery, London. The origins of illustrations 83 and 84 are not known but are believed to be either US or British Crown Copyright. All other illustrations are from the author's collection.

LIST OF ILLUSTRATIONS

One

BACKGROUND

THREE families largely determined Torquay's pattern of urban development and its emergence as a celebrated Victorian watering place and seaside resort. They were the Palks of Haldon House, the pioneers in this enterprise; and, later in the century, the Carys of Torre Abbey together with the Mallocks of Cockington Court. Between them they owned most of the land, comprising three parishes, on which Torquay now stands. As landlords of contiguous estates, as lords of the various manors, together they controlled for many years the physical layout of the burgeoning town: its roads, streets, and buildings.

The bankruptcy of the 2nd Lord Haldon in 1891, followed in 1903 by that of his heir, the 3rd Lord Haldon, led to large auctions of leaseholds and freeholds, and eventually to the disposal of the Palk family's manorial rights. Their land was parcelled out in building lots. Then followed a period of uninhibited construction carried out by numerous developers. The central control once exercised over the estate relaxed and standards were lowered. This was clearly a misfortune for Torquay. Independent builders put up what

1 *Hesketh Crescent – the Palk legacy to the town is there to see.*

they thought the public wanted, without much attention to design or suitable location. But the Palk legacy to the town is still there to see: one has only to view Hesketh Crescent at Meadfoot or the Higher Terrace above the Strand.

The taste of these members of gentry or aristocratic families was not faultless, but they put up few shoddy or worthless buildings; and nearly all the splendid ones – individual houses, terraces, churches, public and other large buildings – were mainly of their creation: inspired, financed, or supported by them. They gave Victorian Torquay an elegant appearance that strongly appealed to the upper classes, to members of the gentry, aristocracy and nobility, as well as to titled and opulent foreigners. Torquay was also much approved of by the *haute bourgeoisie* and by a host of comfortably-off spinsters and widows and especially by a large number of Scottish ladies who, as the century progressed and travel became easier, sought a warmer, more congenial and more social resting place than their austere homeland could provide. They came south to the English Riviera. One may mention, as exemplars of this group, the novel-writing Findlater sisters, both of whom were good friends of Henry James and of his brother, William, the celebrated psychologist and pragmatic philosopher, and they entertained the latter on several occasions at their home in Torbay.

2 *Built by the Harvey brothers in 1848-9, on Lincombe Hill the Regency crescent by the end of the century was enveloped in greenery planted by the Victorians.*

Victorian Torquay had no wish to attract the plebs or the lower middle classes, except as servitors. It sought as residents and visitors only the well-off. It did not attempt to emulate popular resorts such as Margate and Southend, the haunt of *hoi polloi*, or Brighton after the Prince Regent had forsaken his Royal Pavilion. And needless to say the town never aspired to rival Blackpool, a holiday town catering to a Northern proletariat. At mid-century the Victorian upper classes regarded Torquay as one of the grandest, most tasteful, and most salubrious places in all England. It was particularly admired and sought after by those who relished a life of quiet days spent among equals. Tucked away in their secluded villas, nearly all built on hilly or rising ground, they entertained their friends with tea and polite conversation or paraded gracefully around their scented gardens, waited upon by servants. In those tranquil mid-century years, the high summer of a great and peaceful era, some must have felt close to Eden.

The town then was in no way raffish. It was certainly less rakish and adulterous than Brighton, already notorious for its gambling and immorality, its kept women and strumpets, although Torquay, like all Victorian cities, also had a secret and subterranean side – a world of low life. Torquay remained upper-class, or, more precisely, upper-middle-class in attitude and spirit until the turn of the century, and maintained this reputation well into the 1920s, although increasingly its clientele should more properly be described as plain middle-class. Yet in some circles in the 1930s it was still being pilloried for its exclusiveness and snobbishness, for its gentility. Then, after the Second World War, it truly fell from grace, a victim to democratic progress in the age of the common man. Once the habitat of the well-to-do, it steadily became a resort for the less well-off, for countless holiday makers on low incomes. The affluent started to desert its great hotels and rented villas and went instead to the Continent and to far off and exotic places or they simply took winter cruises to the Mediterranean.

Torquay is situated on the northern coast of Torbay, whose waters measure around four by three and a half miles in length and breadth. Paignton is on the western edge of the bay and the town proper. The original nucleus occupies a relatively flat area, whereas Torquay is built on seven hills, with ravines and valleys criss-crossing its expanse and presenting a walker with some steep climbs. The hills at Paignton lie behind the town and gently surround it. From a distance Torquay has an Olympian air; Paignton a not too displeasing run-of-the-mill look.

As a resort town Paignton developed much later in the century and its growth owed much to, and may be correlated with, the arrival of the railway from Torquay in 1859, which meant that there were now direct links with London and other large conurbations. The spelling of Paignton varied until the Great Western management, a strong believer in standardisation, declared that its sign boards henceforth should read 'Paignton', and not 'Paington', as it was commonly spelt by local people. Following this edict the GWR's orthography became standard and has remained so.

Paignton's transformation accelerated in the last four decades of the 19th century when a number of shrewd businessmen, property developers and land speculators concluded that the town had much potential as a future seaside resort, since it was adjacent to Torquay, had finer stretches of beach, and now was linked by rail. Land could be bought cheaply because it was mostly wasteland along the shore and of little value to local farmers. These vanguard entrepreneurs were W.R. Fletcher and Arthur Hyde Dendy, both Birmingham men, and the Singers, an expatriate American family, whose founder, Isaac Singer, had made a fortune with his inventions and improvements for the sewing machine named after him. He had come to Paignton from Paris to seek a home and to build a family mansion, to establish a 'seat' (though it is doubtful whether Singer would have used that particular word) for his transposed family.

These new men were neither peers of the realm nor of old stock. As a consequence, there was no aristocratic influence that could be exercised over the planning of Paignton as a seaside resort. A number of businessmen, acting independently, mostly have shaped its urban landscape. The Templer family of Stover, once lords of the manor, withdrew from any active participation in the town's affairs in the 1820s when George Templer lost the greater part of his fortune. Thus, there was no single person in the parish with the requisite power to prevent fragmented development. Paignton's development has been almost entirely piecemeal, with the exception of the seafront area. It is not in any way a planned town as is much of central Torquay. Today it looks as though it grew without design: a rather haphazard putting together of ill assorted buildings. It is a town that so obviously mirrors the bad taste and the quirks of a number of developers, and of numerous jerry builders, if one excepts the Esplanade, the area along the seafront.

The old town centre of Paignton comprised a warren of streets, lanes, and alleys surrounding St John's, the parish church. The hub of the town, over time, has been engulfed by swarms of undistinguished houses and shops, which run down to the seafront and along all roads that exit from the town, in several places just dingy or uninspired rows of houses. Over the years the centre of gravity has moved seaward, away from the area around Church Street. Apart from the church, a Norman foundation, and Oldway, the former Singer mansion, Paignton has little to boast of architecturally. It does have fine stretches of sands and beaches at Preston, Paignton, Goodrington and beyond, and a bijou harbour, now given over not to commerce but pleasure craft; but that is about the best one can say about its physical appearance. Nikolaus Pevsner, a severe critic of bad architecture, comments bleakly on

Paignton: 'Not much of note in the town'. Another writer declares that it is 'visually depressing'. Torquay still retains a degree of chic: Paignton lacks style in almost all parts.

The two form an interesting contrast. Each has had a different history and pattern of development. And the contrast highlights certain themes and makes plain the virtues of the aristocratic developer with taste, someone who had gone on the traditional grand tour of the Continent and had viewed the architectural treasures, the splendours of foreign cities. With much wealth behind him, the aristocratic landowner could afford to wait until he received a return on his invested capital. On the other hand, the speculator, the developer, wanted a quick return on his outlay: he had no wish to tie up his working capital in bricks and mortar for a decade or so. Again, this contrast reveals the effects of different methods of land management and land use. There is, generally speaking, an advantage for a town, at least in its earlier stages of development, for control to be vested in as few hands as possible for a monopoly of control may permit a grand, all-encompassing design or, at a lower and more usual level, some degree of planning; and of the towns being studied neither fully experienced the former, and only Torquay the latter.

Brixham, the third of the Torbay towns, faces Torquay and is at the apex of the southern arm of the bay. It was once a noted fishing port, but it has never experienced the high rates of population growth registered in certain periods by the other Torbay towns, although in the summer season it is always congested with visitors. Brixham's retarded growth, comparatively speaking, is mainly a consequence of its lack of obvious tourist attractions: no first-class beaches, no delightful promenades or esplanades to saunter along, no pier (*a sine qua non* for a seaside resort 'going places'); the streets narrow and mostly running uphill, and with plenty of mean dwellings. It interests the sightseer principally for its nautical atmosphere and 'quaintness', an example of which is the much photographed Old Coffin House near the harbour. Its main attraction for the visitor has always been its congested quays and its quayside pubs.

These three coastal towns, each of which can claim an ancient birth and a history going back beyond Domesday Book, have been taken over administratively by the Torbay District Council, a new unit of local government. This all embracing body was created in 1968, following which the name of the parliamentary constituency of Torquay was also changed to Torbay, a more appropriate name for the division. This measure of unification was not popular with all, especially Paigntonians, for each town believes it has a special identity which should be preserved. Local loyalties still appear to be strong among certain sections. But to treat Torbay as a single unit for planning purposes makes sense. These once separate towns are now being fused inexorably together by encroaching housing developments and welded together by an expanding road network, so that sometimes it is difficult for a stranger to determine where one ends and another begins. Sooner or later, one may predict, Torbay will emerge as one large residential district, a huge collocation of houses, overtaking in scale and population even Plymouth. The Palks, Carys, and Mallocks may be blessed or blamed for this outcome: it is certainly a prospect they never envisioned. But W.R. Fletcher and Arthur Hyde Dendy, the early promoters of Paignton, probably would not have been dismayed by this evolution: they were of a far different breed from the old aristocratic landowners; they were tomorrow's men.

An analytical study of the rise and decline of Torquay as a prestigious resort cannot confine itself to a relatively small area delimited by the Rivers Dart and Teign and bounded by the outpost towns of Dartmouth, Totnes, Newton Abbot, and Teignmouth. The Torbay littoral and its immediate hinterland must of course be of primary interest; but Torquay also forms part of an area historically known as South Devon, which for a short period after the 1832 Reform Act was a separate parliamentary constituency. Exeter was the largest town in this district, after Plymouth, and the county seat. Before the arrival of the Railway Age ordinary Devonians did not travel far afield and typically only to the nearest market town where goods not found in the village shop could be purchased. A visit to Exeter from the coast was an event and only the wealthy could go by coach or packet boat to London. North Devon was cut off from South Devon, above all in winter, by the desolation of Dartmoor, then an inhospitable region. Even townsmen seldom travelled long distances except on urgent business. What this suggests is that most social interaction occurred within a restricted space, within small communities or neighbourhoods. Robert Fraser's report to the Board of Agriculture and Internal Improvement written in 1794 and entitled *General View of the County of Devon* contains an apposite passage: 'So great is the extent of the county, and so little intercourse is there between the people in different districts, that it is very rare to find a man who is acquainted with any part of the county, except in his immediate neighbourhood, and I have scarcely met with any who possess a general knowledge of the whole county.'

To study Torquay also as part of South Devon makes sense, for it was the area in which most of Torbay's inhabitants spent their lives, did their business, were employed in, and formed alliances. Before the coming of the railway this was the real world for most of them. So the larger focus in this book will be on South Devon; and the narrower on Torbay, in particular Torquay, the main subject of this study.

Exeter ceased to be Devon's most important commercial and industrial city by the early 19th century. By mid-century Plymouth was Devon's most industrialised, economically active, and populous town and its largest port. Yet Exeter continued to remain the county's banking and financial centre. The traditional professions tended to cluster there: physicians and surgeons, barristers and solicitors, and a flock of clergymen, for the Bishop of Exeter managed church affairs from the city for the whole of Devon and Cornwall. The Devon quarter assizes were always held at Exeter and malefactors guilty of a capital offence committed in Devon were hanged in the local prison.

At Exeter the more important London banks had their branches, agents and representatives. It also had one of the earliest savings banks, the Exeter Savings Bank (better known later as the Exeter and Devon Savings Bank), principally established through the exertions of Sir John Acland, a leading county member. This bank served the poor, for extremely small sums could be deposited, and its real aim was to encourage thrift among the poorer classes. John Baring, a merchant banker, one of the famous Baring Brothers, retired from London to his home at Exeter, in the late 1760s and established a private bank, the Devonshire bank. Torquay itself had no local bank until 1832, when the Torbay Bank was established on the Strand. Before that date, Exeter banks (which could draw upon London banks) channelled funds and advanced credit for early building operations and other developments in the town. Haldon House, the Palk family seat, was but a few miles from Exeter and the family banked there as well as in London. Once the Torbay Bank opened its doors it took over this role, for William Kitson the solicitor was its promoter and director, and in 1833 was put by Sir L.V. Palk in sole charge of the Palk Estate Office. He held that responsibility until 1874, when he resigned. Exeter, it follows, played an important part in Torquay's transformation, certainly in the early years.

The Palks, Carys and Mallocks have been mentioned as the leading families in the Torquay district, as they had much patronage to dispense, including a large number of church livings. But there were other gentry families on the fringes of the district who also played some part in the town's history and growth. There was, for example, a scatter of family seats and country houses in South Devon; and in particular along the waters of the Dart, notably Mount Boone, Greenway, Sandridge, and Follaton. Inland from the river were to be found Lupton and Churston Court. All these mansions were occupied by members of aristocratic or gentry families. One should also mention Haccombe, the seat of the Carews, about two miles from Newton Abbot, and Forde House on the road to Torquay.

The inhabitants of these country houses met as equals; some, if not most, were commensals. They formed an educated and cultivated élite, whose sons usually were sent away to be educated, and then on to one of the ancient universities or into the army. They tended to intermarry. The Palks and Mallocks, for example, formed alliances. West Country gentry families were to a large degree interrelated, with a few conspicuous exceptions. Religion was usually a bar to a marriage contract being signed, and therefore negated the practical advantages of a union between two estates. The Carys, recusant Catholics, had necessarily a more restricted choice when it came to marriage partners and at times selected brides or grooms from Continental Catholic families.

These and other local families must be among our cast of characters, if only with walk-on parts. This is also true of the Seales, Cliffords and Yarde Bullers, the Lopes, Champernownes and Carews. These gentry families exercised much political power in South Devon, a region that was strongly Tory and truly conservative, representing as it did the agricultural interest. The Whigs and later their successors, the Liberals, had numerous adherents in Devon, above all in North Devon, where the Aclands were politically active, and also in its large towns and cities, such as Plymouth, Devonport, and Exeter. The Liberal tradition is still very much alive in these areas. But in South Devon conservatism has always been strong, deeply entrenched in some parts. Since 1910, with one very short break in 1923, the Member of Parliament for Torquay has always been a Conservative or of that complexion.

The names of these locally prominent families, once familiar to all in South Devon, are enshrined in many a Victorian guidebook, directory, and gazetteer of Devon. Octavian Blewitt, author of *The Panorama of Torquay*, published in 1832, visited most of the family seats in the vicinity of Torquay and some further afield in Devon and describes and comments upon them in his guidebook. Together they formed an élite of country gentlemen, which was not entirely closed. This élite did not form an immutable caste: to some degree it was able to assimilate petitioners, new entrants. For example, the founder of the Palk dynasty, Sir Robert Palk, was a nabob (which may be translated here as a *nouveau riche*) of humble birth, but the majority of prominent families in Devon were of old stock. Such was the situation, in the 1820s and 1830s, when Torquay was undergoing modernisation. In Torbay the Palks, Carys and Mallocks held sway. Professor Lawrence Stone has demonstrated how remarkably adroit this élite was in maintaining its privileges and power and in fending off intruders. Historians generally agree, though the debate is not over, that mobility between social classes in England was less than once believed, but in the main greater than in continental Europe.

* * *

The prehistory and recorded history of the Torbay district before 1800 need not be discussed in any great detail since the emphasis in this book is on Torquay's transformation in the 19th century. In most general histories of England one normally finds few specific references to this area. Those that do figure in such works are as a rule the seizure of Dartmouth by royalists in 1643 and its recapture by parliamentarians three years later; the landing of William of Orange and his army at Brixham in 1688, the precursor to the Glorious Revolution; and the destruction by fire of Teignmouth by the French

3 *Invited by prominent Englishmen, William of Orange landed at Brixham in 1688 – within two days 15,000 men and their provisions and 600 horses were ashore.*

in 1690. The most important role that Torbay played on the national scene was its use as a base by the Channel Fleet during the Napoleonic Wars. Torbay then witnessed the end of the saga, when the *Bellerophon* entered its waters with the French Emperor on board, whereupon a fleet of small ships, crowded with sightseers, went out to glimpse Boney on his way to exile. He in turn, it is reported, was much flattered by his reception and the marked attention paid to him.

Torbay was far distant from the centre of affairs in London and difficult to reach before the railway era. It was a thinly populated mainly agricultural region, and was not to become well known until Torquay's rise to eminence as a fashionable winter resort, when such distinguished people as Disraeli, Lord Lytton, and the Baroness Burdett-Coutts graced the town. Torbay, of course, is given far greater prominence in naval and maritime histories for it had been home over the centuries to scores of mariners, explorers, travellers to foreign parts, and to fishermen, some of whom went as far afield as Labrador for their catches. Brixham, in particular, engaged in much carrying trade, especially the fruit and wine trade, with Portugal and Spain and the Mediterranean countries.

Evidence of settlement by prehistoric man has been found abundantly at Kent's Cavern, Torquay, and in the limestone cave at Windmill Hill, Brixham. Both sites were diligently explored in the 19th century by geologists and local residents, mostly amateurs with a scientific bent or great curiosity, such as Father McEnery and William Pengelly. In that period there was a vogue for fossil collecting and for digging up the past, a vogue which reached its peak in mid-Victorian times, when earnest groups of enthusiasts chipping away at rock faces or engaged in excavations were common sights.

There is some evidence that Roman soldiers were resident (we do not know for how long) in the Torbay area, at, for example, the rectangular earthwork above Stoke Gabriel on the River Dart. It is also probable that at times they landed on the coast for short stays; but this is conjectural and we know little about their presence in the Torbay district. There is no dispute that they occupied South Devon and that extensive Roman remains have been uncovered at Exeter, which was the legionary headquarters for the West Country. At Topsham there have been several finds which indicate the site of a fort, probably used as a supply base for the legionary fortress at Exeter.

With the Saxons local historians are on slightly firmer ground, but the exact date of their arrival in Torbay, some time in the fifth century, is not known. After the Saxon victory over the Britons at Penselwood on the Wiltshire/Somerset border in 658, they moved into Somerset and in considerable numbers continued their advance into Devon, which, once occupied and settled, became part of the Saxon kingdom of Wessex. W.G. Hoskins argues that such ancient villages as Paignton and Brixham were probably among the earliest settlements founded by the invaders, but he agrees that both could have been previously occupied by the Britons. Moreover, Britons and Saxons appear to have lived alongside each other after the invasion without friction. This is, once more, conjecture, since records for the area are scant; but nearly all the villages whose names are recorded in Domesday Book were founded by the Saxons, and these would include all those in South Devon. The county's history starts, then, properly speaking, with the Saxon hegemony. And it is not unreasonable to affirm that in 1800 the majority of Torbay's inhabitants were either of Saxon ancestry or had a good dash of Saxon blood.

On the other hand, the sea-roving Danes were pillagers, not settlers. For many years they ravaged coastal regions, capturing Exeter in 876; and in 1001 they sailed up the Teign, plundering the district as they went, burning among other villages Teignton (probably Kingsteignton). In the year 1016 Devon passed for a time with the rest of Wessex under Danish rule under Cnut. W.G. Hoskins writes: 'The Danes, during all this time, had made no permanent settlements in Devon … On the mainland of Devon there is not a single Scandinavian placename.' The Normans who became the ruling élite in Devon some years after the Conquest did not add greatly to Devon's population. They did not enter the county as a horde of freebooters or settlers. Devon's population at that time has been estimated at between sixty to eighty thousand and Exeter, the largest town in the county, had around 1,448 living within its walls. Berry Pomeroy, about five miles from Paignton, became the symbol of the Norman presence for those who lived in the Torbay area. The great Norman family of de la Pomerai owned the manor from 1066 until 1548 and in the 13th century built the castle. At the turn of the 18th century it was an ivy-covered, picturesque ruin standing in romantic surroundings with its own distressful ghost. There was also Totnes Castle, now partially restored, with its motte and circular keep intact, which was built by another Norman, Judhael. The Normans have left their architectural impress in many parts of Devon and in Torbay at Torre Abbey, once a Premonstratensian house, founded in 1196 by William de Brewer.

This extremely sketchy outline of Torbay's past has been introduced as a backcloth to the rapid changes that took place in the 19th century and after, when Torquay was utterly transfigured. Hoskins' magisterial *Devon* should provide an interested reader with all the facts. Much of modern Britain's social fabric, its system of government and its social institutions, was created in the centuries following the Norman Conquest. At the end of the 18th century the configuration of contemporary Britain can be partially discerned. In Devon, as in most parts of England at that date, the gentry owned most of the land and as a body exercised great political power, but not always over some large towns, such as Exeter. Sir Robert Palk who owned over 11,000 acres at Haldon and Torquay was a member of this class and his career will be examined in chapter 2.

* * *

Torbay much charmed the Revd John Swete on his horseback tour of the South Devon coast in 1793 and this is revealed in the account he gave of his journey and the many small water-colour sketches he made of the district. Lush combes, rustling with birds, then ran down to the sea; streams broke cover from woods and meadows to wander across the shore; wooded hills at intervals traced the contours of the bay. The upland in many places was covered with apple orchards and the lowland given over to the cultivation of the outsize Paignton cabbage and to mixed farming. The rock pools, investigated at a later date by the naturalist Philip Gosse and his son Edmund and also by Charles Kingsley, were replete with marine and plant life. The bay was filled with men of war and merchant vessels when a storm was blowing up and there was always a bustle at Berry Head and the approaches to Brixham, home to a great fleet of merchant vessels, fishing boats and other craft. Torquay and Paignton each had small but dilapidated harbours, the jetties in good weather home to loungers, old fishermen and children. Most of them would have been conversing in the Devonshire dialect, now rarely, if ever, heard in Torbay.

The line of the bay, with its red sandstone cliffs, was indented with coves, caves and caverns and there were long stretches of sand ideal for bathers, though few people except fanatics then took a dip. The sea bathing craze had yet to reach Torbay. There were practically no tourists – the term was not in common use and the first sighting of the word is given as *c.*1800 in the *Oxford English Dictionary* – but Teignmouth and Dawlish, nearer to London, had already

4 Babbacombe Bay and Anstey's
Cove. The line of the bay, with its
red sandstone cliffs, was indented
with coves, caves and caverns.

become popular with invalids and hypochondriacs, romantics and spinsters, and with townsmen who simply sought a quiet retirement near the sea.

In 18th-century Devon communications were extremely poor, and were not to improve until an efficient turnpike system was developed, followed by macadamised roads. As there were few good turnpike roads but many meandering lanes and tracks, usually either muddy or rutted, a stranger was a comparative rarity and an object of curiosity in villages. The pace of life was slow, with spurts of activity when harvests were gathered. Farmers, fishermen, artisans and labourers congregated at night in the numerous inns, cider- and alehouses, some squalid but most warm and friendly. Market days were the major events that interrupted this humdrum and uneventful life; then crowds gathered from neighbouring villages and hamlets and from the scattered houses and farms in the district. From a poet's point of view, it was a beautiful and romantic land, for Torbay had great natural beauty. This was the district that Sir Robert Palk must have surveyed before he bought the manors of Tormohun and Torwood, and with them the little fishing village of Tor Key, in 1768. This is clearly too superficial and poetical a picture of Torbay in the late 18th century: it did have darker sides – poverty and squalor and bad housing; alcoholism, infanticide, and illegitimacy; as well as witchcraft and stark village tragedies and shipwrecks and men lost at sea. There were always bankruptcies, distraints, and ejectments; and epidemics removed not only rude mechanicals but the better off. Childhood was hard and brief for the poor and old age one of tribulations for the property-less, but since life expectancy was low far fewer survived to old age than would have today to become a burden on their families and their communities.

The population of Torquay (i.e. Tormohun and St Marychurch) was 1,639 according to the 1801 census (the first of its kind held in England); Paignton was given as 1,575; Brixham, 3,671. Thus Torquay had fewer inhabitants than the other towns and was outranked demographically by both Dartmouth and Teignmouth, with populations of 2,398 and 2,012 respectively, and by Totnes with 2,503 inhabitants. In 1801 there was no road that followed the coast from Torquay harbour to Torre Abbey sands. Torre itself was a small disorderly collection of houses centring on Tor Church, with outlying cottages and farmsteads. The Cary family of Torre Abbey could gaze from their casements at an expanse of grass and oak trees – parkland – that sloped down to the open beach. There was no road, no promenade, needless to say, to spoil this view. The scene was pastoral, sylvan, and entirely delightful for the Carys. The town proper (Tor Key as it was commonly spelt), spreading somewhat awry uphill from the harbour, contained a number of small houses with garden plots in front, a sprinkle of cottages on the Strand, and some newly-built terraces. Building of late certainly had taken place, but not on any imposing scale. These were merely intimations of future progress. The urban develop-

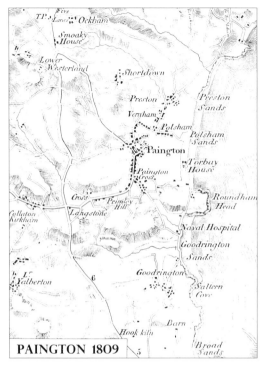

PAINGTON 1809

5 *Map of Paignton, 1809. Paignton was really a large village and its denizens led a village life.*

ments that were to transform Torquay were still some years off.

In 1801 (the starting point for this study) Paignton was largely a maze of narrow streets and alley ways mostly to the west of the parish church. Winner, Church and Duck Street were the main thoroughfares. There were also huddles of houses along the Totnes Road. Paignton had plenty of inns, as one would expect in an age when there were few recreational facilities for the lower classes. The old town was separated from the sea by a wilderness of marshes and willow beds. The sea, in the season of high tides, overflowed the low barrier of shingle and grassy knolls to flood the seashore area now called Paignton Green and its precincts. From a distance the one prominent feature of the town that stood out was always the church steeple, the focal point of many early prints and sketches of the town. Paignton in 1801 was really a large village and its denizens led a village life. Local grandees did not reside in the town proper but outside in country mansions. Consequently there were few large houses or mansions of note. The one residence of consequence, Torbay House, built sometime in the 18th century, was situated on the seashore (roughly where the Festival Theatre now stands on the seafront), then a desolate and rather lonely place in winter. There were few other substantial brick or stone houses standing at that time. Brixham, south of the bay, was the largest parish in the Torbay area. In the second half of the 18th century its population had steadily increased, to reach 3,671 in 1801, most of whom lived in Lower Brixham where the harbour and quays were located. It was then the largest town in Torbay waters and it remained the largest fishing port in Devon until overtaken by Plymouth in the 1870s. It also specialised in shipbuilding, net-making, rope-making and associated marine trades and crafts. The village of Higher Brixham lay about a mile up the valley from the harbour. This was the original Saxon settlement. Its church, St Mary, built in the late 14th century, was the third erected on the site.

Over time Lower Brixham became the town centre, for trade and business gravitated there, and people too. The taverns along the quay were much frequented by sailors, fishermen and trawlermen, all those who went down to the sea in ships. Visitors to Brixham remarked that the town always stank of rotting fish, tar, and much other effluvia, for drainage and sanitation were practically non-existent and most cess pools leaked into the harbour and creeks, over which seagulls constantly wheeled, whirled and dipped. Worth in his *Tourist's Guide to South Devon* (1880) dismisses the town in these words: '7 Streets irregular buildings in the main unarchitectural, and including the most hideous church in Devon; it rarely loses its "ancient and fish like smell"'.The church referred to by Worth was All Saints, built 1820-4, which has fortunately since been considerably altered.

The old harbour, an estuary locked in and completely sheltered by cliffs, was the best and most secure in Torbay, though small. Later it was to be much enlarged and a breakwater was thrown far out to sea. Brixham was considered one of the finest nurseries for seamen in the British Isles and large numbers of Brixham men served in the Napoleonic and other wars. It also had a reputation for smuggling, an activity rife in South Devon. The headland of Berry Head was hardly built upon. There were some ramparts and military buildings and a few private houses, but most of the plateau was occupied with a common of grass and furze. This long open area provided locals with good walks and fine views in all directions – up and down the Channel, across to Torquay with its Thatcher, Orestone, and Shag rocks standing sentinel off its coastline. On a clear day Brixham residents could see Torquay harbour, the houses on the Strand and a scattering of newly built villas on its hills. Torquay was then not as wooded as it became later. It was the Victorians who planted so many trees to beautify the town and to provide shelter for villa gardens. Daddy Hole and its environs and also Meadfoot were practically treeless, as can be seen in early prints. It may well have been that much timber had been used over the years as fuel by Torquay's poor. But we do know that many of the great oaks had been cut down during the wars with France to provide masts for the fleet.

As the 19th century opened few would have predicted the shape of things to come. With hindsight, we now know that Torquay was to become in a few decades or so a rich man's resort; and, much later in the day, Paignton the common man's holiday home; and Brixham to remain largely a fishing port and to keep its smells and attract sightseers. In Torbay's halcyon days, the mid-century years, old residents versed in the classics might well at times have murmured: 'Et in Arcadia ego'. In that era pictorially it was a lovely place – serene, quiet and not over populated and rightly called the English Riviera. It had even pleased Napoleon, a much travelled soldier and head of state, who likened it to Porto Ferrago in Elba. Others were to call Torquay the Queen of Watering Places. But that was well before a mass of housing began to scale Torbay's hills and to cut swathes through woodlands, meadows, and fields.This

6 *Brixham looking over Torbay. Brixham, south of the bay, was the largest parish in the Torbay area. On a clear day residents could see Torquay harbour.*

blight was to be reserved, in its fullest form of suburbanisation, for the next century. Osbert Lancaster's ironical remarks in *Pillar to Post* may be quoted as obituary: 'Notice the skill with which the houses are disposed, that ensures that the largest possible area of countryside is ruined with the minimum of expense.' The jerry builder has always been with us, but conspicuously so after the First World War. He has certainly left his spoor everywhere in South Devon. This contrast between the past and the present is a dismal one and geographers now refer to the Torbay district as a metropolitan area, an urbanised area taking in much of the bay.

* * *

There is a well-known dictum by L.P. Hartley that 'the past is another country: they do things differently there'. It is not always easy to understand the idiom of the past, nor is it any easier to uncover the assumptions that influence people's conduct and thought in another age. This is particularly true of how people relate to others in any historical social system. It may therefore be useful to interpolate here some comments on the subject of class.

The main concept in sociology is class; for social anthropologists it is kinship. These terms are seen as explanatory devices for the study of societies at different stages of development. Thus, it is generally agreed that 19th-

7 *Brixham Harbour, seen here in the early 1900s, was considered one of the finest nurseries for seamen in the British Isles.*

century Englishmen viewed the social order as a natural hierarchy, with, broadly speaking, lower, middle and upper divisions. In reality it is always far more complex than that. Problems arise in allocating people to an appropriate place in a pecking order; there are obviously always elements of flux in any class system. This comes about because new social and occupational groups emerge in response to changes in society and economy. And that was especially notable in the 19th century, with the rise of a large and diversifying middle class.

As the 19th century progressed new professions, activities, and groups evolved. The numbers of people involved in industry, trade, commerce, and the professions increased so that fortunes were now being made in ways unknown in the past, a past that was bound by tradition and to varying degrees stationary compared with the present. How, for example, did one rank new occupations and professional groups: accountants, civil engineers or company directors? Insurance agents, bank managers and local government officials? This is a difficult question to answer because many variables are involved: facts of birth, background, education, wealth and occupation. Any position in the social hierarchy has meaning only in reference to others. Why did some professions grow in esteem, such as medicine, and others decline, as with the Church? Figuratively speaking it may all be viewed as a game of snakes and ladders, a game where positions on the board are apt to change as time goes by. Nothing stays the same in the long run.

The family histories of the nobility and aristocracy are recorded in numerous books of genealogy; but even these soberly written volumes contain pitfalls, for there was much make-believe in the composition of pedigrees: as a general rule the further back the more suspect. But such books, extremely popular with the English middle and upper classes, testify to the Victorian passion for matters of birth, position, and rank. Debrett, Cokayne, Burke, and a host of lesser genealogists produced a quantity of books, in some cases only available to subscribers, that sold well, for most were constantly revised and from time to time brought up to date in new editions, Debrett and Burke in particular, both of which later were issued annually. Copies were to be found in the libraries of most gentlemen.

An interest in genealogy has always been with us as any reader of the Bible knows, with its long listing in the Old Testament of the names of ancestors; but in England a vogue for genealogy began to flourish in Tudor and Stuart times, more so in the 18th century, and was to reach its apogee in the 19th century. Arthur Collins's *Peerage of England* came out in 1709 and was the basis of many later compilations. This trend culminated in George Edward Cokayne's eight-volume *Complete Peerage*, 1887-98, although of course many genealogies and critical works have been published since.

In this study, which is focused principally on the resorts of Torquay and Paignton, there are numerous references to questions of class, status and power, and to rank, position and standing. This reflects reality and it is also mirrored in much Victorian fiction, in Jane Austen, Mrs Gaskell and George Eliot, and in the novels of Dickens, Thackeray and Trollope, and also in Surtees, a superb observer of social differences. Victorian England is very much a different country and we still must try to make sense of its sometimes outrageous differences and not sniffily dismiss the importance it placed on class in social relations.

The primary aim of this book is to describe *how*, rather than *why*, Torbay changed. Answering the first question may throw light on the second, for the two are related. Impersonal forces certainly hurried events forward but they are not examined at any length here. So the Torquay and Paignton chapters are constructed around the biographies of a restricted number of people: those who took the lead in promoting urban development and who, as a consequence, succeeded in leaving their mark on them. It is, after all, individuals who take particular decisions and not impersonal forces, although that does not dispose of the fact that nearly all of us are caught up in the *Zeitgeist*, the prevailing spirit of our age, and are affected by it. We are all creatures of our time and place, even if we react against them like Marx and Engels, Carlyle or William Morris.

Two

THE PALK FAMILY OF HALDON HOUSE

IN *A Book of the West* (1899), Sabine Baring-Gould has this to say of the Palks: 'A cloud of dust has been stirred up to disguise the humble, but respectable, origins of the family.' Baring-Gould takes to task the genealogist Sir Bernard Burke, Ulster King of Arms and editor of the famous *Peerage* of his name, for promoting myths about the family's history: that they descended from one Henry Palk of Ambrook, Devon, in the reign of Henry VII, Walter seventh in descent. In his typical no-nonsense way Baring-Gould demolishes this piece of fiction by adducing the true facts, stating that Ambrook (or Ambrooke), which is at Staverton, a village on the River Dart, near Totnes, never did belong to the family and that Robert Palk, when created a baronet in 1772, received a grant of arms, as the family was not previously entitled to them.

In another passage, he writes of the Cary family as being 'as ancient and noble as that of Palk is modern and humble'. Baring-Gould was very Victorian in discriminating between a true (old) and a factitious (new) gentry. When he penned these words, in the late 1890s, Lawrence Hesketh Palk, 2nd Lord Haldon, had been declared bankrupt. One surmises that he had little respect for a family fallen on hard times of their own making. He regarded the later Palks as spendthrifts who had brought their family down by their unconscionable neglect of duty and their incapacity to manage a great estate. Baring-Gould was correct in insisting that the Palks were parvenus for the facts support him (although all great families at one time must have been labelled 'parvenu'). Sir Robert and succeeding generations of his family had either faked their family tree, their ancestry, or had given credence to an apocryphal past, as have so many families that have translated wealth into status by acquiring land as a means of setting themselves up as members of the landed gentry. Historically, this was the route taken by so many aspirants to the upper classes. As Oscar Wilde remarked of the *Peerage*: 'It is the best thing in fiction the English have done.' Printed genealogies are rarely without error; and purported family links may be difficult to prove, as Tess of the Durbervilles was to discover.

The facts are these: originally the Palks were small farmers, the proverbial yeomen of England, in the Ashburton district. Sir Robert's father, Walter, had married Frances, daughter of Robert Abraham, a prosperous farmer residing in the same locality. Ashburton in the early 18th century was a flourishing and prosperous centre of the clothing trade, procuring yarn from Cornish and also Tavistock spinners with which to produce serge, a worsted fabric, for a wide market. Walter Palk, as well as farming on a small scale, made a living by carrying serge by pack horse from Ashburton over the Haldon hills to Exeter, the main distribution centre for the finished product. He was a well known carrier in those parts. Walter had two sons, Robert (named after his uncle Robert Abraham) and the younger Walter, who took his father's Christian name, and a daughter, Grace. The future Sir Robert, born in 1717, was educated at Ashburton Grammar School and sent with his uncle's help to Oxford as a sizar, which meant that he paid reduced fees but was expected to perform some menial duties. Ordained a deacon, he accepted a curacy in Cornwall, a 'hardship post' in those days. He was poor and greatly bored with the stark and miserable life he was forced to lead as a Cornish curate in the back of beyond, in a stark land of much superstition.

The story goes that one Christmas he walked from Cornwall to Ashburton to visit his parents and on his way back, while he lingered on Dart Bridge gazing abstractedly at the river, he was accosted by a passing horseman with the words: 'Is that you, Palk?' The rider turned out to have been at Oxford with him. This gentleman listened patiently to Palk's drab tale of woe and suggested, in turn, that Palk's way to fortune was to enter the service of the East India Company, which was just the sort of place for a bright young man without means or an influential patron. He volunteered an introduction to the Company, whose headquarters were in London. Palk did not take up this offer at once. Whether this story is fanciful or not, soon afterwards he did change direction. Forsaking Cornwall, he joined the navy as a chaplain, serving on several ships, including the *Namur*, and he was present at Anson's victory over the *French* at Cape Finisterre in 1747. In November of that year he sailed for the East Indies in the same ship,

8 *Robert Palk (1744-1783), portrait by Tilly Kettle. He was born in Ashburton, the second son of Sir Robert Palk's younger brother, Walter. Like his uncle, the great Sir Robert Palk, he joined the East India Company and amassed a fortune in India. Following a bad fall from his horse, while hunting wild boar, he suffered from epileptic fits and died on the voyage home.*

which went down in a hurricane off the Indian coast whilst the Admiral and his staff, including Palk, were still on shore. Soon after this event he joined the East India Company, being appointed a chaplain at Fort St George in 1751. He was to stay in India for over twenty years and to become a rich man by so doing.

In 1757, after performing important official work for the Company and having proved himself an excellent negotiator, he resigned his chaplaincy and returned to England, whereupon he renounced holy orders and married Anne, daughter of Arthur Vansittart and sister of Henry Vansittart, who became Governor of Bengal during Palk's period of Indian service. In 1761 Palk finally entered the Company's civil service, a step that was to be his making. In 1763, while he was kicking his heels in London, he was offered appointment as Governor of Madras and returned to India. Thereafter he was involved in numerous negotiations with the Deccan and other Indian powers and with the French. Some of the actions he took were heavily criticised in his day. His signing of a treaty at Hyderabad in 1766, by which Palk hoped to protect his own territory – Madras – by siding with the Carnatic against Tanjore, was debated as unwise. The *Dictionary of National Biography* declares: 'This treaty is reprobated by all historians as a grave act of pusillanimity.' Soon after, in 1767, he resigned his governorship and was on his way back to England, out of the tiger's den so to say, with his great fortune intact. The Company's servants were permitted to engage in trade on their own account and most, if not all, accepted bribes, sometimes enormous sums in gold, jewels, or specie.

Palk, like so many others, went to India to better himself. There was a long tradition in the West Country of seafaring, wayfaring and travelling and a surprising number of nabobs came from or settled down in Devon. Devonians were not stay-at-homes. Devon and Cornwall were also noted for their eccentrics and adventurers. Of the latter group, the most extraordinary is probably Bampfylde Moore Carew (1690-1758), the son of the rector of Bickleigh. Educated at Blundell's School, Tiverton, he became a gipsy and was elected their king. After committing various misdeeds, including horse-stealing, he was transported to Maryland, escaped back to England, and in middle age followed Prince Charles Edward's army to Derby. Eventually he returned to his home at Bickleigh and died there in 1758.

Palk's great friend and patron in India was Major-General Stringer Lawrence, 1697-1775, who warmly returned his loyalty and affection. They were certainly great chums, if nothing else; but the strength of their ties suggests it was a deep, a sentimental friendship. Stringer Lawrence, whose origins are unknown, never married, had no children. Like Palk, he was of humble birth and a self-made man. An older man, he recognised Palk's qualities at an early stage and no doubt saw him as the son he never had; or, perhaps, as a younger brother. When Stringer left India, he went to live with Palk at Haldon House and frequently stayed in Palk's London house, where he died.

Palk built, around 1780, a great shrine to his memory in the form of a castellated three-storey Belvedere, each tower marking the point of a triangle. It is now called the Haldon Belvedere, though occasionally referred to as Lawrence Castle. The Belvedere still stands on one of the highest points of the Haldon hills, on an eminence above Haldon House, a landmark for a great part of Devon. It is 70 feet high. Both the main stairway and the spiral one in the tower are of Indian marble donated by the Nizam of Hyderabad. There is a ballroom above, which was used by the Palk family for special celebrations. The East India Company also put up a monument to their old servant in Westminster Abbey. Stringer left Palk his entire estate, a testimonial to their great and enduring friendship.

When Palk retired from his service in India he was an extremely rich man, for he had been eminently successful as a merchant and trader on his own account; and he was to inherit £80,000 from Stringer Lawrence in 1775. Like most wealthy returned Anglo-Indians (nabobs as they were pejoratively or derisively called) he looked around for land to buy – an estate – preferably in Devon. He aspired to become a landed gentleman, as other nabobs had done, and to found a dynasty. This could only be achieved in the 18th century by laying out his gains in land and by acquiring a seat – a place in the country in which to live like a gentleman. His father might have been a carrier: he meant to place his family on a far loftier plateau.

In Devon, as elsewhere in the agricultural counties of England, there were few vacant estates on the market, for the majority of the larger were heavily entailed by the legal device of strict family settlement, an arrangement designed to prevent estate fragmentation or sale by an incumbent. In theory at least, this meant that an estate should pass from generation to generation, passing to the eldest surviving male heir (if there were one) in the direct line of descent, failing which, to the eldest male in a collateral branch of the family. The normal procedure was for lawyers to draw up a family settlement when the heir came of age. The control over inheritance was then placed in the hands of trustees who guaranteed the descent of property to unborn heirs. In this way the role of the eldest son or heir was limited to that of a life-tenant. Under the terms of settlement he was prevented from selling off all or parts of an estate in order to meet current expenditure.

In most cases the settlement provided jointures for surviving wives and an income for sons and daughters, though younger sons were usually kept on short commons. This legal device may be illustrated with reference to the Palk family. There was a family settlement in 1841 between Sir Lawrence Vaughan Palk and his eldest son Lawrence (later first Lord Haldon); and in 1868 between the latter and his heir Lawrence Hesketh Palk (later 2nd Lord Haldon); but there was no family settlement in 1890 when the heir to the Palk estates, Lawrence William Palk, came of age for by then his father had broken the entail (originally set up by Sir Robert's lawyers in the 18th century) so as to pay off a mountain of debt, the trustees having given their approval. He did this by selling off most of the leaseholds and freeholds he held. This could only be achieved, as the law then stood, by the passing of a private Act of Parliament, an expensive business for the petitioner. Consequently a bill was introduced and became law as Lord Haldon's Estate Act, 1885. The Palks in a few years were practically landless. But all that was far in the future and the sanguine Sir Robert, one imagines, never supposed that his heirs would dissipate their patrimony.

From the 13th century onwards most of Devon's large landed estates were produced by a succession of judicious marriages. There is a relevant and important passage in W.G. Hoskins and H.P.R. Finberg's *Devonshire Studies* (1952) which should be quoted:

> Marriage has been by far the most important single factor in the successful accumulation of estates (in Devon): more so even than the cloth trade, the tin trade, and the law, those other fertile sources of large fortunes in land in the Devon countryside, for marriage operated in every generation, century after century, whereas the other factors were intermittent in their working. It is true that the giving of a daughter in marriage took away land, just as a son brought it in. The estates of the landed families, large and small, therefore fluctuated in extent and whereabouts from generation to generation ... A considerable proportion of the squires and gentry of Tudor and Stuart Devon descended from the small – almost peasant – freeholders of the thirteenth and fourteenth centuries. They represent the successful survivors, those who had accumulated around their own nuclear tenement the estates of other freeholders who had either failed to produce male heirs, or who had produced too many daughters for their economic health, or had encountered misfortune in some other guise.

The manor of Tormohun, which Palk was to buy, had formerly belonged to the Ridgeway (Londonderry family), but was neglected in later years when their interests shifted to Ireland, where they took root and flourished. The male line of the Ridgeways failed in 1712 when the 4th earl died. His widow then retired to Torwood Grange (in Torquay) as a dower house. When she died in 1724, the estate passed to her son-in-law, Arthur Chichester, 4th Earl of Donegal, from whom it went to his nephew. In 1768, Palk succeeded in buying the whole property, then in chancery. He paid £12,000, which perhaps seems cheap, but it was land mostly uninhabited and not much sought after by local farmers since it was mostly hill ground, with many rocky outcrops. It included the manorial estate of Tormohun, the barton of Torwood, and the manor of Ilsham. Later, in 1803, his son Lawrence was able to acquire the manor of Combe Pafford in the parish of St Marychurch. Sir Robert, it seems, intended to develop Torquay as a port to rival Dartmouth and with that end in mind, some time before his death, set in motion plans to construct a modern harbour and this work was continued by his son and grandson.

In essence, the Palks became the landowners of the major part of what was to become Victorian Torquay, an extremely valuable inheritance, once the town became a fashionable watering-place and a popular place of residence for the well off. Included in the purchase price, then, was a beautiful coastline, with several beaches, a coastline that ran from Anstey's Cove to Hope's Nose and from that small protuberance along Meadfoot and around Daddy Hole to the harbour. The Palk estate at that point concluded at the Cary boundary at Waldon Hill. Palk also became owner of the palaeolithic Kent's Cavern at Ilsham and many acres of land suitable for future development, especially housing. But, as Oscar Wilde warned in his usual paradoxical style: 'Land gives one position, and prevents one from keeping it up.'

A gentleman needed not only land, usually a minimum of around 1,000 acres – there were exceptions: the Mallocks owned 850 acres – to secure his status but also what was then known as a 'seat', a country mansion within its own grounds or demesne.

This Palk first envisaged would be the Torwood Grange, a Tudor edifice, the ancient Ridgeway family seat, now badly in need of repairs and refurbishment; but below the house lay a rocky hill and some fields, part of the Braddon property owned by the Carys and sold to them by a Ridgeway long before Palk came on the scene. If any Cary built on this land, Palk's marine view from Torwood Grange would be spoilt. This Cary-owned piece of land was later to become the location for both the Torquay Natural History Museum and the Wesleyan Church in Torwood Street. Dismayed by the prospect of future building by the Carys, with whom he was not on very good terms, he decided to go further afield to find a grand enough seat that would satisfy his ambition. In 1772 he bought Haldon House and its large estate. Haldon House, only part of which survives, is in the parish of Kenn and situated on the Haldon Hills, some 4½ miles from Exeter. Finally he had acquired both a seat that satisfied his needs and a perfect rural retreat. He quickly set about the task of improving his new estate.

The building of Haldon House was begun by Sir George Chudleigh in 1735 and completed in 1738 after his death. Palk added much to it and greatly enlarged the fine timbered park. His chosen model was Buckingham House (later Palace), which gives some idea of his social ambitions, but he was always prepared to do things on a grand scale when necessary and his entertaining at Haldon was sumptuous. He did not stint guests. In time Haldon House became one of the most notable and palatial homes in all Devon and would come to rank among the most imposing mansions in England, certainly in

9 *Haldon House. Palk's chosen model was Buckingham House (later Palace); he was always prepared to do things on a grand scale.*

scale and setting. As such, it was included in Sir Bernard Burke's book on the seats of the noblemen and gentlemen of Great Britain, published in 1855. A lithograph of the house done by the topographical illustrator Thomas Allom around 1828 depicts it against a background of wooded hills with huntsmen and hounds racing across the greensward in the foreground. Allom's picture reveals how vast the house once was. Palk, whose boyhood home had been a modest farmhouse at Ashburton, had advanced far in his domestic arrangements, as attested by Sir Bernard's fulsome listing of the splendours of Haldon House. The Palks were to live there, with some breaks, until 1892. Because of its vastness an extremely large staff was needed to run the house efficiently and the cost to the Palks of living in such state must have been onerous, and too much of a burden for future and mostly improvident generations, when the family's disposable income began to shrink.

It seems likely that Palk spent most of his time on his Haldon estate, supervising building operations and the laying out of new parks and woodlands, with only occasional visits to Torquay, where as yet he had no mansion. As the Member for Ashburton, a pocket borough, from 1767 to 1768 and from 1774 to 1787, he needed to pay frequent visits to the metropolis, where he had his own town house in Hanover Square, Mayfair. He always retained a great interest in the East India Company's affairs and in events in India, and that is revealed in his correspondence. Palk, a self-made man and now a Devonshire magnate, was a Tory, but demonstrated his independence on occasions: he was his own man, neither placeman nor toady.

Percy Russell writes of Torquay, 'There is nothing to show that Palk regarded his purchase as anything other than the acquisition of valuable lands in his native county.' This statement is soundly based, since for some years Palk did little about his Torquay property apart from granting a few leases and there is no evidence to suggest he dreamed of becoming an urban developer on a large scale. He was, in those early years, a rentier rather than entrepreneur, living off his invested capital and the rents from his Haldon and Torquay estates. The idea of turning the town into a watering-place like Bath or Brighton clearly had not entered his head.

The Carys of Torre Abbey were the leading gentry family in Torquay. The fact that Robert Palk claimed descent from one Henry Palk of Ambrook in Henry VII's time cut no ice with them; nor did the fact that Palk was knighted in 1772 for his services in India, and granted arms. In Cary eyes Palk was a parvenu, a *nouveau riche*. In an era of No Popery, epitomised by the Gordon Riots of 1780, the two families were divided by religion. The Carys were Papists, recusant Catholics; the Palks staunch supporters of the Anglican Church. Moreover, the Carys were of ancient lineage and had played a leading part in Devon's earlier history. Another branch of their family resided at Follaton House, Totnes. Cary influence had always been strong in South Devon and they viewed the Palks as interlopers, now throwing their weight around in Torbay, a district in which the Carys had been paramount for generations. Sir Robert Palk had to battle against a degree of social prejudice from some quarters and to face up to the proud Carys, one of the most ancient families in South Devon.

Palk initially had been exasperated by the matter of the Cary ownership of the Braddon fields, which as we know occasioned his retreat from Torwood Grange to Haldon House in 1772; and over the years he suffered from a number of other vexations which he believed emanated from the Cary family or their agents. Among the Kennaway papers at Exeter City Library, as Percy Russell reports, is a case for counsel's opinion in 1789, in which Palk attempted to demonstrate that the Torre Abbey estate was not a separate manor but only a barton (a large farm) and historically part of the manor of Tormohun. The case was finally dropped since the issues were opaque and demanded far too much fine historical research into the available records. There were repeated territorial and other disputes between the families throughout the 19th century, which ended of course when the Palks sold their holdings and left Torquay for ever. These disputes had unfortunate consequences for Torquay's development and will be referred to in more detail in a later chapter.

Palk, a far richer man than any Cary and the largest landowner in the Torbay region (the Carys and Mallocks each owned under a thousand acres

10 *Torre Abbey was bought by a famous Devon Catholic family, the Carys, in 1662, and it remained in the family until 1930. The monastic buildings and gatehouse were extended by the building of a three-storey house on the site of the old refectory.*

11 *Follaton House. The Carys were of ancient lineage and the leading gentry family in Torquay; a branch of the family resided at Follaton House.*

12 *Henry George Cary (1800-40), portrait by James Ramsay. The Carys maintained their leading position well into the 19th century.*

and are not listed in the New Domesday Book of 1873), had to take second place socially to George Cary (1731-1805), the accepted leader of Torquay society at that time. The Carys maintained their leading position well into the 19th century. In 1814 Colonel Cary (1769-1828), George Cary's son, was the steward of the first regatta held in the town and afterwards hosted a dinner for 80 gentlemen at Torre Abbey, a resplendent occasion; and in 1833 when the Princess Victoria and her mother, the Duchess of Kent, visited the town, it was again a Cary – Henry Cary (1800-40) – who was the head of the committee of prominent citizens and gentlefolk that received her. As G.M. Young claims of the Victorians: 'In a money making age opinion was, on the whole, more deferential to birth than to money.'

The Carys, it should be emphasised, also had some disagreements with the Mallocks, their neighbours on the western fringes of the Torre Abbey estate. 'Fallings-out' would perhaps be too strong a term since both parties always acted, at least in public, with dignity and an appropriate degree of decorum or hauteur. The Carys had once been lords of the manor of Cockington; but Sir Henry Cary, ruined by his extravagant support of the Royalist cause in the Civil War and much fallen in debt, was forced to make a general sale of his properties in 1654, and Cockington was then bought by an Exeter merchant, Roger Mallock. Thereafter 12 Mallocks were to be lords of the manor, until the last sold the entire estate in 1932. These contentions between Carys and Mallocks in Victorian times, mostly conducted in a distant, gentlemanly way through their agents, afflicted all three of Torquay's landowning families and they provided, on occasion, diversion and amusement for the quality and some nice gossip in the clubs.

Carys and, in particular, Mallocks (some of whom would fit nicely into a novel by Thomas Love Peacock) wished to shield their estates from outside intrusion. The Mallocks wanted to maintain Cockington Court and its demesne in its early 19th-century guise, as a Georgian mansion contained in an ordered landscape, enshrined in a pastoral setting, all ugliness concealed or glossed over. To this end old cottages near the church were pulled down and new

13 *Cockington Court and Church. The Carys had once been lords of the manor of Cockington but Sir Henry Cary, ruined by his extravagant support of the Royalists in the Civil War, was forced to sell the estate in 1654.*

14 *Cockington was bought by an Exeter merchant, Roger Mallock, and there were to be 12 Mallocks as lords of the manor until the entire estate was sold in 1932.*

15 *The Mallocks wanted to maintain the estate in its early 19th-century guise and to this end old cottages near the church were pulled down and new thatched ones put up in the village.*

thatched ones put up in the village. The Mallocks imposed a symmetry that nature had not intended. The little settlement was much prettified, so that the place looks artfully rustic and picturesque as can be seen today, the sort of village beloved by Christmas card designers. The Mallocks did not follow Sir Robert Palk and his heirs, who put up villas on their property and thus enriched themselves; the Mallocks resisted the onrush of urbanisation, the growth of suburbia. In the early years of the century the Revd Roger Mallock had permitted the erection of two houses, Livermead House and Livermead Cottage, near the shore, but these were put up for close personal friends, the Earl St Vincent and Sir John Colbourne. Thereafter he refused to permit any more private building on his land. A solitary exception was made in 1867 when William Froude, a kinsman, was granted a lease and he built a commodious villa, Chelston Cross, in Seaway Lane (it is now the *Manor House Hotel*). Of course the Mallocks' attempt to keep things as they were was not to succeed once the ambit of local government expanded and local officials had been granted greater powers of regulation and improvement. Autocracy at Cockington was steadily eroded by the effects of a rising democracy.

The Cary family were marginally more successful in withstanding the winds of change; and there is still a Cary estate office on Marine Road, just by the harbour; but members of the family no longer live in Torquay, nor do the Mallocks. At mid-century Torquay's population had risen from 803 in 1801 to over 11,000 in 1851 and was to reach over 24,000 in 1901. Because of this population growth landlords were under great pressure to grant leases and free more land for housing and other purposes. The Palks had invested so heavily in the development of Torquay that they were prepared to join, with certain reservations, the march of progress, since they assumed they would benefit from improved land values and thereby increase their revenues.

It has been suggested by some writers that relations between the Cary and Mallock families might well have been soured by religious differences, as had happened, it is speculated, between the Carys and Palks. The Mallocks were pillars of the Anglican Establishment. They controlled 16 livings and it was quite common for members of the family to be in holy orders. The Revd Roger Mallock (1772-1846), the creator of Cockington Court and its grounds as they presently exist, was squire of Cockington for over sixty years, and his father before him had been a clergyman. But we really do not know the reasons for the coldness that existed between the families and even R.H. Mallock, the Revd Roger's grandson, author of the once famous satire, *The New Republic*, does not throw much light on the matter in his autobiography, *Memoirs of Life and Literature* (1920).

Torre Abbey and Cockington Court were perhaps too close to each other for harmony always to prevail. Distance does lend enchantment. These adjacent estates were like tiny principalities governed at times by quarrelsome and autocratic rulers. But the Palks resided at distant rural Haldon until their Manor House on Lincombe Hill, Torquay, was completed in 1864 by the 4th baronet, another Lawrence Palk. Before that, the family resided on occasion at Torquay in a rented or borrowed villa or in one or other of the houses they owned. Only in 1864 did they shift their base, for all intents and purposes, from Haldon House to the New Manor House. The Mallock family did not cause the Palks any problems for they were always on good and courteous terms and, of some importance, also related by marriage. Their estates, in any case, were not contiguous. Neither did religion impose any barrier since both families were Anglican. Around 1846, when discussion as to the direction the railway should take beyond Torre – a line that would necessarily cut across one or the other's land – both Cary and Mallock experienced perturbation and anguish and each conspired to have the new line constructed on the other's land. There was a sharp correspondence between C.H. Mallock and the South Devon Company as to the proposed route: Mallock wanted it to run through the Abbey grounds. It is interesting to note that he contacted the Company and not Robert Cary in a matter that would affect both proprietors. The Palks had always backed railway developments in the Torbay region and had even sold a strip of land under Chapel Hill when the Newton Abbot to Torre line was constructed. Top dogs in the region for several centuries, the Carys and Mallocks were finding their ascendancy also under challenge from a rising, prosperous, and assertive middle class.

After 1803, the year in which Sir Lawrence Palk purchased the manor of Combe Pafford – the last of the Palk purchases of land – the land-owning map of Torquay remained fixed until Lawrence Hesketh Palk, 2nd Lord Haldon, was forced to make sales of his estates in 1885 and of his manorial rights in 1894. During this 80-year period, the Palk and Cary estates were contiguous, with the for-mer mostly encompassed by the latter, apart from the small Cary enclave at Braddon Hill. The Palks owned almost the whole of the harbour area, the focal point of the nascent town, and the Flete stream which, when covered over, became Torquay's main thor-oughfare (today's Fleet Street, con-tinuing into Union Street), until

16 *Babbacombe. The Carys were the landlords of St Marychurch and Babbacombe, with its lofty cliffs and magnificent sea views.*

Torbay Road was constructed in the 1840s, running under Waldon Hill to Torre Abbey sands and on to Paignton. The Carys owned an area which became known later as Belgravia, an area much built upon and developed in the second half of the century, and also Waldon Hill, by then mostly bereft of its oaks and truly a rabbit warren. They were the landlords as well of St Marychurch and Babbacombe, with its lofty cliffs and magnificent marine views. The Torre Abbey grounds, which ran down to the sea, terminated at Corbyn Head, a small grassy headland; at that point ownership changed hands, with the Mallocks in possession of Livermead. Their estate ended at Holla-combe, now the gateway to Paignton. Both families had an unobstructed coastline to the east of their properties.

The Mallock-owned vale of Chelston, running inland from the sea, was a separate manor, mostly given over to agriculture. The actual settlement of Chelston was a mere hamlet. Chelston manor, adjacent to Torre Abbey, was ripe for development once the railway came to Torquay, since Torre and Torquay stations were close by. This Mallock-owned land was mostly flat and would provide excellent building sites. At that time, Chelston was a kind of buffer zone between Torre Abbey and Cockington, thus an area of great interest to Mallocks and Carys and one which gave rise inevitably to disputes about rights. Chelston was somewhat cut off from the manor of Cockington by a range of low hills, hills which shielded Cockington Court from Torre Abbey and preserved Cockington's comparative isolation from the outside world.

Now we should return to Lawrence Palk. Little has been recorded of Sir Robert's heir, Lawrence, born at Madras, India, in 1766. It was a condition of Stringer Lawrence's bequest of £80,000 that the eldest son in each succeeding generation should be christened Lawrence; and this condition was honoured until the last of the Palks – Lawrence Bloomfield Palk, 4th Lord Haldon – died in poverty in 1938. Lawrence, the 2nd baronet, appears to have remained much in his father's autocratic shadow until Sir Robert's death, aged 81, in 1798. Of Sir Robert, Charles Worthy enthused: 'Robert Palk's touch seemed to turn everything into gold. He realized it for himself, for his children, for his relatives, for his friends, and for his surroundings.' Written in 1889, Worthy's words are a sad encomium, for

17 *Sir Lawrence Palk (1766-1813), Lady Palk and their three children, painted by one of the circle of Richard Cosway. Sir Lawrence led the conventional life of a country gentleman, managing his estates, engaging in rural pursuits and riding to hounds.*

by that time Sir Robert's descendants had frittered away much of his wealth, a fortune acquired not by inheritance but by hardwork, with the exception of Stringer Lawrence's legacy.

As the eldest son, Lawrence inherited the estate and continued to reside in Haldon, for he had no house of his own in Torquay. In 1787 he took over his father's constituency of Ashburton and then succeeded Sir John Rolle in 1796 as MP for Devonshire. His first wife died childless in 1791 and soon after he married Elizabeth Vaughan, daughter of the 1st Earl of Lisburne, by whom he had eight children. In his lifetime he was not celebrated in any way, unlike his father who was very much a public man, and he has no entry in the *Dictionary of National Biography*. Lawrence led the conventional life of a country gentleman, managing his estates, much engaged in rural pursuits, and riding to hounds. In Parliament he was a staunch supporter of Pitt the Younger. Like most of the Palks he was neither a connoisseur nor a dilettante; he exhibited no great interest in the arts, in collecting or in the world of learning. Sir Robert had a cabinet of medals and a good library on the history and topography of Devon and some fine paintings by Cuyp and Rysdale and, according to Burke, 'some masterpieces by Rembrandt'. As one would expect, he had brought back from the East numerous oriental gewgaws. But the more expensive pieces and pictures at Haldon House were, one feels, regarded

more as 'furniture', as the normal accoutrements
of a rich man's house.

Lawrence was also slow to recognise Torquay's
potential as a resort and there is no evidence to
suggest that any systematic development of the
manor of Tormohun was undertaken before 1803,
in which year he secured an Act of Parliament for
the improvement of the harbour. The Scottish civil
engineer John Rennie (1761-1821), who later
designed London Bridge and improved the harbours and dockyards at Portsmouth, Chatham,
Sheerness, and Plymouth, was engaged to draw up
plans for Torquay harbour, including plans for
streets and roads in the vicinity. This, on a relatively
small scale, was urban planning, the first of its kind
in the town; and the main purpose behind the
enterprise was to make the harbour a more attrac-

18 *John Rennie. A Scottish civil
engineer, he was engaged by Sir
Lawrence Palk to draw up plans
for Torquay harbour. He was
later to design London Bridge.*

tive and efficient place for passenger and cargo vessels to berth, and to promote
commerce and trade. There was even a proposal at this time to construct a
canal to Newton Abbot to bring stone and other heavy building materials to
the Torbay district, but nothing came of it. These surely were signs that Palk,
or his surrogates and agents, had realised at last that Torquay was likely to
bloom as a watering-place, following in the wake of Dawlish and Teignmouth,
both now attracting substantial numbers of invalids, visitors and residents.
Since local roads were in an appalling state many preferred to journey by sea,
if possible. Better harbour facilities might encourage this sea-borne passenger
traffic, to the benefit of the town and its chief landlord.

These developments involved him in great and mounting expense. As is
common with construction work, it is never easy to determine with exactitude
the final cost of a project: there are usually unforeseen contingencies that
crop up to force up the price; nor can anyone predict the vagaries of nature,
such as storms, not uncommon in Torbay, and other disasters. Dr Henry
Beeke, eminent both as a divine and political economist, calculated in 1814
that Lawrence Palk had expended around £27,000 on harbour and associated
works. This estimate is given in a letter he wrote to James Lambert, the Palk
family's London solicitor. But even the clever Beeke had difficulty in ascer-
taining the true costs, for Palk's solicitor in Devon, Robert Abraham, whose
office was at Ashburton, and Palk's steward at Haldon, Beard, had been dilatory
in settling accounts and in the passing on of papers. His business affairs had
got into a great mess. Neither Abraham nor Beard was up to the mark. In
retrospect this signals the origin of the family's future financial embarrassments
but the *dénouement* would come much later in the century. Sir Robert had been

19 *Torquay Harbour* c.*1848 (above), with the Strand open to the sea, after the new quays had been built in 1803 by Sir Lawrence Palk at a cost of £27,000. Nearly seventy years later Lord Holden spent a further £70,000 on harbour improvements. Quantities of stone and debris from the construction of the Baths above Beacon Cove were used for the quays and wharfs.*

an astute merchant; Lawrence, on the other hand, seems to have lacked his father's drive, his flair for business – his 'golden touch' as Worthy expressed it – but he must have experienced some training at his father's side. There is evidence, as Beeke hinted, that in old age even Sir Robert, the founder of the family's fortune, had begun to lose his touch and had grown a trifle slothful. But the nub of the problem then was indifferent, negligent auditing of the estate books.

At that time the profession of accountancy was in its infancy and there was no great demand for specialist accountants. Accurate accounting techniques had yet to be invented and when they were, the impulse came mainly from large-scale enterprises, such as railways, which daily handled large sums of money, and from joint stock companies. Even as late as 1822 there were only 75 persons to whom the label of accountant properly could be attached in all England and Wales. On the other hand there were scores of book-keepers in various enterprises and firms, in nearly every case people who had received no training in accountancy: they simply learned on the job, and the qualities their employers most treasured were honesty, diligence, and fine copperplate handwriting. And so Palk's true financial position always remained cloudy, masked by an accumulating mass of paperwork. Country solicitors like Robert Abraham were not always the best people to prepare complex statements of accounts; and Beard, the Haldon estate steward and also Palk's manager for the harbour works, seems to have lacked the ability to see things in the round and to advise Palk on such complicated matters: the arcane world of law and accounting. Palk was therefore much in the dark. This came to Beeke's notice and he was soon to be invited to step into Beard's shoes. Sir Lawrence Palk, the 2nd baronet, was enmeshed not so much in a tangled web of deceit as of incompetence.

The return to a landowner from improvements would normally accrue – and that was often problematic – only in the long run. Urban development was a risky business, as so many aristocratic landowners in the 19th century were to find, though a few did make fortunes. Of course there was a degree of prestige attached to those benevolent landowners who spent money on improving a town. Big spenders as such were applauded but not emulated by many members of their own class. There were too many cautious or uninterested landowners. The price paid for modernisation was so often a bankruptcy. Those in Torquay who obviously benefited from improvement schemes were, above all, the 'shopocracy' (a very special interest group) and members of the professional classes, specially doctors, always in great demand in a watering-place or where an affluent middle and upper middle class had congregated in large numbers. Palk, as we know, used his own resources to improve Torquay, with little help in the early years from the Carys. The 4th baronet, another Lawrence Palk, was to spend another £70,000 on enlarging the harbour. It has been estimated that over the years the Palks spent around £100,000 on harbour works; and the harbour as revealed today is principally of their making. It was the hub of the town, to which all major roads eventually led.

The extremely able Henry Beeke, doctor of divinity and son of a clergyman, was born at Kingsteignton, a village near Newton Abbot, in 1751. Elected a scholar at Corpus Christi College, Oxford, in 1769, he became a fellow of Oriel at the age of 24, Regius Professor of Modern History in 1801, and received the lucrative post of Dean of Bristol in 1813 for political services to the Tory Party. Beeke acquired a great reputation as a financial authority and pundit on economic affairs following the publication of his *Observations on the Produce of the Income Tax* in 1799. J.R. McCulloch, a noted political economist of the time, observed of the work that it was 'the best example of the successful application of statistical reasoning to finance that had then appeared'. His reputation as an economist established, Beeke was frequently consulted by Sir Robert Vansittart, son of a former Governor of Bengal and Chancellor of the Exchequer from 1812 to 1823. Vansittart was also a relation by marriage to the Palks, for Sir Robert had married his sister. The Palk family often sought Beeke's advice on Torquay's affairs and on financial matters in general. Later in life he bought a house in Beacon Terrace, adjacent to the harbour, and resided there until his death in 1837, at the age of 86, an octogenarian, as had been his good friend, the much lamented Sir Robert.

20 *Torquay from the Beacon. Beacon Terrace had been completed in 1833 and was viewed as 'a fine example of Regency Marine building'. Henry Beeke was later to live there until his death in 1837.*

Beeke, as we know, had evinced great interest in the harbour works, from their inception in 1803. As he observed the work progressing he became critical of and alarmed by the quality of the workmanship. He suggested to Sir Lawrence that the plan could be completed in a less costly fashion and that certain economies could be made. At the same time, he offered to take over direction from Beard, the agent on the site, and also the supervision of the laying out of roads, streets, and terraces, as well as the other ancillary structures to be put up in the harbour vicinity. Sir Lawrence, who had much confidence in Beeke's abilities and acumen, readily accepted the offer. Without any increase in cost, Beeke made the harbour twice as large as Rennie and Sir Lawrence had originally envisioned. This he achieved mainly by lengthening and rebuilding the head of the former pier, which had fallen down only five years after it had been put up.

Thus the early development of the town and the harbour area, the nucleus from which modern Torquay emerged, was essentially of Beeke's own design and owed little to Sir Lawrence (who of course paid for all the work) or to Beard and his nephew, Joseph Beard, a Somerset architect employed by his uncle to draw up plans for some of the houses and other buildings to be erected. Joseph Beard and Jacob Harvey, another architect, were soon busy at their drawing-boards under Beeke's guidance and direction. The result of their labours was to be seen in the Higher Terrace (erected in 1810 onwards), in Park Place (a row of five Georgian-type houses), and in Beacon Terrace, Vaughan Parade, and some other houses on the Strand. All these structures were completed by 1832 and are mentioned in Blewitt's *Panorama*. The harbour by that date was circumscribed with habitations, offices, and hotels (the *Royal* and *Marchetti's*, roughly where the *Queen's Hotel* stands today). A bijou resort had arisen, outclassing in attraction, chic, and popularity its former peer – Teignmouth. Torquay was now the premier watering-place in the West Country; and would continue to outstrip all its rivals in Devon and Cornwall.

In 1813 Sir Lawrence died at his London residence in Bruton Street (where Stringer Lawrence had predeceased him) and was interred in the family vault at Dunchideock Church near Haldon House. He was succeeded by his eldest son, Lawrence Vaughan (usually referred to as Sir L.V. Palk), born in 1793, who at the early age of 20 now became the 3rd baronet. Lawrence Vaughan was totally unfitted by his youth, education, training, character and temperament to have control over and to manage a large estate. Three generations of Palks – Sir Robert, Sir Lawrence, and Sir Lawrence Vaughan Palk – followed a familiar pattern in the rise and fall of many wealthy Victorian families. There is an old saying that the third generation makes the gentleman. F.M.L. Thompson, commenting on this piece of folklore, writes: 'Irrespective of the origins of a fortune there was a regular pattern of development, in which the sons of the founder continued to take some part, probably intermittent, in

21 *Torquay in 1832, a fashionable resort outclassing its former peer at Teignmouth. By the late 1820s regular coaches reached Torquay.*

the original business, and the grandsons severed themselves from it altogether.' This pattern fits the Palks. As a dynasty they are an interesting example of downward social mobility.

Sir Robert had acquired a large fortune in India and had even survived, for many did not, its torrid and unhealthy clime. He achieved this by his cleverness, hardwork, and by sheer grit. Returning to England he invested most of his wealth in land, as a result of which he acquired gentry status and his sons aristocratic pretensions. Sir Robert made the right moves. He was a shrewd man. On his road to riches in India he was forced to mix with all classes and races, with people of all sort and condition. But Lawrence his heir did not inherit his father's instinct for business nor his shrewd mind, and had not been greatly exposed to the hurly-burly of making a living, as his father had been. But Lawrence must have learned something merely from living and working at times with his father. He was, for example, involved in the early planning for the new resort and he certainly was no great spendthrift. His son, Lawrence Vaughan, was of a different species: he was a 'gentleman', with a gentleman's tastes and cast of mind – a member of Veblen's 'leisure class'. Matthew Arnold would have correctly termed him a Barbarian, a class whose attributes, according to Arnold, consisted principally in 'outward gifts and graces, in looks, manners, accomplishments, prowess'. The 3rd baronet had inherited an estate of 10,109 acres, including valuable lands at Torquay. This meant that his income could, within bounds, well support a gentlemanly and leisurely existence. So Lawrence, now Sir Lawrence Vaughan Palk, was destined to become a drone, as we would perhaps view him with our modern, more censorious eyes, for it is now a commonplace that all should work or make some contribution to society. In the early 19th century people saw things differently.

Except for one short break, the Palks represented the pocket borough of Ashburton from 1774, when Sir Robert took over the seat from the earls of Oxford, to the year 1831. Only freeholders at Ashburton having land and tenements in the town had the right to vote, and there were not many of them. Ashburton lost one of its two seats with the passing of the 1832 Reform Act and the other in 1867 when the town was finally disfranchised. Sir L.V. Palk, one of the MPs for Ashburton until 1831, did not distinguish himself as a parliamentarian. He has left behind no echo of his presence, for his interests lay outside the Commons. Like both his grandfather and father, he was a Tory; but he showed no great enthusiasm for politics and public affairs. A clubman at heart, he used the Commons, when in attendance, as a club rather than a debating chamber. He was bent on a life of pleasure.

If work was the curse of the drinking classes, as a wit remarked, then gambling was the curse of the upper classes. L.V. Palk inherited an estate in 1813 not overburdened with debt but one that needed careful husbanding and management, after the debts incurred by the 2nd baronet in establishing a sound harbour at Torquay. L.V. Palk took over estate account books that were in a muddle from his stewards, Abraham and Beard, when he reached his majority in 1814. Did he ever glance at them? Did he ever make an effort to understand their contents? But Lawrence had no aptitude for financial affairs and always left such matters in the hands of his agents, his stewards and lawyers. He was by nature a gambler, a gamester, a spender, as well as a great womaniser, also an expensive habit. He exhibited all the traditional vices, including drink. To put it euphemistically, he was a poor manager of money. Thus he fell into debt, slowly but ineluctably over the years. Threatened by the imminent approach of the tipstaff, the bum-bailiff, and the prospect of a spell in a debtors' prison, Lawrence was impelled to leave England in 1846 for Dieppe. Lawrence's debts could have been paid in full but that would have meant impoverishing the family estate, an entailed estate under strict family settlement. This could not be allowed. So Lawrence was destined to become an exile in France living on an exigent allowance.

For ten years Sir Lawrence was not seen in Torquay. But during that period Torquay grew rapidly under the aegis of his agent, William Kitson, who because of the prolonged absence of the chief landlord had sole control over Torquay's urban development. He was to do a remarkably good job and to create a most pleasing and fashionable resort.

Three

THE MAKING OF A RESORT

WRITING in 1861, the French historian Jules Michelet acclaimed Dr Richard Russell as: 'L'inventeur de la mer'. Russell, an English physician, had published in 1750, in Latin, a *Dissertation on the Use of Seawater in Diseases of the Glands*, a book which had an immense success with both lay public and members of the medical profession. The Latin first edition was soon followed by Russell's own English translation and by five editions of the pirated English text, all issued in the 1750s. The history of sea-bathing as a treatment for various disorders goes back to early times and was advocated by folk medicine – 'alternative medicine' as we now term it – as a remedy for scrofula and various skin conditions, most of which were then caused by dietary deficiencies or malnutrition. This practice was common in northern counties, above all in Yorkshire. But it was not as yet advertised as a beneficial treatment by orthodox medical practitioners. That was to come as Russell's fame spread across the land.

Russell succeeded in convincing his fellow doctors that sea-bathing – or simply being dipped in the sea – as well as imbibing sea-water (a practice regarded as analogous to drinking spa-water), were both therapeutic and prophylactic in their action. This belief encouraged the 'sea mania' of the 18th century, the vogue for travelling to and lodging in a coastal village or town where sea-water was close to hand. This fascination with the sea, with seascapes and storms – with nature in the raw – was also, from the 1770s onwards, stimulated by the rising tide of Romanticism, a movement which drew people to the scenes of nature and the picturesque, to wild landscapes – and what was wilder than the sea in stress?

Brighton by the end of the 18th century had become England's most fashionable resort, and was patronised by royalty in the portly shape of the Prince of Wales, later Prince Regent, who paid his first visit to Brighton in 1781. Soon the town became as celebrated for the life of pleasure it offered visitors as for the sea-water cure it purported to effect. Seaside resorts, like the older spas, found it necessary to supplement treatment with entertainments and diversions. Bath was the pioneer in this field with its assembly rooms, pump rooms, public rooms, and circulating libraries and its balls, soirees, theatres, and Master of Ceremonies, normally a portentous figure, who set the rules of behaviour. It was Beau Nash, the great regulator of conduct, who first developed this public role, at Bath.

Spas and resorts were places where intrigue was wont to flourish, where gentlemen sauntered and strutted and ogled and ladies flirted and blushed, had the megrims or the vapours and the lucky formed alliances with the opposite sex. A spa, in order to prosper, therefore needed to provide entertainment for both sexes and all ages, to encourage social life as much as medical treatments for the gout and other ailments. A spa needed to reduce the boredom necessarily attendant on the pursuit of medical regimens and hydropathic remedies and cures. Patients – invalids and hypochondriacs – needed 'jollying up' to some degree. The answer to that was a congenial and relaxing environment, so that sufferers would come to forget their woes.

The watering-place or inland spa, a gathering place which pre-dated the seaside resort proper, introduced the notion of a health cure away from home, for the sick, the hypochondriac, and even the obviously moribund. These cures included the drinking of water from local mineral springs and bathing in spa-water. By extension, the imbibing of sea-water and immersion in salt water became fashionable in the later 18th century and as a much touted cure was to overtake the spa in popularity, so that by the 1840s the older watering-place – the spa – had begun to decline in favour, whereas its rival, the seaside resort, with its particular natural 'cure', flourished. At one time both competed for the same clientèle – wealthy invalids, husband-seeking women, adventurers and adventuresses, and plain pleasure-seekers – but the race was won finally by the seaside resort, which became the predominant form of resort town in the second half of the 19th century. The sea, the seaside, sea-water and sea-air, all became associated in the Victorian mind with health and good spirits, and this association is still entrenched in the majority of minds. As Michelet observed, the seaside was essentially an invention of the English, and was then exported to other countries, in particular to France and North America. Brighton was the first important English seaside resort on the Channel coast, where resorts were to spring up throughout the 19th century, reaching westwards in Victorian times to Devon and Cornwall. Devon became the homeland of the so-called English Riviera, that is to say, Torbay and its environs.

Torquay does not fit neatly into this summary account of spas and watering-places, for a special type of sufferer at first was attracted to the town in the 19th century – the consumptive. Consumptives did not come for a sea-water cure. Torquay had no mineral springs with advertised medicinal properties; and in those days no sea-front. Sea-bathing as such could hardly have been the great attraction when the stony beaches of Beacon Cove and Meadfoot alone were available for the bather or dipper. As late as 1841, Dr Granville claimed 'Torquay ... offers no resources in the way of sea-bathing. Near it the coast is rugged and broken masses of red sandstone gird the sea'. Granville, of course, was writing before the Torbay Road had been constructed, thus opening up easy access to Torre sands, now the main bathing beach for visitors to the town.

We do not have accurate mortality and morbidity statistics for the 18th century; medical statistics for the 19th, although far better, need to be used with care. Social and medical historians agree, in the main, that pulmonary tuberculosis was a major cause of death, above all for young people, especially women, and that there was no effective treatment in those days, only spontaneous remission of the symptoms on occasion. Keats, who died at the early age of 25, symbolises the hopelessness of those so afflicted in the 19th century. Most died. Others lingered on to become chronic cases, never quite well enough to lead an active life. They remained in limbo till their eventual death. The well-off consumptive was drawn to Torquay because going there was less enervating than taking a long journey by sea and road to the Continent or some other warmer clime. Despite the poor condition of English roads, travelling along them by coach was preferred by sufferers from this debilitating, wasting disease. And so Torquay became their last resort because of its reputed Mediterranean climate. Charles Kingsley spoke of Torquay's 'delicious Italian climate'; Ruskin declared it was 'the Italy of England'. By 1850 Torquay had even earned the proud title of 'The Belle of Health Resorts'. It was also widely known as 'The Modern Montpellier'. Numerous other tribute are to be found in contemporary guidebooks. Torquay had, therefore, acquired a reputation for being a very healthy place. Dr Granville, a matter-of-fact fellow, quite brutally referred to it as 'the south western asylum of condemned lungs', perhaps at that time a fitting epitaph for the town. However, it should be emphasised that Torquay was not a summer but a winter retreat – 'a sort of winter Brighton', as one visitor commented. It became a haven for invalids because the town had acquired a reputation by the 1820s for very mild winters compared with most of the British Isles.

In spite of its lack of convenient facilities for bathing, the tubercular came in numbers to Torquay to seek a cure, a cure induced not by sea-water but a mild climate. In the early stages of tuberculosis, a contagious disease, bed rest, fresh air, and good food may effect a cure or stabilise the condition (it was the only efficacious method, generally speaking, until the introduction of chemotherapy in the 1950s); but the vast majority of those who ventured to Torquay in the early 19th century had left it too late. They were chronic cases, with damage to their lungs entrenched and irreversible. The journey to Torquay must also have had a weakening effect on invalids and the moribund sometimes came from remote places like Scotland.

The fact that TB patients chose Torquay in preference to other English towns in which to convalesce or achieve a cure, however forlorn that hope, tells us little about why or how the town originally acquired its reputation as a health resort. It was once generally believed that naval officers of the Channel Fleet brought their wives and families to Torbay during the Napoleonic wars and that they were the first to discover the district's special qualities – its great natural beauty, its mild climate, its vaunted sunshine and health-enhancing sea-air. This thesis has been strongly disputed by Percy Russell in his fine book on Torquay, who has brought forward a number of telling points to contradict it, arguments that demolish a well entrenched fiction, advanced by, among others, J.T. White in his 1878 history of the town, and repeated *ad nauseam* by lesser writers on Torbay. The myth seems to have originated in Blewitt's *Panorama of Torquay*, in which this passage may be found:

> About the close of the century, when Torbay became important as a naval rendezvous, the salubrious climate of Torquay appears to have attracted attention; and it is, we believe, from that period that we must date its rise and progress. When, therefore, subsequent observations had confirmed the testimony of public opinion in its favour, houses were erected for the accommodation of the invalids, who annually migrate from the colder parts of the Island to Devonshire.

The navy's influence on the rise of Torquay must have been small. Earl St Vincent, who commanded the British Channel Fleet, only stayed at Torre Abbey – George Cary was his kinsman – for a single winter, in 1800; and although he set up quarters at the Abbey, his real base was the port of Brixham where the fleet established most of its necessary shore facilities: there, his ships watered: near Berry Head was the Officers' Hospital, and at Goodrington, just to the south of Paignton, another hospital was constructed close to the beach; the navy also built a stone quay at Brixham for improving watering arrangements and victualling. No buildings, it seems, were erected at Torquay or nearby. No doubt some naval wives and families came to the little town, but one must remember there was a shortage of houses to rent in the area, hotels were practically non-existent and the few lodging-houses were mostly unappealing to well-brought-up wives and sisters.

The reasons for Torquay's growing popularity in the early 19th century are simple. Visitors at the turn of the century no doubt would have praised its mild winter climate, its unspoilt beauty and have recommended the place to friends and acquaintances as a delightful retreat: and so Torquay and Torbay became better known by a process of 'hearsay'. More and more people came to savour its special qualities; the demand for accommodation mounted and local people responded by making more available. Apart from the truce that followed the Treaty of Amiens – a short lull that only lasted from March 1802 to May 1803 – the English could not travel on the Continent. Their wanderlust was bottled up and could only find an outlet in journeying within the British Isles. Foreign parts were virtually closed to all but the intrepid.

Some comments on Devonshire resorts close to Torquay may throw further light on Torquay's own evolution. A decisive influence on Devonshire resorts was the arrival of royalty. Sidmouth, for example, was frequently visited, from 1809 onwards, by the nobility and in 1819-20 the Duke and Duchess of Kent, with their young daughter, the Princess Victoria, took up residence at Wood-brook Cottage; later the Duke of Connaught spent four years in Sidmouth. This put a stamp of royal approval on the seaside hamlet (for such it then was) and gave the place social cachet, a quality that attracted middle-class snobs.

Dawlish began to attract visitors in the early 1790s and Jane Austen knew and liked the place, but it was always eclipsed by Teignmouth, where Keats stayed and finished *Endymion* and where Fanny Burney much enjoyed herself. This ancient town began to attract visitors as early as the middle of the 18th century, but only became markedly fashionable as a resort at the turn of the century. It is, after Exmouth, the oldest resort in Devon. Construction of a bridge across the River Teign in 1825, linking Teignmouth with Shaldon, speeded its progress and at the same time benefited Torquay, for the bridge obviated the roundabout route – via Newton Abbot – that travellers between these towns once had to take.

Since George III introduced the fashion of visiting the seaside for health reasons numerous little resorts had sprung up to cater for health-seekers. But Torquay was not put on the map by a royal visitation or by residence in the

22 *Teignmouth, from the Ness. Teignmouth and Dawlish, nearer to London, had already become popular with invalids and hypochondriacs; with the building of wider turnpike roads, coaches were encouraged to venture further.*

23 *Babbacombe Bay and Watcombe, near Torquay. Visitors came to Torquay to discover its marvellous location, balmy climate and the great cliffs with their superb sea views.*

town by a royal personage, and the Princess Victoria did not visit it until 1833, when the place where she landed was renamed Victoria Parade. The answer to our original question as to how or why Torquay acquired its reputation as a watering-place is plausibly given by Granville:

> London and other doctors have been in the habit of recommending to those who cannot or choose not to go abroad, the same description of residence (i.e., the seaside) in all cases of individuals of consumptive habit. The particular spot designated for this purpose has varied from time to time, having extended west and south, farther and farther every eight or ten years; from Weymouth to Sydmouth [*sic*], from Sydmouth to Exmouth, and so on to Dawlish and Teignmouth, and lastly and now to Torquay.

Torquay, following after Teignmouth, was next on the list, as it were. Then visitors came to discover its marvellous location, balmy climate and its great cliffs with their superb sea views. One has only to read Edmund Gosse's *Father and Son* with its descriptions of Watcombe and Babbacombe in the 1850s to realise the great impact they must once have had on those in poor health, who came seeking peace and quiet. These factors far more than any naval presence during the Napoleonic Wars pushed Torquay into the limelight.

* * *

Dr Henry Beeke commanded the first phase of Torquay's development. The solicitor William Kitson (1800-83) the second phase – there was some overlapping of roles – when in 1833 he was put in charge of the Palk estate office, a position he occupied, with the help of his brother, until resigning in 1874. Kitson's mother was Robert Abraham's sister and nepotism probably played some part in the decision to appoint Kitson as the new agent, thus taking over the post formerly occupied by his uncle. The Kitsons originally came from Hengrave in Suffolk; but one of the family acquired Shiphay Manor, adjacent to Torre, in 1739, and a branch of the family took root in Devon. William, second son of the Revd William Kitson, was sent to Blundell's School, leaving in 1817 to study law in the Ashburton office of Robert Abraham. Working with his uncle must have familiarised him with the affairs of the Palk estates, of which his uncle was steward. The family had had a long connection with the Palks, for Abraham's grandfather had been Sir Robert Palk's maternal uncle and godfather, and his adviser long before Sir Robert became a rich man.

In 1823 Kitson began practising in Torquay and the firm was known as Messrs Abraham and Kitson, Attorneys-at-Law, though Kitson was really the senior member of the firm. His offices were at 10 Vaughan Parade but transferred to 1 Vaughan Parade in 1854 and are now at 3-4 Vaughan Parade. There were, in the 1820s, two rival solicitors in Torquay, James Cosserat and

Thomas Atkins, but Kitson soon outshone both, as neither left a great mark on Torquay. Abraham, who probably put up the money for the newly established office on the Strand, was mostly a sleeping partner, for he was kept busy running his Ashburton office and he continued to reside there.

Then Kitson became a banker. In 1832 he established the Torbay Bank, with rooms in his own law office at 10 Vaughan Parade. His partner was Edward Vivian, eight years his junior, whose family helped with financing the project. Banking was still a risky business in the 1830s. It is estimated that out of over 400 country banks established in the 18th century no fewer than 100 failed by 1782, and they continued to fail in considerable numbers well into the next century. But the Bank Act of 1832 to some degree helped in stabilising the banking system, an unsophisticated one to modern eyes. Before that date, embarrassed country bankers had to send panic messages to the Bank of England for gold when a run was on and customers were clamouring for their deposits. Now, for the first time, banknotes were made legal tender and they could be sent more expeditiously than gold to any bank under siege, a fact which allowed banks to discharge more speedily their obligations. In 1847 the Torbay Bank itself faced a nasty crisis following the collapse of a Newton Abbot bank; but Kitson survived. Eventually the Torbay Bank building was taken over by Lloyds, the great combine that evolved from the original Lloyd's Bank in Birmingham.

When his uncle Abraham died in 1833 Kitson was put in charge of the Palk estates. At later periods his brother Charles and his son acted jointly with him for he was always an exceedingly busy fellow. In the future, all was to go well with him; although socially Cary was the leading figure in Torquay, Kitson soon established himself as Torquay's most prominent citizen and the town's civic leader. Percy Russell claims that William Kitson (known as 'darning-needle' or 'penny bun' Kitson from his well known parsimonious habits) was already the leading businessman in Torquay by 1828. As director of the local Gas Company he ruled that to save money the lamps must not be lit on the night of a full moon. Unhappily, the full moon once fell on a Sunday in the middle of winter. It was a cloudy, misty night, visibility extremely poor. After Evensong the congregations pouring from Torquay's churches found themselves in almost pitch darkness. Pandemonium broke out as people blindly searched for their carriages or for members of their families. Afterwards, Kitson relented to some slight degree: henceforth, the superintendent and his staff were allowed at full moon to light the company's lamps if weather conditions made this necessary. Kitson was a man who always believed in making small economies whenever practicable; he hated any waste of money, and in this he differed vastly from most of the Palks, whom he regarded as senseless spendthrifts. His career may be summarised in Ogden Nash's cynical couplet: 'Professional people have no cares. Whatever happens they get theirs'.

Abraham had been called the steward of the Palk estates: Kitson's title was that of land agent for the property. F.M.L. Thompson writes: '... the "steward" of £150 to £300 a year became the "agent" of £750 to £1,000 a year.' But Kitson was more than a mere agent: he pursued three professions: law, banking, and estate management. He was also Palk's auditor although in no way a trained accountant as we now understand the word. In Victorian England there were many solicitors who acted as land agents or bailiffs as they were originally termed; but in fact most were no more than receivers, for they lacked any professional training in land management. Kitson was in a better position since at an early age he had acquired intimate knowledge of the Palk estates from his uncle, Robert

24 *William Kitson. He pursued three professions: law, banking and estate management; he was also Palk's auditor. He became known as the man who made Torquay.*

Abraham, and there were close ties between the families. Once he was instituted agent for the estate, he was to suffer little interference from Sir L.V. Palk who was somewhat lackadaisical about financial affairs so long as he received a steady income. This combination of professions or roles was very much to Kitson's benefit – that is obvious – but it can be criticised as morally ambiguous in its particular context. Sir L.V. Palk's heir complained in the 1840s that Kitson was leasing villa sites too cheaply and yet, in his role as banker, making profitable loans to lessee builders.

Before we examine the important part Kitson played in Torquay's development, we should continue with the saga of Sir L.V. Palk, for the story of his ups and downs throws light also on the way Kitson operated in his three professions and on his handling of the Palk estates and the family itself. By 1841 Sir L.V. Palk's affairs were in a mess and in December 1844 he was forced by his financial circumstances to execute a comprehensive settlement with his solicitors, Kennaway and Kitson, by which they were to act as trustees and managers to the estate. In sum, this meant that he was put on a fixed allowance and the major portion of his income was retained by his trustees to meet outstanding debts and for other purposes. By this settlement his eldest son, Lawrence, and a few other members of the family were provided with fixed annuities on which to exist in some comfort. By the end of 1846 Palk's finances were again in a parlous state. Kitson speeded up the sale of land at Chapel to the South Devon Railway Company, which they needed for their line from Newton Abbot to Torre, and with the proceeds Palk fled abroad with his wife, Anna Eleanor. They went to Dieppe. J.T. White, the author of the first detailed account of Torquay's history, published in 1878, is reticent about these events and merely states that the baronet resided abroad 'for many years'; but White could hardly relate the true facts about the exiled baronet since the Palks were still the leading family in and the major landowners of Torquay.

Dieppe became very popular with the English after 1815, when this old medieval city and port was developed into an attractive seaside resort. Soon a small English colony took root and a British Consul was appointed. Dieppe was reputed to be a very cheap place to live in and for this reason alone appealed to those on short commons. Sir L.V. Palk and his wife were short of cash, but his wife was not to be so for long, for she died in January 1846 shortly after arriving in the town. Her husband was now alone in licentious France and, as usual, got himself into trouble. The source of his future predicament was probably the casino, which had opened its doors to the public in the summer of 1822 and attracted the attentions of English gamblers, of whom he was one. In June 1848 Palk inevitably complained to Kennaway that he was 'perfectly destitute'. Palk, financially, was now on his last legs and there are, perhaps, sound reasons for the fix he found himself in.

Sir L.V. Palk had remarried. Neither Sir Bernard Burke nor any Victorian compiler of *Peerages* mentions this fact. This was certainly a *mésalliance* for why else should this event have been suppressed – expunged – by so many genealogists? All we can deduce is that Palk had set up house in Paris with Phillipine-Anne-Victoire; and, as a consequence, had run up debts, for his yearly allowance was only £2,000, not enough for a spender like Palk.

The baronet lingered on in France for a few years, a broken man. His eldest son, the future Lord Haldon, was enraged by his father's follies and in the autumn of 1858 took legal steps to have him declared a lunatic and incarcerated in a private asylum, of which there were then many in England, and where inconvenient relatives could be nicely sequestrated and forgotten. Kennaway and Kitson stopped this move by relinquishing their trusteeship and agreeing to the appointment of trustees more to Lawrence Palk's liking. This satisfied the heir, but Kitson was still retained as the family solicitor. Arrangements were then made to bring the widowed, infirm father back to England to be placed in the care of one of his daughters.

He returned to Haldon House in 1857, after more then ten years of exile. Shortly afterwards, he presented himself to his tenantry and then paid a much-advertised visit to Torquay where he was received, local newspapers inform us, with great acclamation and much cheering. A public address was presented to him outside Torre Station by five of his old tenants. Then a procession formed and moved on, headed by a large banner on which were blazoned the words: 'Welcome Sir L.V. Palk to Torquay'. Included in the procession were the sub-steward, George Pearce, aged 89, the Drum and Fife Band of the Torquay National Schools and the Torquay Subscription Band. Then came the ageing Sir Lawrence, like a returned Bourbon, in a carriage drawn by four greys. Sitting with him were the Revd Wilmot Palk, his uncle, and, oddly in the circumstances, the two solicitors, Mark Kennaway and William Kitson, who were no doubt wryly amused by the proceedings, for they knew the background story. Tradesmen, two abreast, preceded the carriage and also mounted tradesmen (perhaps a better class of retailer?). It seems that the long procession included representatives from all social groups and occupations, a cross-section of Torquay's population. Down Union Street the celebrants went, to stop at the Town Hall, from a window of which hung a silk banner bearing the arms of Torwood and Torre – a nice touch – and the inscription 'Union is Strength', a reference of course to the Palk and Cary families. The procession then moved down the street to the Strand, where speeches were delivered from the balcony of the *Royal Hotel*. Much cheering broke out among the assembled landsmen and from the ships in the harbour. It must have been a memorable day for the citizens of Torquay. Sir Lawrence Vaughan Palk's odyssey was now over. He had come safe to port. It was a remarkable day altogether. The old buck – the old roué – was home at last, if not totally reformed now at least quiescent, under heavy chaperonage. Until he died at Haldon House on 16 May 1860 he appears to have led an exemplary life. His gambling days were over.

* * *

Kitson had been in charge of the Palk estates since 1833, when his uncle Abraham died, and his power grew when Sir L.V. Palk was forced to abscond from England in 1846. He was the virtual, or de facto, master of the estate for the ostensible landowner was so troubled by his penurious (in his eyes!) situation that he rarely interfered in business affairs, except at times to write petulant letters home. When Kitson had declined to meet his draft for £100, Palk wrote back that this refusal had deprived him (Palk) 'of all Character for Honour and Uprightness'. This is typical of his style of writing. Kitson was also widely accepted in the town as the Squire of Torquay, for he headed nearly every important committee and his position seemed unassailable; only the 4th baronet, Sir Lawrence Palk, it seems, stood up to him. When Sir L.V. Palk died it was discovered he had mortgaged property to the value of over £118,000 mostly for his own use, borrowed money on which the estate was paying four per cent annually. There were no ways by which these mortgages could be liquidated except by the sale of lands, and that was out. Sir Lawrence was to inherit this burden and so, too, was his heir.

Victorians had mixed feelings about the law's practitioners: attorneys, notaries, solicitors, lawyers, and the rest. Dickens in *The Old Curiosity Shop* depicted with relish the rascally Sampson Brass and his beastly sister Sally; and in *Bleak House* we come across the sinister, insinuating Tulkinghorn. Philip Collins in his *Dickens and Crime* cautions that:

> Neither Parliament nor the Law was quite as bad as Dickens intemperately thought, but again he expresses the common man's view. Lawyers, as a profession, neither warm the heart nor excite the admiration of the great British public ... His friend Douglas Jerrold was writing well within this popular tradition, when he said that 'Turkey has her eunuchs, Russia her Cossacks, and England her attorneys'.

The reason for this ambivalence was, I believe, that people knew full well that solicitors were privy to family secrets and sometimes with stigmatising details of their lives: solicitors (or attorneys as they were commonly called in those days) as a class were feared and often distrusted, for the home was regarded by Victorians as a sacrosanct private domain. Moreover, the language of law was obscure – so arcane, so opaque – that few laymen could understand the meaning of legal documents they read; as a consequence, bewildered clients supposed they were likely to be humbugged by smooth-tongued solicitors who hoped to inflate their fees with yet more hocus-pocus. However, in the annals of crime we discover that the commonest crime committed by solicitors – white-collar criminals – was embezzlement of a client's money, forgery or fraud, and in the eyes of the propertied classes these were always seen as peculiarly heinous offences since they tended to undermine the institution of property; moreover, such crimes were seen as a serious betrayal of trust, destructive of the confidence which should exist between lawyer and client.

There is no attempt here to impugn Kitson's reputation for honesty. The preceding paragraph was designed to stress the strategic position solicitors occupied in society, certainly in early Victorian England, and which they could use to their financial advantage: law could be a most lucrative profession, for all people of wealth necessarily had recourse to them at times. Similarly, from Tudor times judges as a group did particularly well, not a few acquired great fortunes and were able to establish their sons as members of the gentry or aristocracy. In South Devon we have the example of the Yarde-Bullers (Lords Churston) of Lupton House and Churston Court, whose fortunes derived from the 18th-century eminent lawyer and judge, Sir Francis Buller. In 1883 the 1st Lord Churston owned over 10,000 acres in Devon and Cornwall.

Kitson's three coterminous professions of law, estate management, and banking have been mentioned; but, after 1832, it was the last that transformed this ambitious young solicitor into Torquay's leading businessman. But one should remember that in Victorian England solicitors, as well as bankers, often advanced money on mortgage to builders direct. H.J. Dyos refers to '... that discreet civilian figure, the solicitor, whose financial operations were sometimes vital in maintaining him [the speculative builder] at the front ... Lending on mortgage was the passive, safe-as-houses, five percent, way of taking part [in building]; going into the land market, getting some suburban land ripe for development, making it go, was the active, all-or-nothing way of doing so'.

As Torquay grew and prospered, so too did the Torbay Bank. So many of its new residents were wealthy rentiers or people of substance: there was a flow of funds into the town and bank deposits tended to rise over time at a steady pace. The booms and slumps of the Victorian age, a dread cycle that afflicted tradesmen and workers above all, did have an impact on Torbay, but was rarely as cataclysmic in its results as in the industrial Midlands and the North.

Kitson, who had almost unrestricted control over the Palk estate, largely determined where building was to take place, and what type and quality of housing should be sanctioned. There was, at that time, no working-class housing contemplated in the Palk manors of Tormohun, Torwood, or Ilsham. Kitson was the man who planned and directed the processes of urban development. On behalf of the absent Sir L.V. Palk he administered the granting of leases and the sale of sites and it was his bank – the Torbay Bank – that raised money for 52 mortgages and supplied credit to the numerous developers, builders, and sub-contractors active in Torquay. The Palks did not own a fragmented or dispersed estate but a large block of land – the manors of Torre, Torwood and Ilsham – and had no need to relinquish freehold rights to land, unlike some landowners in other developing towns who had only a series of dispersed plots to lease or sell, not plots over which they could easily enforce covenants relating to the type of housing to be put up. Sir L.V. Palk, or rather his agent Kitson, wished to influence all subsequent development by retaining the title to land and by encouraging building as the resort became fashionable. Kitson wished to augment the value of land and, its corollary, housing. This meant that quality was of the utmost importance in a town where the wealthy congregated. The type of housing permitted must be clearly specified in the leases he granted, although of course certain land was allocated for shops, churches, public buildings and other necessary appurtenances of a town. Kitson wanted no cheap or jerry-built houses in Torquay. As a banker he was greatly to profit from the sale of leaseholds rather than freeholds. He was in a happy situation. While the Palks waned, Kitsons waxed, though this was not known to the generality. We should add to Kitson's curriculum vitae his fourth avatar, that of accountant, for, together with Mark Kennaway of Exeter, his firm audited the Palk estate accounts and exercised a tight control

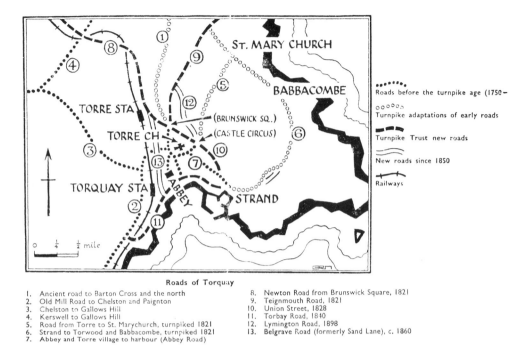

Roads of Torquay

1. Ancient road to Barton Cross and the north
2. Old Mill Road to Chelston and Paignton
3. Chelston to Gallows Hill
4. Kerswell to Gallows Hill
5. Road from Torre to St. Marychurch, turnpiked 1821
6. Strand to Torwood and Babbacombe, turnpiked 1821
7. Abbey and Torre village to harbour (Abbey Road)
8. Newton Road from Brunswick Square, 1821
9. Teignmouth Road, 1821
10. Union Street, 1828
11. Torbay Road, 1840
12. Lymington Road, 1898
13. Belgrave Road (formerly Sand Lane), c. 1860

25 *The creation of Torquay's roads infrastructure: a new Dartmouth, Torquay and Shaldon Consolidated Turnpike Trust was formed in 1821.*

over the estate finances, especially when Sir L.V. Palk was marooned in France for over a decade.

Local government was also effectively dominated by Kitson for over a quarter of a century. He was the chairman of the Select Vestry, a type of appointed parish council, which appears to have been set up around 1815 and about whose operations not much is known; for only one document relating to its work appears to have survived. John Pike writes that 'in some areas the Select Vestry was synonymous with a select band of rogues who appointed themselves for life'; but he optimistically concludes: 'It is however unlikely that this appertained locally when one reads the list of the early vestry.' This body functioned as the organ of local government until 1835, when the adoption of the Improvements Act was approved. Kitson's firm of solicitors promoted the change and he was appointed the first chairman of the Improvements Commission, a position he occupied until the granting of much wider powers under the Public Health Act of 1848; again Kitson acted as chairman and continued to do so until he resigned voluntarily in 1860. The Commissioners had found that the provisions of the former Improvements Act were too limited in scope for the needs of a rapidly expanding Torquay. When Kitson withdrew as agent for the Palk estates in 1874 the senior magistrate March Phillips declared in a testimonial speech:

Mr William Kitson took over the administration of the manor at a critical time; when a guiding hand was needed to direct and encourage improvement, and in a variety of ways to advance the interests of the town. To Mr Kitson's discrimination, foresight and judgement should be ascribed whatever attractions art has conferred on the town … In short, Mr William Kitson had before him the building up of a new town. How far he had succeeded, those who knew Torquay forty years ago could best testify.

The creation of Torquay's infrastructure – its permanent and costly installations, such as roads – was again mainly of Kitson's doing. Sir Lawrence, the 2nd baronet, was persuaded by a friend to build a new road to Newton Abbot and there join up with the county's main road system. Newton Abbot already had links, over the Haldon Hills, with Exeter, with Totnes and Ashburton and other points west, and with Teignmouth. The new road constructed, west of Chapel Hill, displaced the ancient ridge road from Torre village by Barton Cross, Haccombe (where the Carew family resided) and Milber Down. This had been maintained by the Keybury Turnpike Trust, formed by an Act of Parliament around 1765, but the Trust had been unable to keep it in good repair. A new Dartmouth, Torquay Turnpike and Shaldon Consolidated Trust was formed in 1821, but most of the work on the district roads took place after 1826. In 1827 the Shaldon Toll bridge was opened, which brought the road from Teignmouth into Maidencombe and then followed the line of the Fleet stream from Combe Pafford down into Torquay proper. Percy Russell writes: 'These two roads, from Teignmouth and from Newton Abbot, were of great importance to the rising watering place of Torquay and were regularly used by coaches and by carriers.' The Trustees then made an entirely new road, the cutting of Upper and Lower Union Street, from the junction of the Newton and Barton roads, north of Torre

26 *Torquay from Park Hill. The great oaks had been cut down for ships' masts during the war with France. Kitson involved himself with the planning of the Warberry and Park Hill sections of the town.*

27 *Vane Tower Villa. During the 1860s villas of various styles were built on Park Hill, where there were limestone quarries. Vane Tower Villa, buit in 1871, was a copy of an Italian villa on the shore of Lake Lugano.*

village, which met the Flete stream at Castle Circus. The perambulating Flete stream was then culverted over; extended to the harbour, these two roads – Union and Fleet Street – now bisected Torquay town. They became the main shopping streets, and still are.

The firm of Abraham and Kitson were the first clerks of the Torquay Turnpike Trust; but Kitson, not Abraham, was the person most involved with the detailed planning of the road system and with supervision of the work being carried out. Kitson also involved himself with the planning of new residential districts – the Warberry, Braddon, and Park Hill sections of the town. As well as that, he was active in promoting the putting up of public buildings and churches and in generally beautifying the place: all this was achieved of course in the name of the principal landowner of Torquay – one or other of the Palks. The commemorative plaque put up by the Torquay Civic Society on the front of 2 Vaughan Parade reads: 'The home and offices of William Kitson 1800-1883. solicitor, land agent, local authority chairman, banker and churchwarden. THE MAKER OF TORQUAY.' That Kitson largely 'made' Torquay is beyond dispute.

Four

RELIGION AND POLITICS

T HE early Victorians in the main were a church- and chapel-going people and zealous sabbatarians. Compared with us, more often than not they were excited and exalted by religious controversy and doctrinal disputes. For them, religion was not the opium of the people but a stimulus to thought and passion. Later in the century the picture changed when a general loss of belief among Victorians occurred, a loss which affected particularly the educated classes, and this gave rise to the questioning of orthodox religion and the tenets of Anglicanism. The Church was forced on the defensive. After 1900, fewer churches and chapels were built; and congregations in some places, particularly cities, started slowly to decline.

In 1800 Torquay had two churches – St Saviour's, the parish church of Torre, and St Marychurch, from which the parish took its name. Tormohun's population was small so there was not much demand for extra stalls or seating at St Saviour's. The 14th-century St Marychurch at that time was in poor condition and had been much patched up and altered over the years, but was large enough for the size of its congregation.

A demand for new churches, and chapels-of-ease, grew steadily in the 1830s and 1840s, the decades when the town became popular as a place of residence and its population much expanded. This need was especially felt in central Torquay, for that was the district the Palks were steadily developing, laying out roads and building terraces and villas up the hills. Both Torre and St Marychurch were some distance from the harbour area – the focal point of the new town – and pedestrians found the older churches sometimes inconvenient to reach since most of Torquay was hilly. Even those fortunate enough to own a private carriage could not always drive comfortably to church since many roads were pitted, some even rutted, and the level stretch of the Torbay Road, skirting the shore from the Strand to Livermead, a convenient route to Torre, had yet to be constructed.

Before commenting on Church of England foundations, some account should be given of the places of worship of other denominations. In the 18th century, the local community of Roman Catholics attended mass at Torre Abbey, for Torquay had no Catholic church. However, as a result of the Catholic Relief Act of 1778, George Cary (III) was now permitted to convert the old monastic guest hall into a chapel for his co-religionists. Before the Act, the practice of Catholicism in Torbay had always been a hugger-mugger affair and the Cary family had been obliged illegally to construct a secret garret chapel in which to celebrate mass at the Abbey, to which the Catholic faithful discreetly came. The Carys always employed a resident chaplain (a practice common among Catholic gentry) and in the early 19th century he was Father MacEnery, an enthusiastic amateur geologist and a celebrated pioneer explorer of Kent's Cavern, at that time owned by the Palks, who had railed off its entrance to prevent vandals from despoiling its contents. At first, Father MacEnery's paleolithic finds were displayed in cabinets at the Abbey but later, after they had been moved to a succession of homes, they were transferred finally to the Natural History Museum in Babbacombe Road, built in 1875, where they are to be seen today.

In 1853, a Catholic church – the Church of the Assumption – was erected in Abbey Road on a small plot, on ground then covered with a plantation of beech trees. The site – part of the Torre Abbey estate – was the gift of Robert Cary, scion of one of Devonshire's most ancient Catholic families, and now the patron and leading representative in Torbay of the Catholic community. Cary also gave land for a church – The Church of Our Lady – at St Marychurch, a parish of which he was the chief landowner. This is an impressive building, with its lofty spire rivalling that of the nearby Anglican parish church, and it can be seen from a great distance. At that time the majority of Catholic parish priests in the West Country were Irish or of Irish extraction, poor exiles in an anti-papist England. They formed a kind of ecclesiastical underclass and were obliged to subsist on a pittance, for their Church had been stripped of its wealth at the Reformation and its properties sequestrated and sold. The Catholic Church remained poor in England and only grew richer later in the 19th century when the Catholic revival took place, greatly encouraged by the ultramontane Cardinal Manning. Beneficed Anglican clergy, and even curates, lived comfortable lives compared with the majority of Catholic priests.

In the West Country, Catholic communities were typically small in size and were usually served by a parish priest who had to spend much time visiting a number of scattered congregations, to which he would bring the Blessed Sacrament. Only Plymouth and Exeter could boast of substantial numbers of Catholic communicants. At mid-century, it follows, the county of Devonshire was still overwhelmingly Protestant, Anglican and Nonconformist in complexion: Catholics were few, and had to put up with much prejudice and hostility, and abuse from Protestant bigots and zealots.

The Anglo-Jewish community was also represented in Torquay, although, again, in comparatively small numbers. Most were in business or the professions; a few were retired people or rentiers. Their synagogue, later in the century, was in Abbey Road, at the former Congregational church, a building erected in 1853, which at one time served as the Nonconformist British School, then was converted into a synagogue. Expelled from England in 1290 by Edward I, Jews were formally readmitted by Cromwell in 1655, but long before that date many Jews had been living covertly in England. Most appear to have been Sephardi Jews of Spanish or Portuguese descent who had come to England from Amsterdam. A Plymouth congregation was founded as far back as 1754, when a Jewish cemetery was also opened in the city. The synagogue, built at Plymouth in 1762, is one of the oldest Ashkenazi houses of worship still standing in the English-speaking world.

We do not have figures for Torquay's Jewish community but we do know that the town became a place of residence for several wealthy Jewish families. Probably the best known is Disraeli's fervent admirer, Mrs Brydges Willlyams, an elderly widow of Jewish extraction, the daughter of a certain Abraham da Costa of Bath. Mrs Willyams, who died in 1861, left Disraeli about £30,000 in her will in recognition, she wrote, of his 'work in elevating the Anglo-Jewish community in the eyes of the world'. She was devoted to Disraeli: she also had, it seems, an obvious *tendresse* for the great man.

In Devon the most distinguished and influential Jewish family was probably the Lopes. Its founder was Sir Manasseh Masseh Lopes (1755-1831), a descendant of an ancient and opulent Portuguese family from Jamaica. He was a Christian convert, of necessity, for Jews were only admitted to the House of Commons as late as 1858 and Sir Manasseh's ambition was to enter Parliament and join the ranks of the landed gentry. In 1819 he was accused of electoral corruption – a common enough practice in pre-Reform days and to which little stigma was attached – tried at Exeter, convicted, fined £1,000, and sentenced to two years' imprisonment. But this mishap did not seriously impede his public career for on his release from gaol he was again returned for the pocket borough of Westbury – a borough very much in his own 'pocket' – despite the fact that its electors did not care much for him; and he only relinquished it in 1829 in order to provide Peel with a safe seat after his rejection by the University of Oxford.

When he died in 1831, childless but very rich, he left £800,000 in Government and East-India stock to his nephew, on condition that he changed his name from Franco to Lopes. The second baronet, Sir Ralph Lopes (1788-1854), became a prominent Devonshire figure as MP for South Devon from 1849 to 1854; and his son, Sir Massey Lopes (1818-1908) followed in his wake. Perhaps it is wrong to speak of Sir Massey as Jewish for by a process of assimilation he, like his father, became anglicised and he had also married into a local gentry family. Sir Ralph married Elizabeth, daughter of Sir Ralph Trehawke Kekewich of Exeter and his heir, Sir Massey, in 1854 married Bertha, only daughter of Sir John Yarde Buller, who was raised to the peerage in 1858 as Baron Churston. The Lopes family became renowned in South Devon for their philanthropy and, most notably, for their generous donations to the young University College of Exeter (now Exeter University). Sir Moses Montefiore (1784-1885), whose ancestors were also Portuguese Jews, was the most prominent 19th-century Anglo-Jewish philanthropist and led the campaign to remove Jewish disabilities; but in South Devon it was the Lopes family who were always celebrated for their munificence.

It should be stressed that in the 19th century the Anglo-Jewish community, although small, formed an important component of English cultural and economic life with its support for and involvement in artistic endeavours, music and painting in particular, and it was strongly Anglophile. A significant number of Jews were engaged in banking, finance, and stockbroking, as well as commerce and trade. With their more cosmopolitan outlook, Jews also helped to diminish English insularity, so strong an element in Victorian England. In most cases their families had come from Europe and they usually maintained contact with a network of relations and friends there.

Dissent and Nonconformity had established strong roots in Devon. Puritanism, for example, had attracted much support not only from farmers, husbandmen, craftsmen, and artisans but from prominent county families like the Fortescues, Strodes, and Yardes. W.G. Hoskins states that 'Devon as a whole had become one of the mostly firmly protestant counties in England within two or three generations of "the great commotion" of 1549'. Yet Charles Wesley, the great apostle of 'enthusiasm' as the instrument by which to re-awaken and revive a flagging Anglican Church, did not achieve much from his missionary labours in Devon. It was only much later, in the 1850s and 1860s, that Methodism began to flourish in the county.

Although there is no mention in Wesley's *Journals* of his having visited the Torquay district, oral tradition insists that he preached at St Marychurch on several occasions and that he held meetings at Barton at the home of one of his followers. George Whitefield, another pioneer of what became called Wesleyan Methodism – a coalescence of a number of 18th-century evangelical bodies – also visited the district and attempted to spread the word; but Wesleyanism, or Methodism, did not flourish in South Devon until the mid-Victorian period. Wesleyans worshipped at first in the Union Hall, but in 1873 a large Wesleyan church was built in Babbacombe Road, just above the Torquay Natural History Museum; and in 1877 they erected a Chapel in Lower Union Street.

By the turn of the century Torquay had a remarkable number of churches, chapels, and meeting-places, representative of almost the entire spectrum of Victorian creeds and faiths though, needless to say, the size of the respective congregations tended to vary markedly. Little space can be given to these disparate churches and groups – for example, Pentecostals, Bible Christians, Primitive Methodists or Baptists, Unitarians and Friends – but one sect should be singled out: the Plymouth Brethren. Like the Mormons, they called themselves 'Saints', which suggests they knew not what hubris was.

In Torquay there was one notable family of Saints: the Gosse family. In 1852 Philip Gosse and his family came to Torquay and he was to reside there for over thirty years. He was a distinguished man of science, an eminent marine zoologist and writer, whose son Edmund was also to become a celebrated man of letters and the author of the masterpiece, *Father and Son*, the book which describes life with his father, an uneasy relationship at best, and it also includes a vivid picture of Babbacombe. Edmund was not a great poet but 'In The Bay' speaks of his youth: 'When full of life and youth and careless mind / We dashed and shouted in the sunlit bay.' These lines express something of his feeling for sparkling Babbacombe Bay. His father was a fundamentalist Christian who was unable to reconcile the growing scientific evidence in support of the evolutionary hypothesis which appeared to undermine the biblical account of Creation. Unable to reconcile science and religion, he lived in a considerable state of intellectual and emotional tension.

Gosse lived in a small villa at Oddicombe (close by Babbacombe) and there he continued with his researches into marine life and with his writing. A small body of Plymouth Brethren resided in the village or in the neighbourhood and they met for worship in a room above a stable; the room was called by them the 'Public Room' (their word for a chapel). In this room was enacted their Sunday communion service. Philip Gosse was appointed its administrator. At that time, his son tells us, the Torquay Brethren included 'jobbing gardeners and journeymen carpenters, masons and tailors, washerwomen and domestic servants'; also 'peasants', by which he must have meant poor farmers or smallholders. In later days the Saints attracted to their congregation a few 'retired professional men, an admiral, even the brother of a peer'. The sect, which by then had split into two (the Exclusive Brethren and the Open Brethren) had another Public Room in Warren Road, Torquay. Over the years their membership became more exclusive, respectable, and middle-class, which tended to happen with some other sects, such as the Quakers.

The name has little significance for it derives from the accident that the first congregation was formed in Plymouth in 1831. The Brethren were evangelical in spirit and made no distinction between clergy and laity; and the Open Brethren, in particular, resisted any idea of a central authority. The sect came into being as the result of the activities of a number of pious evangelical Anglicans who wanted to distance themselves from High Church principles, from the dead world of formalism.

Philip Gosse made a living from writing popular accounts of marine life, for which Victorians had an insatiable appetite, as they also had for natural history in general. Father and son often worked side by side exploring the rock pools which then were plentiful along the shores of Babbacombe Bay and Torbay. Gosse would describe and illustrate his findings in works such as *A Naturalist's Rambles on the Devon Coast* (1853) and *A Year at the Shore* (1864). These sold very well and were popular. And so he became known to a wider public as an explorer of the sea-shore and a describer of its miracles. He may be compared today with a travel writer who by extolling the charms of some remote secret place leads to its future destruction by hordes of holiday makers.

The Revd Charles Kingsley, a great admirer and friend of Philip Gosse, and influenced by him, also published a number of books on natural history. Thus he, too, inadvertently encouraged the spoliation of Torbay's numerous rock pools. Kingsley's wife in 1853 suffered a bad miscarriage and her doctor advised wintering in salubrious South Devon. And so they came to Torquay, where they rented Livermead House from Charles Mallock, and stayed there for much of the following year. Livermead House, situated just above the beach, was an ideal place for convalescence and for studying marine life, and husband and wife spent many happy hours exploring the long narrow strip of beach and neighbouring sands and coves. One result was a long article entitled 'The Wonders of the Shore', an enthusiastic, appreciative review of a number of Gosse's works. Soon after, the article was expanded into a book for children celebrating the miracles of nature. It was called *Glaucus: or the Wonders of the Shore*. Published in 1855, it soon became extremely popular not only with children but with the general reading public and went into numerous editions. One passage from it should be quoted for it provides a vivid description of Torbay in the 1850s:

> Follow us, then, reader, in imagination, out of the gay watering place [Torquay], with its London shops and London equipages, along the broad road beneath the sunny limestone cliffs, tufted with golden furze; past the huge oaks and green slopes of Tor Abbey; and past the fantastic rocks of Livermead, scooped by the waves into a labyrinth of double and triple caves, like Hindoo temples, upborne on pillars banded with yellow and white and red, a week's study, in form and colour and chiaroscuro, for any artist; and a mile or so further along a pleasant road, with land locked glimpses of the bay, to the broad sheet of sand which lies between the village of Paignton and the sea …

Charles Darwin, whose epochal work, *The Origin of Species by Means of Natural Selection* (1859), so rattled the Victorian orthodox, especially evangelicals and fundamentalists, and caused Gosse, inevitably, so much spiritual perturbation by implying that the biblical account of Creation was a fairy tale, arrived in Torquay on 1 July 1861. He stayed there with his family for eight weeks, at No 2, Hesketh Crescent, Meadfoot; but he did not, it seems, disturb Torbay's miraculous rock pools. He was not engaged in field-work of any type and was mostly preoccupied with revising his great book and with preparing a paper on the fertilisation of orchids for a scientific journal. It is not known whether he met Gosse during his stay, although he must have been well aware of

Gosse's numerous publications on marine biology. Darwin from early days suffered from certain psychosomatic or nervous ailments – he was a great hypochondriac – and the main reason for his coming to Torquay was his health. Some time before his visit he wrote to a friend: 'I believe I shall have to go soon for some winter cure. I cannot sleep and my heart is almost palpitating.' The family elected to go to Torquay: the resort had, by this time, acquired a reputation as a marvellously quiet place for invalids, above all for those who stayed at one or other of the many villas scattered over its hills and slopes, and remote Meadfoot, an area adjacent to the sea, was greatly esteemed as a haven of repose. From the gardens fronting the curved row of houses at Hesketh Crescent one looked right across the bay.

* * *

The Anglican Church was dominant in Torquay – in numbers, in wealth, and in social prestige, as was usually the case in nearly all watering-places and resorts, places where middle- and upper-class residents were plentiful. Worth's *Tourist's Guide to Devonshire* (the 1886 edition) declared of Torquay that 'in proportion to its population [it is] the wealthiest town in England'. In Victorian England those who were rich, or had achieved that happy state, tended to attach themselves to the Establishment, to the Established Church, for membership in that institution was taken as a sign of respectability: but there were conspicuous exceptions among the better-off: such as the Quakers with their chocolate-manufacturing millionaires and bankers, and also Scots Presbyterians, who tended to remain loyal to their austere Church.

The history of Anglicanism in Devonshire, and in the Torbay area in particular, was overshadowed in Victorian times by the towering presence of Henry Phillpotts, nominated to the See of Exeter in 1830. Bishop Phillpotts, it is worth mentioning, was a good friend of the Palk family and of their old advisor, Dr Henry Beeke, whose career has been discussed earlier. In 1830, the Bishop came to reside in Exeter, in the medieval Episcopal Palace, which is situated on the south side of the choir, near the old chapter house. The Palace was then in a dilapidated, rather tumble-down condition and it suited neither the Bishop's sense of dignity nor his ideas of comfort (much of the structure was later rebuilt by him); so he removed firstly to a rented villa at Teignmouth and then in 1840 to Torquay, where he commissioned a local architect named Gribble to build him a grand house at Babbacombe, on a site behind Anstey's Cove. This new house had extensive grounds, which sloped upwards to wooded cliffs, about 200 feet above sea level, that overlooked the cove.

This palatial villa he appropriately called Bishopstowe (now the *Palace Hotel*) and he resided there, apart from necessary visits to Exeter or the House of Lords, until his death in 1869. The Bishop's presence in Torquay meant that its inhabitants were often at the centre of a storm, for he was

28 *Bishop Henry Phillpotts. The history of Anglicanism in Devonshire, and in the Torbay area in particular, was overshadowed in Victorian times by his towering presence.*

often irritable and acerbic, combative when the dogmas and privileges of the Church were under attack, and despotic with his clergy. Clergymen, especially those inclined to low church beliefs, to evangelicalism, came to fear his wrath and his thunder. They feared his intrusion into parish affairs. Bishop Phillpotts was a frightening man to confront and the weak and the supine shuddered before him. He was inclined, like an enraged bull, to rush straight into a fray, knocking people aside with his furious partisanship; moreover, equipped with a most powerful mind and acute reasoning powers, he was a superb controversialist. He relished having his own way; he relished exercising authority. A small man – so too were Napoleon and General Montgomery – he liked to make his presence felt, as small men often do. Sydney Smith, although disagreeing with him over most things, confessed in a letter to Lady Grey: 'the Rogue [Phillpotts] is a sensible agreeable man.'

Henry Phillpotts was born at Bridgwater, Somerset, in 1778. A few years later his father removed to Gloucester, where he kept the *Bell Inn* and at the same time acted as land agent to the Dean and Chapter of Gloucester Cathedral. The young Henry, after attending Gloucester College School, entered Corpus Christi College, Oxford, at the age of 13, and graduated four years later. In 1795 he was elected a fellow of Magdalen, taking Holy Orders during his residence. In 1804 there was a decisive event for his future career: he married a niece of Lady Eldon and in consequence of his marriage had to vacate his fellowship. His first preferment, probably due to his wife's connection with Lady Eldon, was the living of Kilmersdon near Bath, though there is no evidence that he ever lived in the place. In 1806 he became one of the chaplains to Shute Barrington, Bishop of Durham, and held that post, together with several livings and a prebend at Durham, for 20 years. He was rewarded with the Deanery of Chester in 1828 for his defence of Tory causes and measures. When in 1830 he was nominated Bishop of Exeter, he found that it was worth only £2,700 per annum and involved much expense, so he insisted on retaining his rectorship of Stanhope, Durham, which was worth £4,000. In 1832 the

Whigs, who were not in favour of plural livings, came to power and Phillpotts was challenged about this. Eventually, he gave up the rectorship for a stall at Durham Cathedral, which was worth less, but he was under great political pressure to do so.

Trollope incorporated some of his more notorious traits in Archdeacon Grantley. Employed first as a clerk in the General Post Office in London, Trollope was sent early in 1851 as a so-called postal surveyor to reorganise their services in the South West of England. He began his work in Devonshire and travelled almost everywhere on horseback, which was unusual for an official. Thus he visited Exeter on numerous occasions and lodged in the city; there he picked up much gossip about Bishop Phillpotts and information about the life and politics of the Cathedral Close.

By the late 1830s the Bishop had become a national figure, pilloried in the Radical press for his well advertised public controversies and extraordinary behaviour. Some described him as a bully and an ogre – a view shared by Radicals and Liberals – but many came to admire him as a pillar of the Established Church and as a sound and trusted Tory. Whatever view was taken of him, few would deny that he was an extraordinary man, a prelate with numerous quirks.

Soon after his installation the Bishop was to become the most unpopular man in Exeter, a city with a large flock of Radicals, Reformers, and Dissenters, people who were mostly hostile to the city's ancient corporations. The politically disaffected, as well as the rancorous and turbulent, were all agreed that the Church was the most baneful, anachronistic, and corrupt of these corporate bodies, and its chief representative in Devon, Cornwall and the Scilly Isles was now Bishop Henry Phillpotts. He was roundly disliked for several reasons but principally for his vehement opposition to the progress of the Reform Bill, as a result of which the Exeter mob threatened to attack his Palace. On the eve of Guy Fawke's Day 1831, the city was placarded with the message 'Woe to the Bloody Set, on Saturday the common enemy will be burned' (this was a coded message that the Bishop was the intended victim). His son garrisoned the Palace with a posse of coastguards, who stood sentry overnight within its grounds, and the streets were filled with troops of yeomanry and patrols of constables. This show of force aborted any riot, and the mobs dispersed.

Many among the local Anglican clergy were evangelical in temper and distrusted his High Churchmanship; but it was true that a certain slackness had crept, over the years, into the diocese, which the Bishop, always a disciplinarian in Church affairs, sternly reprobated. The lesser clergy were mostly given to evangelicalism and low church practices. They certainly could not be numbered among his supporters. The higher clergy feared his tightening the screw. Some revealed their antipathy. This the Bishop well knew and it may, in part, have conditioned his decision to vacate his Palace and reside firstly in Teignmouth and then in salubrious Torquay, where Dissent was much weaker or, at least, less organised and rancorous.

His conduct during the 1832 cholera epidemic, when over 400 people in Exeter alone succumbed to the dread disease, also affected his popularity. It was common knowledge that he did not remain behind in the city but, adopting a policy of *sauve qui peut*, had scuttled off on a tour of rural Devonshire, ostensibly to hold confirmation classes for village children. During the plague's visitation he paid only one very brief visit to the city, when he attended a special service of prayer and humiliation at the Cathedral. When he was asked to consecrate a new church he wrote to the Mayor of Exeter and attempted to excuse himself on the ground that there was the danger of contagion. The Bishop in abandoning the city – the plague raged from early July to October 1832 – was sternly admonished by newspaper editors and other scribblers for leaving his post. But it seems very sensible for him to have done so, since he was neither a physician nor an apothecary and, on rational grounds at least, he could just as well pray for the afflicted from afar as from the Cathedral, for God is everywhere, Christians believe.

One anecdote – there are many to choose from – may reveal why the Bishop became so notorious a public figure not only in Devon but nationwide. In the 1840s his authoritarian character was further displayed in the matter of the Revd George Gorham. This elderly clergyman had already been presented to the living of Brampford Speke in the diocese of Exeter when the Bishop refused to institute him. Gorham, it seems, had twice previously offended his Bishop who, as a consequence, regarded Gorham's conduct as contumacious and his theology unsound. Before instituting Gorham, he declared, he must assess the clergyman's orthodoxy.

Gorham was summoned to Babbacombe. Seated in the Bishop's study at Bishopstowe, a house which by now substituted for the old Episcopal Palace at Exeter, he underwent a *viva voce*, a verbal examination which extended to 75 questions, and was cross examined by the Bishop for eight hours a day on five successive days. Gorham did not, it seems, pass his oral, since he was recalled three months later to Bishopstowe, to undergo a further disputation, when now 150 questions were to be put to him. At this point, the aggrieved clergyman refused any further inquisition and said so. The Bishop promptly responded by summarily pronouncing the offender unsound in doctrine (and possibly in mind!). Gorham was not instituted to the living. Commenting editorially on what seemed to be a spiteful persecution of a harmless cleric, John Latimer, the radical editor and proprietor of *The Western Times*, thus commented: 'This conduct of the Bishop in endeavouring to establish a sacerdotal tyranny, would strike at the root of all freedom of thought and action, whether religious or civil.' In the end, though, the Bishop was dis-comfited. On appeal, the Judicial Committee of the Privy Council in March

1850 ruled that Gorham's views were neither unsound nor heretical, and the Archbishop of Canterbury was rumoured to have given his support to the judgement. In turn the furious Bishop protested by letter that the Archbishop was supporting heresies and he threatened to break off communion with Canterbury.

The inhabitants of Torquay evinced more interest in parochial affairs. As in Mrs Gaskell's little provincial town of Cranford, the better-off formed a small, closed world of shared interests, through which gossip, rumour, and scandal circulated. Tittle-tattle among the leisured and retired classes was rampant in Torquay; many of its citizens had little with which to occupy their minds, apart from the buzz of daily events. Once the Bishop settled in their midst he rapidly became the talk of the town. From the early 1840s, he spent much of his life at Bishopstowe, his Italianate villa on the Babbacombe Road. It became his habit to walk from its grounds either uphill to Wall's Hill and to continue along the Babbacombe Downs or, choosing an opposite direction, to walk from Anstey's Cove along a crude footpath to what is now the Marine Drive, and then if time allowed continue down to Meadfoot Beach, returning by way of the Ilsham valley. It was a most agreeable walk (and still is) that pleased those who wished to commune with nature or simply enjoy fresh air. This pathway along the cliffs, traversed so many times by Henry Phillpotts, became celebrated locally as the 'Bishop's Walk', and is so gazetted today. Yet the Bishop did not lead a reclusive, contemplative life in Torquay; he was frequently to be observed seated in his carriage, being driven to and from his villa. On Sundays he would always attend one of the several Anglican churches, but his favourite place of worship was mostly St John the Evangelist's, above the Strand, easy to reach from Bishopstowe and popular with the Torquay élite, though he did display great affection for St Marychurch. St John's had become the resort's most fashionable place of worship, which its leading citizens, such as the chief magistrate March Phillips, Edward Vivian the banker, and the Kitsons, mostly attended; it was central and convenient.

St John Evangelist had replaced a chapel-of-ease built in the early 1820s at the same time as the neighbouring terraces. This small building had been erected on land that formed part of the Torre Abbey estate, so that ground rent was payable to the Carys. Between 1861-71 a fine church, designed by G.E. Street, was erected in place of the former chapel. St John's occupies a dominant site, overlooking the Strand, the harbour, and the sea. In 1861 it became the parish church of a large area behind the Strand and was made independent of its mother church at Torre, for Bishop Phillpotts had encouraged the division of Torre parish. Its first incumbent was William Parks Smith, a Puseyite, a Ritualist. Under his guidance and that of his successors St John's became one of the leading centres of late Victorian Anglo-Catholicism, competing with Brighton on that score.

29 *St John the Evangelist and the Higher Terraces. It was easy to reach from Bishopstowe and popular with the Torquay élite.*

In the late 1850s St Marychurch was undoubtedly the most advanced of all the Torquay churches until St John's Chapel became a parish church. On Christmas Day 1837 the service at St John's Chapel provoked the Bishop's ire. According to the Prayer Book it should have included the Athanasian Creed, but the curate in charge had an aversion to using the strong word 'damnation' and substituted the Apostle's Creed, which he started to recite; whereupon the Bishop shouted out, in thunderous tones which made the congregation jump in their seats, the opening words of the Athanasian Creed and obliged all present to follow him. When they came to the word 'damnation' the curate again introduced in it the weaker word 'condemnation' in its place. The enraged Bishop, his dander up, turned towards him and bellowed 'damnation'. The astonished congregation fell silent.

In 1847 took place the first 'Ritual Prosecution' in England of an Anglican clergyman. Bishop Phillpotts was the accuser, Parks Smith, the incumbent of St John's Chapel, Torquay, the accused, and ritual improvisation the crime. The offence was witnessed by a large number of celebrants on Easter Day, 1847. The Bishop was one of the congregation and observed that Parks Smith had placed on the altar a wooden cross, two feet high, decorated with flowers and evergreens, and also two small glass vases, secured to the altar table by string lest they be knocked over by the officiating clergyman. The Bishop did not approve of this Romish display and made his displeasure clear. At the time of the offertory he tried to remove the vases. He succeeded in pushing one vase down behind the table but the other, still secured by string, remained in sight.

The outcome was the appointment of a Court of Inquiry to 'decide whether there were sufficient grounds for the Bishop's directing further proceedings'. The Commissioners mulled over the matter at the Chapter House at Exeter and concluded that there was a *prima facie* case established for the case to go before the Lord Bishop, who after hearing the evidence declared: 'As there is no ground on which the act, admitted by Mr Smith, can be deemed lawful, it is my duty to adjudge that he be admonished, and I do now admonish him not again to offend in the like manner; and I further order that he pay the cost of these proceedings.' After the trial, Parks Smith was ever known as 'Flower-pot' Smith. This might seem less than a storm in a tea-cup, but people took such controversies seriously in mid-Victorian England when any attack on the principles, forms, or practices of the Church was usually zealously rebutted by its adherents. We have simply grown slovenly in such matters in an age in which deeds rather than beliefs are seen as important.

Parks Smith continued in his office and when in November 1861 St John's was constituted a parish he remained its incumbent. In July 1870 he mysteriously and precipitously departed from Torquay. R.J.E. Boggis, the historian of St John's, states:

> The closing events of Mr Parks Smith's history are lamentably sad. Having preached his last sermon in St John's on Sunday morning, July 17th, 1870,

30 *Interior of St John's.*

and celebrated for the last time early on Sunday, July 31st, he soon afterwards suddenly and hastily resigned his benefice, and left Torquay, never to return. The remainder of his life he spent in Brighton, afflicted by blindness in his last few years, but in comfortable circumstances financially, for his estate was valued at nearly £6,000. When his powers were waning, he joined the Church of Rome, and was disappointed that none of his family would do so.

Boggis, unfortunately, does not tell us why Parks Smith exiled himself. His sudden resignation invites conjecture. Yet his indulgence in private confession (called 'auricular confession' by Tractarians) may provide a clue. Early in 1850 a young clergyman, who had been slighted by Parks Smith, published a pamphlet in the preface to which he averred that Parks Smith had built a room in the chancel for 'the purpose of hearing confessions and giving spiritual advice to such as need it'.

It is possible that Parks Smith succumbed to the charms of one of his parishioners, when closeted with him in his confessional, and by so doing caused grave scandal, a scandal which was evidently hushed up. Torquay, just like Brighton and other south-coast resorts, always had a superfluity of unmarried women who did not work. An examination of the census returns for 1871 reveals a marked disparity between the sexes in high-class resorts, a ratio of over 3:2. Torquay had 8,885 males to 12,772 females listed for that year. This disparity can partially be explained by high numbers of female servants. But even in 1901 about 60 per cent of females living in fashionable resorts were listed as retired or unoccupied, a proportion of whom would have been spinsters living in reduced circumstances or on small annuities. In 1871 the majority of unattached women from this social stratum were obliged to stay at home as dutiful and, in time, ageing daughters.

Now we should return to the Bishop. He died at his home in Torquay in 1869 and was buried in St Marychurch, where he shares a double grave with his wife, close to the east wall of the churchyard. A cross raised above his tomb carries the inscription: 'Henry of Exeter'. The lofty tower of St Mary-church was raised as his memorial. He left behind, one feels, no great cemetery of regrets. To the end of his life he remained a High Churchman, a prelate who to the end fiercely resisted any attempt to dilute the doctrines of the Church or to water down its privileges. He was never a popular man: he made no attempt to be. He was, nevertheless, an excellent administrator and always keen to promote the building of churches. St Mary Magdalene in Upton Vale was erected in 1848-9; St Mark's, near Meadfoot Road, 1856-7; St Mathias, Ilsham, 1858; St Luke's, Warren Road, 1863; All Saint's, Babbacombe, 1865-7; and Christ Church, Ellacombe, 1868. He was active in creating new parishes, as in Torquay, where under his sponsorship St John's Chapel was made a parochial church and split off from Torre. Let the last words on Bishop Henry Phillpotts be those of a fellow clergyman, the witty Sydney Smith, a

Whig in politics: 'I must believe in the Apostolic Succession, there being no other way of accounting for the descent of the Bishop of Exeter from Judas Iscariot.'

* * *

It is not surprising to find that the Torbay district is a stronghold of Con-servatism. It has never been home to a proletariat, it completely lacks working-class traditions and memories; but that is not to say it has been without its quota of poverty and the hard-up. In recent years a number of small factories and workshops have opened up, but their workers are still few. Unlike Blackpool, or even Scarborough, it has no industrial hinterland. Historically, farming and seafaring have always been its main occupations. In the 19th century it was mostly inhabited by the wealthier classes, their servants, and by shopkeepers. There were Liberal revivals in the area – it was 'touch and go' at times for the Tories – but the dominant political ideology has always been Toryism or Conservatism. In the 1930s and '40s it could boast of a handful of Communists and Blackshirts; occasionally one would see a young man on the Strand, or at Palace Avenue, Paignton, trying to sell *The Daily Worker* or *Action*, but purchasers were scarce. Even 'save Spain' rallies on the seafront were not well attended and those by Mosleyites were usually well-behaved.

Before 1832, the richest man in Devon, the Tory Lord Rolle, was the county's political patron. At his great house at Stevenstone the county's landowners arranged matters to their own satisfaction and Sir Robert Palk and his son, in their day, would have been of the company. In 1832 political opinion in Devon was overwhelmingly for reform and on the side of the Liberals. There was a growing opposition to such undemocratic forms, like rotten boroughs and pocket boroughs. It was a time of immense popular enthusiasm and growing disturbance, a mobilisation of the many against institutions that benefited the few. Only a single Tory was returned for the entire county, which gives some idea of the state of feeling in Devonshire.

By the Reform Act of 1832 the county was divided into two divisions – North and South – each returning two members and in the first election held under the new Act two Liberals, Lord John Russell and John Crocker, were returned for South Devon. By the Reform Act of 1867, the county was divided into three, instead of the former two divisions, and the Torbay district incorporated into the newly created constituency of East Devon. Sir Lawrence Palk, as we know, represented this division from 1868 to 1880. The Redistri-bution of Seats Act 1885 again altered the electoral map of Devon by creating eight divisions for the county, each returning a single member, and one of these was Torquay. Earlier, in 1867, it had been proposed that a seat should be created for Torquay, since the resort had become celebrated, grown wealthy, and numbered among its population many titled people. The proposal did not get much support in Parliament. When the Bill was debated in the House of Commons in March 1867, a member derided the notion of Torquay having its own seat and asked what possible interest Torquay would represent. A wit swiftly riposted, 'The pulmonary interest', followed by much laughter.

Richard Mallock, born in 1843, was the ninth Mallock to inherit Cockington Court and the first in later years to become a Member of Parliament. Cockington Court now became the centre of Conservatism for the Torbay region and

at the manor house fêtes were held and meetings of the Primrose League. Mallock was popular in Torquay, principally because he gave up part of his estate – Chelston and Livermead – for development. Afterwards, Chelston was much built over, to become another suburb of Torquay. He fought hard, however, to preserve Cockington Court and village unchanged, as for many years all Mallocks had done. When it was proposed in 1900 that the borough of Torquay should extend its boundaries, he succeeded by adroit diplomacy and reasonable argument in getting his manor of Cockington exempted from the proposed boundary changes. The village was finally incorporated in 1928, long after his death, and the rest of his property, including Cockington Court, was purchased in 1933 for £40,000, which proved to be an excellent bargain for the town.

31 *Richard Mallock was the ninth Mallock to inherit Cockington Court and the first to become a Member of Parliament.*

After his death in 1900 admirers raised money for a clock tower to honour his memory, his public spirit, his work on behalf of the town and its citizens. He was a decent man, a man of integrity. The Clock Tower, a landmark for all who know Torquay, was erected at the foot of Torwood Street and there it remains to this day. In 1895 he resigned his seat in favour of his good friend, Commander Arthur Phillpotts, a grandson of the great Bishop. Phillpotts, a retired naval officer, held the seat until 1900. In the 'Khaki Election' of September 1900 the new Tory candidate, C.R. Rankin, was defeated, though only by 175 votes. The victor was the Liberal Francis Layland-Barratt, a Plymouth man, and he was to hold the seat for nearly ten years. His home was the New Manor House, bought from the Palk family when they fell upon hard times, and he lived there until his death in 1933. Sir Francis Layland-Barratt, as he later became, left little mark on the town and is now forgotten.

The number of non-conformists in Torquay had grown over the years and, such people tending to vote Liberal as much as Anglicans vote Conservative, the first decade of the 20th century marked the heyday of Liberalism in South Devon. The Liberal landslide of 1906, which gave them 400 seats to

32 *Mallock memorial. After his death, in 1900, admirers raised money for a clock tower to honour Richard Mallock's memory, his public spirit and his work on behalf of the town.* Hearder Family Hotel, *built in 1828, has become the* Queen's *and tramlines have been laid for the new (1907) Torquay Tramline Company.*

the Conservatives' 129, seemed to forbode its ultimate triumph in South Devon. Only three Tories survived and the Party was much rattled by this turn of events. They were not to be for long. The two elections of 1910 changed everything for Devonshire Tories: they took eleven of the thirteen seats and a Unionist candidate won Torquay. There was one short break in 1923, which witnessed the last brilliant flash of Devonshire Liberalism; but at the next election, in 1924, the Liberals were extinguished in Devon, all except Hore Belisha at Devonport. The Conservatives held Torquay until 1997 when Adrian Sanders, a Liberal Democrat, was elected. In the 1945 election – a key election in modern British politics and a watershed between the new and the old – the Liberal candidate was Lt Gorley Putt, recently returned from the wars. The votes cast were: Conservatives 25,479, Labour 13,590, and Liberals 13,003.Gorley Putt had clearly split the opposition vote. He was a naval officer, young, dashing, and an excellent speaker. He much appealed to women (all my sisters voted for him). If he had stood down it still seems likely that the Labour candidate would have lost; the majority of those who voted for him, one feels, would have given their votes to Charles Williams, the Member who had held the seat since 1924. Gorley Putt, to digress, went on to become a lecturer in the Department of English at University College, Exeter, and to write about Henry James.

Between the wars, the Church of England and the Conservative Party, pillars of established society in Torbay towns, held their own. There had been, however, a marked decline in church-going among the respectable classes, yet most people continued to believe that religion, in the abstract, was a good thing; even the working classes sent their children to Sunday School. At times Charles Williams was mildly reproved for not speaking up in Parliamentary debates, but he was generally liked. Clearly no orator, he was said to be a useful man on committees. The Masons formed an élite and appealed strongly to businessmen and shopkeepers, and Masonic Clubs were popular and well attended by drinkers, by all those who wanted to escape from home in the evening and enter the magic world of the bar-room. But at the same time they were also responsible for a great deal of unheralded but much needed charity work in the community.

* * *

Advanced thought in South Devon was to be found only at Dartington. The American millionairess Dorothy Elmhirst and her husband Leonard had bought in 1925 the 400-year-old Champernowne estate, with its partly ruined manor house, and they had then transformed it, with the application of much money, into a utopia for craftsmen and artists, writers and poets. At Dartington Hall 'Progress' was ever in the air: they did things differently there. From time to time poetry readings were given at its Little Theatre and local people were invited, to be startled when their eyes lit upon a large placard displayed on the stage, which read 'No Applause'. The performance over, the actor would silently stalk from the stage and the audience as silently file out.

Dartington was a splendidly bogus place: a combination of the simple life and extreme sophistication, a place where the names of Freud and Marx, D.H. Lawrence and Joyce were constantly heard. The Elmhirsts were not attracted to traditional religion; indeed, they believed in Original Virtue. Armistice Day was not celebrated at its co-educational senior school, run on progressive lines, and the national anthem rarely, if ever, heard. What outraged locals most were reports (true) of boys and girls and men and women swimming naked in the 'Salmon Pool', a tiny inlet on the River Dart.

Torbay, on the other hand, was in no way 'advanced' or 'progressive': the hero of those times was the pipe-smoking Stanley Baldwin, who in 1935 had assumed the leadership of the National Government, a coalition formed by Ramsay MacDonald in 1931: its motto was 'Safety First', a catch-phrase that adorned Baldwin's electioneering posters. The idea of a national government perfectly suited the mood and temper of Torbay. During this period the grandees had mostly departed from its towns; they – Torquay and Paignton in particular – had grown more suburbanised; and *The Daily Mail*, *The Daily Express* and *The Western Morning News* – in that order – were the favourite reading matter of most of its population.

Five

DISTINGUISHED PEOPLE

RIGHTON had had its Prince Regent – 'Prinny' – and its Beau Brummell, that great dandy and wit, whose sheer effrontery and contemptuously cool manner much astonished his contemporaries. Brummell, often the Prince's guest at Carlton House, is reputed once to have rudely demanded: 'Wales, ring the bell'. And when asked, on another occasion, whether he liked vegetables replied, 'I think I have once eaten a pea'. Brighton in its heyday was a Regency town, a wicked town with a raffish reputation: Torquay, a much later development, was mostly a mid-Victorian creation. Its authorities never encouraged gambling and never attempted to open a casino.

The good town of Torquay could hardly boast of any such extraordinary or notorious figures as residents. But a number of distinguished men and women over the years did settle in Torquay; and many more lived in the resort for shorter periods, such as Disraeli and Charles Kingsley. The list of foreign monarchs and minor royalty, princelings and dukes, and other titled people, whether resident in or visiting the town, is impressive.

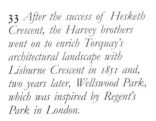

33 *After the success of Hesketh Crescent, the Harvey brothers went on to enrich Torquay's architectural landscape with Lisburne Crescent in 1851 and, two years later, Wellswood Park, which was inspired by Regent's Park in London.*

Throughout Victoria's reign Torquay continued to attract the well-to-do and the celebrated. It became known as the English Riviera, although some other towns, such as Scarborough, also claimed that title.

In October 1868 the Queen of Holland, travelling under the *nom de plume* of the Comtesse Buren, arrived at Torquay and she and her party stayed a fortnight at the *Royal Hotel*. The Dutch Queen was the guest of Sir Lawrence Palk and his wife at Haldon House. In September 1871 the ex-Emperor Napoleon III visited Torquay on the advice of his physicians. He and his party were received at Torquay Station by Sir Lawrence and his son and by a number of Sir Lawrence's friends. Then they all proceeded to the *Imperial Hotel* where apartments had been taken for the Emperor and his suite. The party stayed for five weeks. To begin with, Napoleon was keen to obtain a residence in the neighbourhood, but for political reasons soon after came to feel he should be in London where his agents in France could communicate more easily with him. He left on 18 October 1871, on which day Sir Lawrence escorted the Emperor by carriage through Newton Abbot to Haldon House, where they stopped for a few hours and lunched. Afterwards Sir Lawrence took him around the property and they even ascended the Belvedere Tower from which they viewed much of the surrounding Devonshire countryside. J.T. White relates that Sir Lawrence showed the Emperor his collection of old armour, rare china, paintings, and antique manuscripts, in all of which he appeared to show great interest. Afterwards the party drove off in two carriages for Exeter where Sir Lawrence and the Emperor made their adieux. Then the Emperor and his entourage took the train for London.

It is clear that by the 1860s the Palks had become Torquay's leading family and had taken over the social leadership assumed for several centuries, as of right, by the Carys; though it should be stressed that the latter were not eclipsed: they still enjoyed a large degree of deference from local society and townspeople. At this time the Cary family was represented by Robert Shedden Sulyarde Cary (1828-98) who succeeded his father in 1840. Despite the eminent position he occupied in the town from his birth and the antiquity of his line, Cary had an antipathy to normal social life: he disliked mixing with all and sundry and in later years became almost a recluse, and he suffered from a severe illness; nevertheless, it was during his stewardship that he, through his proxies, developed both the Belgravia and Waldon Hill lands, as well as Babbacombe and St Marychurch, and he also gave or sold on generous terms a number of valuable sites to the town; so that by the time he died, in 1898, nearly half of Torquay's built-up area was to be found on Cary land.

The Mallocks, on the other hand, who spent much time in their very private retreat at Cockington, never showed any great interest in becoming *primus inter pares*. Yet they were much respected by patricians as country gentlemen of good repute and by plebeians as very grand folk indeed, although

34 *Sir Lawrence Palk was Torquay's great improver but Robert Cary was also active and the results are to be seen, after 1840, in Belgravia and on Waldon Hill.*

35 *Kitson's development of 19th-century villas on Park Hill before the building of Shirley Towers (the 'Three Ugly Sisters').*

ranked perhaps a little below the Carys, in these parts commonly recognised as more ancient and distinguished a family. The Palks were the wealthiest of the three families, and that was extremely important in the eyes of the middle classes, who in South Devon, as elsewhere, had a healthy respect for money.

This slight change in the relative social positions occupied by Palks and Carys was mostly the result of Sir Lawrence's reputation as a rising politician; he was MP for East Devon (1868-80), a friend and staunch supporter of Disraeli, and a defender of agricultural interests. These attributes were augmented by a courteous demeanour and statesmanlike conduct in public.

36 *Torquay, c.1871, with the yacht* Evadne, *owned by Sir Walter Carew (8th baronet), lying offshore. These were Torquay's halcyon days as a fashionable watering-place.*

Sir Lawrence, moreover, was held in high regard as the architect of Torquay's continuing prosperity and for its distinction as a great resort; and it was common knowledge that he spent great sums on improving the town and adding to its amenities. Finally, Sir Lawrence lived much in the town, in his New Manor House on Lincombe Hill, where, at times, he would entertain on a grand scale. And now his reprobate father was dead – the one blot on the escutcheon – and this was a bonus for the family. Freed from this awful incubus, Sir Lawrence could relax: now he was his own man, head of the clan, nominally in control of the estate, *pace* William Kitson. Sir Lawrence was now generally regarded as Torquay's leading citizen, the gentleman who met the great, who escorted distinguished visitors around the town and entertained them at Haldon and the Manor House. He had pursued a public career; he had become a public figure; he was admired for his merits.

The years from 1860 to 1870 represented Torquay's finest hours, its halcyon days as an exclusive resort and fashionable watering-place, and notably so in the winter season (summer for high society was out of season), the time when the *crème de la crème* came by coach and rail, even by sea. In his reminiscences W.H. Mallock celebrates these days. He mentions the Dowager Lady Brownlow,

Mrs Vivian, Lady Erskine of Cambo, Lady Louisa Finch-Hatton, Miss Burdett-Coutts, Susan Lady Sherborne, and others, and comments:

> All these ladies were the occupants of spacious houses the doors of which were guarded by skilfully powdered footmen, and which, winter after winter, were so many social centres. Not a few were foreign – vivacious Northerners from New York, with the sublimated wealth of all Paris in their petticoats; Southerners whose eyes were still plaintive with memories of the Civil War; Austrians such as the Von Hugels; Germans such as Countess Marie and Countess Helen Bismarck; and Russians whose figures and faces I remember much more accurately than their names.

Members of the European nobility, as W.H. Mallock confirms, flocked to Torquay; some became residents, others stayed for lengthy periods. The history of the Russian gun throws light on their presence. In 1858 the Local Board of Health (Torquay's directing body) in a fit of patriotic fervour petitioned the War Office for one of the many trophies taken during the Crimean War. The request was granted and in April 1859 a large gun arrived at Torre Station, where a celebration took place. It was drawn to Cary Green and positioned there. But soon after, some members of the town's élite objected on the grounds that the display of captured Russian ordnance might offend members of the Imperial Family living in the town. To this snobbish appeal the Local Board yielded. The gun was removed and placed on Ellacombe Green – Ellacombe was a working-class quarter – where it was unlikely to be seen by any strolling Russian duke. It was not the end of the saga. In 1875 a member of the Local Board, a gentleman who held the Queen's commission, made a great fuss and demanded that the gun be restored to its former glory on Cary Green, for in the intervening 15 years the English had become jingoistic: now foreign sensibilities mattered less. The piece was returned to Cary Green.

In the mid-Victorian period it was not as yet the fashion among the upper classes to frequent restaurants, hotels or other public places, except on ceremonial or official occasions. It was the opening in 1889 of D'Oyly Carte's *Savoy Hotel* that popularised the habit of dining or supping out. Before that, people did occasionally dine out, but such excursions usually meant taking a meal with a host who was staying in an hotel.

It was not the practice for Society to dine out for the sake of dining out. Restaurants were mainly used by travellers, bachelors, businessmen, and by those who happened to work near one; women dining alone were remarked upon and assumed to be *demi-mondaines*, and often were. This was especially true in the starchy provinces, in conservative Devon. In Torquay entertaining among the quality was essentially a private and elaborate affair with plenty of servants in attendance. The town's grandees employed so many servants that entertaining gave their wives little trouble. In the season, in the winter months, there was a round of entertaining and *divertissements*, with people scurrying to and fro by coach and carriage to dinner-parties, soirees, and musical evenings.

For many years – from the late 1860s to the 1880s – the social leader of Torquay society was Anne Duchess of Sutherland (1829-88) – known to her friends as Annie – the wife of Sutherland-Leveson-Gower, 3rd Duke of Sutherland. She set the social tone. Both husband and wife were close friends of the Prince (later Edward VII) and Princess of Wales. Queen Victoria objected to most of the members of Bertie's intimate circle – his notorious fast set – as frivolous; and in particular she disliked the Duke and Duchess of Sutherland. Of the Duke she declared that 'he does not live like a *Duke ought*'. Sutherland had a passion for driving fire engines and even railway trains and the Queen was alarmed that her eldest son might acquire this rash habit and injure himself. She complained of the alluring, lively Duchess, whom she observed laughing at some grand function, that she was 'a foolish injudicious little woman'. 'She would!' riposted the sculptor and art critic Lord Ronald Gower, a friend of the young Oscar Wilde: in Lord Ronald's eyes his niece, Annie, was 'as usual the most beautiful and graceful woman in the place'.

Those who consorted with the Prince of Wales had of necessity to be extremely rich; he was an expensive friend to have and to entertain. The Prince liked most forms of gambling, notoriously so baccarat, and took with him when country-house visiting his own monogrammed playing cards and counters. Fortunately, the Duke of Sutherland was the largest landowner – the eighth richest – in Great Britain with a gross income of £142,000 derived from an area more than a quarter the size of Wales; and, in addition, his rent-roll was supplemented by a personal income derived from investments. His great wealth allowed his wife to entertain friends and guests on a lavish scale.

The Duchess ruled Torquay society from her home, Sutherland Tower, Higher Warberry Road. Her house, appropriately, was located on a commanding site; and at Sutherland Tower she entertained the Princess of Wales. They were such close friends that she named her youngest daughter Alexandra and the Princess gladly stood sponsor for the child. For many years the Duchess spent part of the year in Torquay where she was greatly admired as a sparkling and lively noblewoman and as a fashion-plate in a fashion-conscious seaside resort. When the Primrose League met at Cockington Court, the headquarters of Conservatism in Torbay (Richard Mallock was MP for Torquay 1886-95) it was she, the Duchess, who took the chair. Torquay society bowed before her. Her close friendship with members of the Royal Family gave her the edge over any contender to the title of the reigning Queen of Torquay. The Duchess gave up her 'crown' when she died in 1888 at Torquay. She was immensely popular in the resort and is interred, fittingly, in Babbacombe cemetery.

When Agatha Christie (then Miss Agatha Miller) was living in Torquay in the early years of this century, it was Lady Flora MacGregor who in her widowhood wore the crown and was the social leader. Her late husband, the elderly Major-General Sir George Hall MacGregor, had taken her as his second wife, but he died in 1883 after only four years of marriage. Lady MacGregor was the daughter of the Revd Montagu Oxenden, rector of Eastwell, Kent, and she was left with a daughter and a son and not much else to occupy her mind. She was a kind, amiable woman, who much enjoyed social life and the introducing of the right people to the right people. A bit eccentric, she was also a match-maker. Lady MacGregor lived at Glen-carnock, a large house on St Michael's Road, which lies below Chapel Hill, and close to Agatha Christie's parents's house, Ashfield, on Barton Road.

The change in the composition of Torquay's upper class is illustrated by the fact that, whereas a great Duchess had once set the tone, she was suc-

37 *Anna, Duchess of Sutherland (1829-88), engraving by W.H. Mote after John Hayter. Her close friendship with members of the Royal Family gave her the edge over any contender to the title of the reigning Queen of Torquay.*

ceeded in this role by the wife of a mere Scottish knight; but Torquay in the early years of the 20th century was fast changing and ceasing to attract so many members of the ruling élite as visitors or residents. This process was slow, but steady, and its start may be dated from the late 1880s. When Lady MacGregor died after the First World War, there was no one to fill her role; or perhaps no one chose to do so from what now passed as local society. Style, elegance, glamour, and class had mostly departed from the resort. Torquay was no longer a smart place to live in: as an address it had no special cachet.

Torbay's oldest newspaper, *The Torquay Directory*, founded in 1840, did not provide a gossip or society column of the type with which we are familiar, but it did publish a list of new arrivals in the town, judiciously selected from among the best people. Beverley Nichols' father, retired solicitor and a fearsome middle-class snob, was an anxious and enthusiastic reader of this list of visitors and would always comment to his family on new arrivals to the town. Some, if not most, he thought should have been excluded from the list. This obsession with titles, with rank and class, with the rich, was typical of Victorians and Edwardians. The devaluation of titles began when politicians like Lloyd George started to sell honours – peerages and less prestigious titles – on a stupendous scale. The Duchess of Sutherland and Lady Flora MacGregor both believed titles illustrated something, some tangible or intangible quality, some prized attribute: birth, breeding or great wealth: what did the new titles represent but political chicanery and backstairs influence?

Mr Nichols had a point: there had been a marked decline in the quality of the town's residents compared with Victorian times. A perusal of Kelly's *Directory of Devonshire and Cornwall* 1923 shows that at that date the aristocratic and titled classes were not well represented. 1923 is an excellent year to select since by then English life had returned almost to normal after four years of war. This annual directory always included a select list of 'private residents'. In the Torquay section for 1923 we find only nine titled persons: four men (three of them knights) and five women (three the wives or widows of knights). Included is only one titled foreigner: the Baroness Nordhoff, whose address is given as Haldon Road on Lincombe Hill. There are a few admirals and generals, but more brigadiers and colonels; and numerous majors and captains (mostly war-time commissions); and a surprisingly large flock of clergymen. The point to be made is that in 1923 there were very few people of marked distinction or excellence or the upper class then resident in Torquay.

Of course the town was still home to the comfortably-off, but the unmistakably affluent were now either members of the bourgeoisie or were self-made men who had done well out of the war. For one reason or another, the Palks, the Carys, and the Mallocks had departed; the Sutherland-Leveson-Gowers had abandoned Sutherland Tower; and Lord Sinclair, whose seat had once been Pilmuir, a little westward of the railway at Shiphay, had long since died. His former mansion was now occupied by the wealthy and philanthropic Mrs Ella Rowcroft, daughter of the celebrated cigarette manufacturer, Sir Edward Wills of Bristol. By the 1920s, successful businessmen from many parts of the British Isles, together with army and navy officers, had mostly taken the place of the old oligarchy of landowners and gentlemen. Many of the handsome Italianate villas – spacious residences – and other large houses had been transformed into small private hotels and now a different sort of social life flourished within their four walls, best described perhaps in E.F. Benson's novel, *Paying Guests*. This process of change was happening all over England, especially perhaps to seaside resorts.

* * *

A few of Torquay's most distinguished residents should now be introduced. Sir Edward Bulwer-Lytton (later 1st Baron Lytton), politician and novelist, came to the town in 1856 and took up residence temporarily at the *Union Hotel* in Union Street and soon after acquired Argyll Hall on Waldon Hill. There he continued to reside until his death in 1873. Bulwer-Lytton was once an extremely popular novelist despite his inflated style; but his books are no longer read and all out of print, although his long ghost story – *The Haunters and the Haunted* – continues to appear in anthologies of supernatural stories. It is very good. In his youth he was a 'Heavy Swell', a dandy and a wit. His anonymous satirical poem, 'The New Timon', satirised Tennyson as 'School Miss Alfred'; Tennyson in turn denounced Lytton as 'the padded man – that wears the stays'. Lytton was a versatile and prolific novelist who moved with fashion and the times, producing a string of successful works that were always *à la mode*. His unhappy marriage in 1827 to the Irish beauty, Rosina Wheeler, a marriage which his mother strongly opposed, ended in separation in 1836. As a result of the temporary estrangement between mother and son, Lytton was short of cash and had to rely on his own resources. He plunged into literary composition of all kinds to support himself in style.

At Argyll Hall he did much writing and entertained his London friends. As J.T. White declares: 'His house was the centre of a select circle of literary friends.' Every winter he came to Torquay and stayed the season and continued to do so until his death in January 1873 at Argyll Hall. Lord Lytton was an ornament to the town. But he is now a lost author, not even a cult figure for the few. His once extremely popular historical novel, *The Last Days of Pompeii*, is now totally forgotten. Desmond MacCarthy's opinion was that 'Lytton cashed his cheque on fame for ready money'. In a letter to a friend he admitted, 'I like Torquay very much in a lazy sort of way', which is an odd remark from one who wrote so many of his books at the resort.

The Findlater sisters, Mary (1865-1963) and Jane Helen (1866-1946), were born in a manse at Lochearnhead, Scotland, and were educated at home by their parents, the Revd Eric Findlater and his wife. On their father's death in 1886 the family were forced to leave the manse and moved to Prestonpans near Edinburgh. A decade later the sisters embarked on their literary career in order to support themselves and their ageing mother. Their novels acquired a large readership but their best work was the three novels they wrote together. Their writing was admired by Henry James, Kipling, Walter de la Mare, and Virginia Woolf, among others, which suggests that it did not lack quality. In 1900 they moved south to Devon, for their mother was in poor health, and rented Southfield Mount, 5 Southfield Road, within easy walking distance of Paignton Parish Church and the sea.

The sisters were delighted with their new home at first, which had a small courtyard, a minute garden raised like a balcony high above the road, and with fine views from their windows of orchards and the sea. At one time their neighbour was W.B. Yeats' brother, Jack Yeats, the painter. Unhappily the lease ran out in 1902 and against their will they moved to Torquay and rented a house called Mount Stuart in Lower Woodfield Road on Lincombe Hill. They were at last able to buy Southfield Mount when it came on the market in 1908 and there they lived until 1923, in which year they removed to Rye,

Sussex, for Paignton had become excessively trippery and crowded. In 1940, after nearly forty years of exile, they returned to Comrie in Perthshire, a few miles from from their childhood home at Lochearnhead. Both their literary reputation and popularity began to decline in the 1920s. It is only in recent years that interest in their work has revived.

The Findlater sisters came to know the American novelist Henry James when he was entering his third and final phase. He was not a stranger to South Devon: in 1895 he stayed from early August to late November at the *Osborne Hotel* at Meadfoot, Torquay, and there he completed his novel, *The Spoils of Poynton* and also began work on another. 'I had betaken myself to finish a book in quiet', he wrote later, 'and to begin another in fear.' But Henry James did not meet the Findlater sisters at that time, for they only took up residence in Torbay at the turn of the century. They first met the great man in 1905, in New York, when the writer paid them a visit at their hotel just as they were about to return to England. In England they became further acquainted, meeting at the homes of mutual friends and writers and they also corresponded. The Master always felt at ease with elderly literary ladies.

The sisters also struck up a friendship with his brother, William James, the noted philosopher. In fact, they got to know William before they met his brother, Henry. They stayed with William and his wife at Cambridge, Massachusetts, in 1903, and were present at a dinner party at which the table was strewn with roses in celebration of Mary Findlater's fourth novel, *The Rose of Joy*, published that year. In October 1908 William James and his wife and daughter were invited to Paignton. The two James women were given rooms at Southfield Mount and the philosopher boarded at the *Redcliffe Hotel*. At that time the hotel had an underground passage leading to the beach and one has a vision of the Pragmatist striding manfully along the beach then up to lunch at Southfield House, to be much fussed over by Mary and Jane. The Jameses were of Protestant Scots-Irish ancestry and that further endeared them to the sisters, daughters of the Presbyterian manse.

Despite the many friends they made in the Torbay area, they never forgot their homeland. Their feelings for Scotland are strongly expressed, for example, in Jane's romantic first novel, *The Green Graves of Balgowrie* (1896), which greatly affected Gladstone and was much admired by the late Victorian and Edwardian reading public. Eileen Mackenzie, their biographer, writes:

> They disliked also the red cliffs and heavy, luxuriant vegetation of Torquay. The lush growth represented something wholly alien to their natures. so utterly different was it from the clear cut, stark beauty of the north. The soft climate which helped their mother was enervating and exhausting to them. Mary was assailed by depression, not quite so deep perhaps as that which attacked the Rudyard Kiplings in the spring of '96 when they rented a home in St Marychurch ...

Eileen Mackenzie's reference to Kipling needs comment. When Kipling left Vermont in the summer of 1896, deeply depressed by a series of quarrels with Beatty Balestier, his American brother-in-law, he turned to Devon as a place of repose and a possible future home. As a boy he had spent four years in North Devon at the United Services College at Westward Ho!. It was this school which provided the setting for *Stalky & Co*, a novel mostly composed at Torquay. In late September 1896 the Kiplings rented Rock House in the district of Maidencombe, a hamlet a few miles up the coast from Babbacombe.

Kipling described the house they rented, built in 1863 and once lived in by three spinster ladies, as 'long, low with two stories, stuck on the side of a steep hill falling away ... to a hundred foot cliff of pure red soil. Below that is the sea, about two hundred yards from the window ... I look straight from my work table on to the decks of the fishing craft who come in to look after their lobster pots.'

In his autobiographical *Something Of Myself* (1937) he refers to his sojourn in these words:

> The spring of '96 saw us in Torquay, where we found a house for our heads that seemed almost too good to be true. It was large and bright, with big rooms each and all open to the sun, the grounds embellished with great trees and the warm land dipping southerly to the clean sea under the Marychurch cliffs. It had been inhabited for thirty years by three old maids. We took it hopefully ... The other revelation came in the shape of a growing depression which enveloped us both – a gathering blackness of mind and sorrow of the heart, that each put down to the new, soft climate and, without telling the other, fought against for long weeks. It was the Feng shui – the spirit of the house itself – that darkened the sunshine and fell upon us every time we entered, checking the very words on our lips. More than thirty years later on a motor trip we venture down the steep little road to that house, and met, almost unchanged, the gardener and his wife in the large, open, sunny stable-yard, and, quite unchanged, the same brooding Spirit of deep, deep Despondency within the open, lit rooms.

Kipling soon found Maidencombe uncongenial. He was never to be happy in this apparently idyllic and romantic spot, not far from Torquay town. Quite suddenly he was seized by depression and his black mood darkens the letters he sent from Torquay. Kipling's experience certainly undermines the view that the English Riviera is always good for one's health. He wrote:

> We are a rummy breed – and O Lord the ponderous wealthy society. Torquay is such a place as I do desire to upset by dancing through it with nothing on but my spectacles. Villas, clipped hedges and shaven lawns: fat old ladies with respirators and obese landaus. The almighty is a discursive and frivolous trifler compared with some of 'em ... But the land is undeniably lovely and I am making friends with the farmers.

Those of us born and bred in Torbay know how dank its winters can be, a terrain of dripping trees and evergreens, of moist masses of vegetation, glistening shrubberies and sinister roads, dimly lit at dusk and deserted, as in places like Vane Hill or Waldon Hill. Until some years after the Second World War Torquay was still, apart from its its central built-up core, mostly sylvan and verdant: it was never all bricks and mortar and macadamised road. Kipling, it seems, had been affected by its winter gloom and his experience allows us to modify the usual bland picture of the town portrayed in guide books. Skegness may be bracing but Torquay too often is enervating; but all resorts have their contradictions and how we perceive a town is dependent on our imagination and mood. The Kiplings then moved to Rottingdean where they soon recovered their spirits. Some years later Kipling wrote 'The House Surgeon', a short story included in *Actions and Reactions* (1909). It is an attempt to explain the numbing mystery, the contagion of depression that once affected his family at Rock House.

In late 1892 Oscar Wilde rented for several months a house called Babbacombe Cliff, situated on the steep road that leads down to Babbacombe Beach. It was owned by Lady Mount-Temple, a kinswoman of his wife. In the early spring of 1893 Lord Alfred Douglas came to stay with him. Wilde was engaged in writing a new play and Douglas supposed to be catching up with his Oxford studies. They soon quarrelled and the petulant Bosie went back to Oxford. There is now an Oscar's Bar at Babbacombe Cliff, since transformed

38 *In 1793 the Revd John Swete enthused about the romantic beauty of Babbacombe Downs as he descended to Oddicombe Beach, but made no mention of the tedious ascent.*

into a private hotel, and to this shrine people come to raise their glasses in honour of the great writer.

Wilde, though, did supervise some rehearsals of a production of *Lady Windermere's Fan*, which opened at the Theatre Royal, Abbey Road on 2 January 1893. Professionals such as Lily Hanbury, then well known as an actress and a reputed beauty, and Nutcombe Gould were engaged to provide a degree of glitter and elegance and to draw the crowds; but the cast was mainly composed of local amateurs led by the Mayoress, a Mrs Splatt, whose husband had just been elected Torquay's first Mayor. Mrs Splatt directed the play and took the important role of Mrs Erlynne: she was a mature lady of uncertain age and the part certainly suited her. Hearsay has it that Wilde did not take much interest in the production, that he mostly lolled about the theatre, smoking innumerable Turkish cigarettes and occasionally sipping a glass of hock-and-seltzer. The performance, with the Mayoress much to the fore, was almost a civic event. The cream of local society came to applaud.

There is no information available to suggest that he met any of the local literati. The novelist Eden Phillpotts, the grandson of the cantankerous Bishop of that name, was then living in Barton Road and was neighbour to the young Agatha Christie, whom in later years he was to advise on the craft of writing. In those days, Eden Phillpotts was immensely popular in the West Country. He wrote a few novels with a Torquay setting as well as a great number of romances and stories about Dartmoor and bucolic life in Devon, which is not surprising since he lived to be nearly a hundred. One supposes he was not quite Wilde's cup of tea. No one could ever claim that Phillpotts was a dandy or an aesthete, let alone an intellectual. In any case, he lacked a perfect profile.

One of the most extraordinary women that ever lived in Torquay was surely the Baroness Burdett-Coutts (1814-1906), whose life has been recounted in Edna Healey's biography, *Lady Unknown* (1978). Her father was the Radical politician Sir Francis Burdett and her grandfather the London banker, Thomas Coutts. In 1837, at the age of 23, Angela Burdett-Coutts inherited a vast fortune from her grandfather, such a great fortune that she became the richest woman in Victorian England. Her philanthropy was on a grand scale; she was ever ready to support good works. A close friend of Dickens, she supported his schemes for the improvement of the London poor, such as model housing. In later life, in 1871, she accepted a baronetcy in her own right – the first woman ever to be accorded such an honour.

In the spring of 1857 Miss Coutts (as she then was) rented Meadfoot House, 1 Hesketh Crescent, that splendid long block of houses the Palks had built overlooking Meadfoot Beach, and she stayed there every winter – the winter season – until the early 1860s when she removed to Ehrenberg Hall. As a child, in the 1820s, she had spent an idyllic holiday with her parents and cousins at Torquay. Her father found the district wild and romantic and the mild, warm climate suited his wife. This stay remained a bright memory. Returning to Torquay after so many years she found great peace of mind, away from the hustle and bustle, the ceaseless activity of life in London, which made too many claims on her time and energy. She soon acquired many friends in Torbay, including William Pengelly, the self-taught son of a Devonshire fisherman. Liking Torquay so much, she looked around for a more permanent home in the town and in 1861 leased the newly built Ehrenberg Hall in Belgravia, a district then being rapidly developed by the Cary family. The land in 1860 had been sold to the builders, the Harvey brothers, by R.S.S. Cary. On it they built three Italianate villas of the type popular in Torquay; Ehrenberg Hall in Chestnut Avenue was one. The three villas faced the sea across that portion of the Abbey grounds which at a later date became the site of Belgrave Gardens. Baroness Coutts left Ehrenberg House in 1877; later it was incorporated in the *Rosetor Hotel* and eventually became part of the English Riviera Centre, completed in 1987.

Miss Coutts did not conform to the Victorian ideal of beauty. Edna Healey's description runs: 'tall, too thin, and her complexion was poor'. Even her husband-to-be once referred to her as 'a lamppost of a woman'. Yet, like the plain but not unattractive Charlotte Brontë, there was much passion concealed within her graceless form. In earlier years she had been much smitten by the Duke of Wellington but the heart of the Iron Duke was impenetrable; there were other men to whom she became devoted but none sought her hand. There were a few who would have taken her as a wife, if only because she was immensely rich, but she found she did not care enough for them. In the end, just like Charlotte Brontë, she married a man younger than herself: the American William Ashmead Bartlett, a junior member of her secretariat.

Baroness Coutts was 67; Bartlett 30. Queen Victoria had always taken an interest in the life and work of this enormously rich philanthropist, whom the people of St Pancras called 'The Queen of the Poor.' but was dumb-

39 *Angela Burdett-Coutts, watercolour on ivory by William Ross. She was one of the most extraordinary women that ever lived in Torquay.*

40 *Hesketh Crescent. In the spring of 1857 Miss Coutts rented Meadfoot House, 1 Hesketh Crescent, overlooking Meadfoot Beach, and she stayed there for the winter season.*

founded when a whisper was passed on to her of the impending nuptials. 'Lady Burdett really must be crazy', the Queen expostulated, 'since poor Mrs Brown's death (Mrs Brown was her confidante and companion of many years) she seems to have *lost* her balance.' 'Next to Afghanistan', Disraeli wrote to the Queen, 'I think the greatest scrape is Lady Burdett's marriage.' Undeterred by royal censure, undismayed by family opposition and the general assumption that Bartlett was a fortune hunter, she went ahead with her plans. They were married in London on 12 February 1881. It turned out to be a reasonably happy marriage – probably a companionate one – and the Baroness remained to the end of her days a devoted wife despite her husband's reputed flirtations. But after her marriage she spent little time in Torquay.

It was in Torquay, however, that the Baroness had first set eyes on her husband-to-be, then a schoolboy. His American mother, a Southerner and a widow, had come to Torquay during or just after the American Civil War and had taken up residence in Belgravia, near Ehrenberg House. Miss Coutts met Mrs Bartlett and her son at the annual prizegiving at Apsley House School, Torquay. William Bartlett, who was the Head Boy, gave a speech of thanks in Latin and Miss Coutts was greatly taken by him. His mother was living on a small income and had two sons to educate. Miss Coutts felt sorry for the family and paid for William's education, first in Torquay and afterwards at Highgate School in London and later at Christ Church, Oxford. She continued to support the young man when he read for the Bar. She called him her godson and it is certain that she regarded him as the son she never had. In 1877 she organised the Turkish Compassionate Fund which was set up to provide money for the victims of the Bulgarians – she was a passionate supporter of the Turks against the Russians – and appointed her young protégé as Commissioner to the Fund. Afterwards he continued in her employ. The Baroness died at her London home in December 1906; her husband, who had pursued a successful Parliamentary career with her financial backing, in 1921.

When Miss Coutts first came to Torquay in 1857 she did not relax but busily engaged herself in promoting schemes for the education of the poor and, in particular, for raising the standard of rural education. Her aide in this endeavour was William Pengelly, with whom she became a close friend. Born at East Looe, Cornwall, in 1812, the son of the master of a coasting vessel, at the age of 12 Pengelly went to sea with his father. When he was 16 his brother died and he felt he should come ashore and help his mother who was at home by herself. He became a teacher in a village school and at the same time worked passionately to acquire knowledge.

Sometime in the 1830s Pengelly removed to Torquay and, once established, opened a small school in Braddon Road West. In those days anyone could open a school who had the cash to buy a few old spelling books and a few desks. At this time he had already become an accomplished mathematician and an excellent teacher of various subjects. One task he set himself to was to reorganise the Mechanics' Institute which had originated in 1828 when the first lecture was given, to much applause, by Sir L.V. Palk, the lord of the manor. Since then the institution had lost momentum and subscribers. It needed revitalisation. The first thing Pengelly did was to rename it the Torquay Young Men's Society. Meetings were henceforth held in Pengelly's school-room, adjacent to the *Royal Hotel* on the Strand.

He had always been fascinated by the study of natural history and geology as were so many Victorian savants and amateurs, and, at the request of the British Association, he commenced in 1864 a systematic examination of the deposits of Kent's Cavern; the description of its fossil remains brought him fame, both local and national. Earlier, in 1844, he had been among the committee of 18 people who had set up the Natural History Society, together with its museum, and continued to busy himself with finding a permanent home for the society and its collections. This was achieved, finally, in 1874 when a special building was put up in Babbacombe Road. The Torquay Natural History Society still occupies the site. Such was the man who became Miss Coutts' close friend and special adviser on Devonshire education.

Miss Coutts' plan was brilliantly simple. In a letter to *The Times* in 1865 she wrote that the essence of her scheme 'consisted in the schoolmaster (a trained and certificated teacher) being the ambulatory centre of unity to a group of schools carried on under his superintendence'. The rural poor were mostly educated in tiny schools or classes (at Cockington Court for example, they met in the kitchen) and taught by people who themselves had received little or no formal education. 'Dame schools' they were called, since in most cases they were kept by an elderly woman whose weekly fee for a pupil was a few pence. For many mothers they acted simply as a babysitting service. Typical of this class of school is the 'evening school' kept by Mr Wopsle's great-aunt in *Great Expectations* where Pip learnt the alphabet and precious little else.

Pengelly as a child had also been sent by his mother to a dame school and thus had first-hand experience of their grimmer side and their educational deficits. Miss Coutts, now advised by him, decided that a certificated teacher should be appointed to administer or supervise a cluster of village schools and that once a year all the pupils would sit a common examination at a chosen place. In 1865 the Torquay Group of United Schools was established and it took under its wing schoolchildren from a number of scattered villages, including Barton, Shiphay, and Cockington, all within the Torquay district. This educational innovation was adopted in some other parts of England and also in Scotland. However, the Education Act of 1870, which introduced the principle of compulsory primary education, largely removed the need for dame schools in village England, but in no way lowered the demand for fee-paying private schools which were situated mostly in urban areas, and such schools continued to flourish in class-conscious England well into the 1930s and only diminished in number after 1945. There are still a number of good prep schools in South Devon.

* * *

Oliver Heavyside was not the sort of person you would normally find at a dinner-party in Torquay's villadom. He was no gentleman in the conventional, snobbish sense of the word, which suggests a degree of polish and good deportment. Rather he was the type of dotty scientist much parodied in children's comics and books, a Doctor Doolittle. Over the years Heavyside became Torquay's leading eccentric, a joy to those who relish human diversity.

Heavyside was born in 1850 at Camden Town, London, the youngest of the four sons of Thomas Heavyside, a wood engraver and water-colour artist who specialised in the illustration of archaeological books. This was not a lucrative profession to follow in Victorian England; and Oliver Heavyside received only an elementary education and was not sent to public school nor to university; he diligently studied at home, in seclusion, alternating this with bouts of athletic exercises to keep himself fit. His maternal uncle was Sir Charles Wheatstone, a pioneer of the electric telegraph, and it was through him that he obtained employment, at 20, with the Great Northern Telegraph Company at Newcastle-upon-Tyne. After four years he was induced to resign from his post as a telegraph operator because of increasing deafness and he returned to live with his family.

His elder brother, Charles, at that time employed in Wheatstone's musical instrument shop in Pall Mall, decided to establish his own business at Torwood Street in Torquay, where he knew the rich and the rentier lived, and he also opened another shop in Palace Avenue, Paignton, in the back room of which Oliver Heavyside was to write many of his scientific papers. The elder brother's business flourished and in 1889 he invited his elderly parents and also Oliver to make their home with him in South Devon.

Charles Heavyside specialised in importing pianolas manufactured by the Aeolian Corporation of America; he was their sole agent in Torbay. These were once extremely popular in England. By 1923 about 200,000 player pianos (the American term) had been made and sales continued to increase until the Depression, and that event, together with the growth of other forms of home entertainment such as radio and the gramophone, lessened their popularity. These instruments were built like pianos and had a keyboard, but the secret was in the rolls of perforated paper fed mechanically into the machine which when set in motion simulated the sound of the real piano.

As early as 1868 Heavyside was already engaged upon electrical experiments and in 1872 his first technical article was published in *The English Mechanic*. He found some difficulty in getting his early papers published but slowly his reputation spread and he became well known in scientific circles, where his researches were discussed by the erudite. In 1892 two volumes appeared under the title *Electrical Papers* and he followed these with his three-volume *Electromagnetic Theory* (1893, 1899, and 1912). Heavyside's fame spread at home and abroad: he was awarded an honorary degree by Gottingen University and elected in 1908 an honorary member of the Institute of Electrical Engineers – although some years earlier he had been struck from their rolls for his inability to pay their annual subscription. Heavyside was a disciple of Michael Faraday and of James Clark Maxwell, the celebrated physicist and Professor of Experimental Physics at Cambridge, who developed a theory of electromagnetic radiation. Historians of science now assess Heavyside's place in the pantheon of science as between that of Maxwell and Heinrich Hertz, the German physicist who discovered the existence of electromagnetic waves. Heavyside's achievement was remarkable for a self-taught scientist. He also postulated the existence of an ionised gaseous layer in the atmosphere capable of reflecting radio waves. This is now named the 'Heavyside layer'.

After 1909 he lived with his brother at Killants, Lower Warberry Road and was a neighbour of the young Beverley Nichols. His eccentricities increased. He was a poor manager of money. Although now in receipt of a Government pension, he was never able to pay all his bills. At one stage his gas supply was cut off for nearly two years and, according to Nichols, he used their final demands as wall decorations and festooned the trees in his garden and drive with rate demands. But he was friendly with the local bobby, an understanding man, who would blow his whistle through the letter box to attract Heavyside's attention, for the scientist had become progressively deafer and alienated from social life. Many of his peculiarities could be explained by his inability to hear others. Always a loner, he lived isolated behind the walls of his house, a loneliness only interrupted at times by a blast from the policeman's whistle.

* * *

The lives of a number of celebrated or distinguished Torbay residents have been examined; they are but a sample taken from a far larger group. It is noteworthy that not one was born in Devon, let alone Torbay or Torquay. The rise in the resort's population from over 11,000 in 1851 to over 24,000 in 1901 was caused not by natural increase, by the remarkable fertility or fecundity of its women; nor even by a dramatic fall in the death rate, a factor that demographers believe was largely responsible in the 19th century for Britain's rapid population growth. Torquay's population more than doubled in fifty years but this came about mostly from immigration, from the many middle- and upper-class people who made it their home and who employed a legion of servants. As the population rose the demand for labour correspondingly grew and this resulted in a tide of working-class migrants arriving in the town, many from other parts of the West Country, others from far afield. The 'best' people came to Torquay; and their presence attracted more of their own kind and those who aspired to be taken for ladies or gentlemen.

The arts – artists and musicians – were not well represented in Torbay. There never was a Torbay School of Painters similar to that which flourished at Norwich, or, more pertinently, to the latter-day colonies of artists at St Ives. It is impossible to find anyone of their stature resident, at any time, in Torquay, though droves of painters, watercolourists, and topographical artists visited Torbay on occasion, for its coastline was scenic and picturesque and in parts wild. Torbay's several harbours and the bay's large expanse of water provided an infinite variety of marine views, seascapes, and nautical subjects.

From early days a number of entertainers and musicians came to Torquay, including Liszt in 1840, who gave no performance since on the day he was taken sick. On the whole, the town did not much appeal to musicians. It had no grand opera house and the premises utilised as concert halls or theatres were neither commodious nor comfortable nor imposing. In 1880 a theatre in Abbey Road was erected, largely through the efforts of a member of the Local Board of Health, a Dr Gillow, and at the same time was formed a company of players. The title, *The Theatre Royal*, was acquired when the Princess of Wales and her three daughters, all guests in Torquay of the Duchess of Sutherland, attended a performance in March 1886. But the theatre closed in November 1886 through the bankruptcy of the lessee; soon after it re-opened under new management. In 1912 the front of the building was remodelled in the shape we see today. It was converted into a cinema in 1933 and named the 'Royal'; then in 1933 it was renamed the 'Odeon', one of the chain owned by The Rank Organisation.

After 1900 private gave way to municipal enterprise in the creation of the Pavilion, which opened its doors in August 1912, and this became the home in Torbay not only of theatre but of music with the foundation of a Municipal Orchestra. It never ranked as a great orchestra but it introduced the inhabitants of Torbay to a good range of music and its visiting conductors included Sir Edward Elgar, Sir Henry Wood, John Barbirolli and Sir Adrian Boult. It played comforting or comfortable music; it rarely performed modern music, although it is true to say that innovative music was not, in general, too popular even in London except among the *cognoscenti* and the *avant garde*, the happy few. Torquay was middle-class and middle-brow: it was not sophisticated. Its inhabitants mostly enjoyed symphonies and concertos by the great classical composers, now safely dead, but especially the music of Eric Coates and Edward German.

Torquay did not, could not, support a bohemian quarter and was certainly not the sort of town – it was no Brighton – that appealed to Victorian and Edwardian bohemians, or louche artists, poets and writers, and caddish boulevardiers. Hacks and sponging journalists felt more at ease in Grub Street, *faute de mieux*, and the more successful among them, St John's Wood or Chelsea. It was a characteristic Devonshire seaside-resort town: conformist and, much of the time, sleepy and boring, full of rich elderly residents living in retirement. Not a place for beautiful, imaginative youth. Those who sought artistic licence, adventures and assignations, went off to London, like the ineffable young Beverley Nichols, to revel in the glamour and glitter of the theatre and the ballet.

Oliver Heavyside's eccentricities have been discussed but there were others like him in Torquay. One was Miss Agatha Barrows who lived at Ash Hill Road, above Castle Circus. She rode around the town in a donkey-cart, kept an elderly footman, at night put cake outside her bedroom door for the mice, and was a devoted reader of Beatrice Potter's stories for children. South Devon was a tolerant and understanding, though modern opinion might claim, 'uncaring' place. Each village, as it were, had its spreading chestnut tree under which the village idiot lay. Today, many of these innocent, harmless, eccentric creatures would be classified and committed as suffering from some type of mental disease and given appropriate treatment. It was not so then: only the truly crazed, those obviously unfit to cope in any way with life, were taken from their community and incarcerated in asylums; others stayed where they were, to the merriment of mischievous children.

Six

CRIME AND LOW LIFE

THE world of Victorian high life is well described and documented in numerous memoirs and biographies and in contemporary newspapers, magazines and journals, and today in a continuing stream of popular books on the period. Low life, on the other hand, has few memorialists and is not well documented except perhaps in the fourth and final volume of Henry Mayhew's *London Labour and the London Poor* (1862) or in various blue books, court reports, and works by specialist historians, sociologists and criminologists. Those who lived in the slums and rookeries of the great towns, as well as the great majority of the criminal and dangerous classes who lived in them – Marx's lumpen proletariat – rarely left behind any record of their lives, for they were invariably illiterate and are only commemorated as digits in the statistics of the period.

The publication in 1966 of the once clandestine Walter's *My Secret Life* (written by Henry Spencer Ashbee in the 1880s) has shed some light on how Victorians behaved in private life; public and private personae were not in accord. As far as South Devon is concerned, we must rely mainly on scraps of information mostly taken from local newspapers and court reports. Metropolitan delinquencies were reported at far greater length, in most cases, than those from the provinces. This is not surprising since the criminal classes – the real professionals – were concentrated in London and in a few other large cities, such as Liverpool and Manchester. Torquay, on the whole, was safe from their depredations. It was a town that could not support a cohort of professional criminals, only one or two at times, and these were rarely at the top of their class.

In Torbay those most at risk were always women, especially young women, victims at times of brutal male domination. In *David Copperfield*, Steerforth effortlessly seduces Mr Peggotty's niece, Little Emily, and she becomes his mistress; and then he discards her. Steerforth was typical, as Dickens well knew, of many ruthless, egotistical Victorian males who bedded good-looking working-class girls. A substantial number of such unfortunates ended up on the streets and Mayhew confirms that most street-walkers had at one time or another been in domestic service or low-paid employment. In Torquay servants were mostly recruited from neighbouring villages and small towns and from other parts of rural Devon and Cornwall; but some even as far afield as

Wales, a land where there was much poverty and few jobs available in the valleys for girls; in South Wales coal was king and offered no jobs for women. As Torquay grew, attracting more and more affluent residents, the demand for domestic labour expanded correspondingly. By mid-century it was a town where newcomers or immigrants were in the large majority.

Nineteenth-century censuses reveal that there were always more females than males in Torquay. This marked disparity between the sexes can be explained by a superfluity of female domestic servants in the town but also by an excess of spinsters and widows compared with men. Females tended to outlive males. The whole range of the Victorian servant class was plentifully represented: skivvies, slaveys and drudges, housemaids, parlour-maids, and nursemaids, laundresses, cleaners and cooks; and, and at a slightly higher level, personal servants, nurses, nannies, such as governesses, and paid companions, and in the finer, more opulent homes, imported French ladies' maids who looked after the mistress's *toilette*: they were inclined to put on airs with other domestic staff. There was also a demand for male servants and other male staff, footmen and coachmen, ostlers and gardeners, and the inevitable boy to do odd jobs; and, in richer households with teenage children, tutors were frequently employed, for it was not yet the invariable custom to send children off to school; that only came with the rise of the public schools much later in the 19th century.

Torquay was a land of villas, each employing at a minimum from three to five servants. Many homes supported a far grander establishment since wages were then extraordinarily low and the number of single or married women seeking employment extremely high. In those days, the mistress of the house could pick and choose, and dismiss at will. Supply outstripped demand. Market conditions accurately determined the price of labour and for servants it was always set very low. For the lucky, escape from the treadmill came about from marriage to a respectable young man, but age was seldom a bar if the suitor was in steady employment. Not all could achieve this happy end and so were forced to drudge on into old age.

W.G. Hoskins commenting on working conditions in late Victorian Devon remarks:

> The cost of living was very low for a middle-class or upper-class family. It was no wonder they could afford to keep so many servants. In 1897 there were advertisements in local newspapers for 'A good cook-general' at wages of £12 to £14 a year (living in), housemaids at £18 a year, a nurse-housemaid at £14, and a general servant at £12 a year. A good cook could get £25 to £30 a year, living in.

Although servants worked long exhausting hours and had little time off from labour, they had enough in which to become pregnant, for sexual congress need not be interminable and, indeed, was often brief and furtive, a chance embrace in a villa shrubbery, a public park or common. Then perhaps the cost had to be counted: visible pregnancy was normally followed by outraged dismissal, abuse, and ostracism. Male reaction to the act of creation was mixed: some did the decent thing and married the girl; others reacted with injured innocence, indifference, rejection, or even with violence. Most servants had no family close at hand to give them support, a father or brother who could badger their daughter's or sister's seducer into making some sort of provision for mother and child. A social and cultural chasm separated 'upstairs' from 'downstairs' and was rarely bridged, their respective cultures did not overlap and in the Torbay district there were no trained social workers – a profession yet to be invented – to provide a friendly net when women fell.

In Torquay in 1857, for example, the 19-year-old Jonathan Roose went one evening to see Jane Stone, a servant girl who was carrying his child. They went for a walk. Suddenly he grabbed a heavy piece of wall-coping, struck her repeatedly on the head, and left her lying on the ground, senseless and apparently dead. She was discovered, covered in blood, by a passer-by and taken to the local infirmary where she recovered from her injuries and was able to give information about her assailant. Tried in 1858 at the Devon Spring Assizes at Exeter for attempted murder, Roose was sentenced to penal servitude for life. Later, in 1876, the sentence was remitted and he then left the country for Australia. Even the lower orders had their notions of respectability and Roose acted as he had because he feared to bring shame on his family and on himself if his loose behaviour became known. He was a self-regarding young man.

Abortion, as well as infanticide, was a traditional practice in South Devon and most villages had a knowing woman who would help unmarried women out of trouble. But not all those who found themselves *enceinte* were prepared to use an abortionist's skills, from fear or from moral convictions. Those unmarried women who did give birth to a child found themselves in a difficult position. It was therefore not unusual for those who wished to continue working, or were forced to do so from necessity, to seek a minder or some sort of surrogate mother. Frequently recourse was had to a baby farmer. This became an established and reasonably profitable occupation for women by the end of the century and it served a growing need. Clients of baby farmers came from all classes, but especially from the black-coated lower-middle classes, whose members suffered from an acute sense of conventional respectability, of keeping up appearances on a small income, and from working-class girls. There were baby farmers; and there were murderous baby farmers. Since they were paid a lump sum to take charge of or adopt a child, it was to the baby farmer's advantage that the infant did not live long, and the avaricious saw to it that this was so, either from neglect or, say, from smothering, which could usually be mistaken for the condition now known as 'cot death'.

The larger cities such as Plymouth and Exeter had their slums and warrens, their mazes of mean streets and alley-ways, their stews and brothels, doss houses and squalid inns. Even Torquay had such places, although on a smaller scale, districts where low life flourished and slum property abounded. Such awful living conditions encouraged practices such as infanticide and abortion, as well as incest, cruelty to children and brutality to wives, encouraged by alcoholism.

In the days of the old Poor Law, before 1834, it had been comparatively easy for an unmarried mother to swear her illegitimate child upon the father and then force him to maintain the child and herself. Under the new reformed system magistrates became chary of accepting unsupported testimony from unmarried mothers – the rules of evidence were either tightened or more strictly adhered to – and this change in principle and attitude now favoured the male progenitor. Henceforth it became extremely difficult for a woman to obtain any support from the putative father: and this was another reason why baby farmers flourished. Since Torbay contained such a large servant population, who as a class were prone to conceive out of wedlock, abortionists also flourished. The Victorian servant was subject to much exploitation.

By 1914 the single biggest occupation in Devon had become domestic service and it employed over 55,000 persons. John K. Walton has estimated that in Torquay in 1901 the number of domestic servants expressed as a percentage of the total number of separate households was 42.8. Indeed, as far back as 1851 the census had shown that in England, overall, domestic servants were the largest occupational group and so they remained up to the outbreak of war. In 1901 Torquay had a population of well over 24,000, of whom 59.7 per cent were described in the census as retired or unoccupied (i.e. mostly living on fixed incomes) and 18.5 per cent as domestic servants, an extremely high figure. In that year Torquay was noted for having the highest percentage of domestic servants among all high-class resorts. By then, 1901, the town had become supremely the abode of the rich, of the rentier and leisure classes.

And, of course, as a result of the great boom in the second half of the century in the building and the opening of new hotels, such as the *Imperial, Grand, Palace, Torbay, Belgrave,* and *Victoria and Albert* hotels, the demand for hotel staff increased. These new establishments were mostly newly built or converted from once privately occupied premises. The rising demand for hotel staff attracted employees from all over Great Britain and the Continent (Swiss and German waiters were much favoured and the best hotels and better restaurants usually employed French or foreign chefs). Unfortunately most hotel work was seasonal. The demand steadily rose in Torquay not only for domestic servants but also for chambermaids, waiters, milliners, musicians, cabmen, and other types of service workers. Laundresses were also at a premium and several laundries, some quite large in scale, were established. The number of shop assistants, especially in the grocery and provisions trades, also grew. Gentlefolk who lived in villas and other large houses in the town demanded fine things and good service and those grocers and shopkeepers who catered to this class of customer were apt to do very well, and a few even made a fortune.

* * *

Theft was the commonest offence, particularly larceny by a servant, and there were occasional outbreaks of housebreaking and burglary, which tended to diminish once the culprit or culprits were apprehended. In Torquay there were few professional criminals – except, perhaps, for those on the run from other parts and in hiding. Pickpockets on occasion would come down for the Torquay Regatta when crowded streets provided ideal conditions for the plying of their trade; and sometimes a 'swell mobsman' from the Metropolis would appear in the town, just 'resting' as actors say. There were inevitably some old offenders, old lags and reprobates, as in any town, whose offences were usually not alarming. These were the criminal milieu's pathetic failures, its misfits and oddities. Much petty theft was opportunistic. In rural areas poachers abounded and landowners employed gamekeepers to keep them down. Poachers when caught were severely treated by magistrates, often landowners themselves and keen to protect game. The landowning class, politically ascendant in Devon and all over rural England, was well able to look after its own interests.

Smugglers, once rife in coastal districts, steadily declined in number as the era of free trade opened and duties on goods once profitable to smuggle steadily fell. The introduction of a more efficient and less corrupt coastguard service greatly helped. Coastguard stations were established at Babbacombe and so was a small post at Paignton adjacent to the harbour. Brixham was the main base in Torbay waters for the service. The Brixham station was originally established on Queen's Quay but was transferred to Berry Head Road in 1889. In 1932 the service was taken from the Admiralty and placed in the hands of the Board of Trade. Its great days were now over. Nowadays the activities of drug smugglers who infest South Devon's many small harbours are mostly investigated by agents of the Customs and Excise and the Devon Constabulary.

Most crimes of violence were of a crapulous nature and drink usually the precipitating factor. By modern standards, crime rates were low; there were no crime waves; no sudden outbreaks of mugging or sexual assaults. Habitual law-breakers were mostly known to the police. Throughout the Victorian period Torbay was a remarkably law-abiding district in which to reside and its inhabitant always felt safe in their homes and in the streets.

The guardians of law and order were few and were mostly engaged in routine patrolling. Itinerant labourers and navvies, many of whom were Irish,

were at times imported to carry out heavy construction work on the railways
and on other large projects. They did at times cause concern by their unruly
and drunken behaviour, above all in the mid-1860s, when the Teignmouth to
Newton Abbot, the Newton Abbot to Torquay, and the Torquay to Kingswear
lines were being built. On occasion Brunel, the great railway engineer, employed
over 2,000 workers on particular stretches of the Great Western Railway.
Gipsies – travelling people – could also be a nuisance with their pilfering.
What is now known as Cary Parade or Green, then a patch of wasteland
abutting Torquay harbour, was notorious for numerous strangers who sometimes congregated there and was highly suspect as an area of grave immorality,
of much lewd behaviour. But Torquay night life was normally sedate. Torquay's
body of magistrates always dealt harshly with any disturber of the peace.

William Acton, a Victorian doctor and celebrated veneriologist, declared
in 1857 that: 'Prostitution is a transitory state through which an untold number
of British women are ever on their passage.' In Victorian England women
who elected for prostitution as a career were motivated nearly always by
economic need. This is borne out by Frances Finnegan's study of Victorian
prostitutes in York, published in 1979. Torquay could not support a large
contingent of prostitutes since, compared with York, its population was small,
but nonetheless they did exist. They plied their trade in a number of public
houses in the lower part of the town and the precincts of the harbour. In
1853, according to a report in the *Torquay Chronicle*, the Chief Constable,
Charles Kilby, complained to the local Bench of the 'unbecoming manner
that young women of the town wander around the thoroughfares without
bonnets and shawls' and requested advice as to what action he should take.
The magistrates responded by pointing out that a statute already existed which
gave full power to commit persons of this character – loose women – who
were 'indecent or guilty of unbecoming behaviour'. Even as late as the 1950s

41 *Although a popular walk
by day, the dimly lit Rock
Walk, at the foot of Waldon
Hill, had a dubious reputation
at night.*

a few ageing tarts could be found at night, the last survivors of a long tradition, loitering around Cary Green, who took their clients, most of whom had been out drinking, to the dimly-lit Rock Walk on Waldon Hill for recreation and pleasure.

Torquay always had a small circle of upper-class homosexuals and such a group appears to have been well established by the end of Victoria's reign, a number of whom lived on Warberry Hill, the site of many comfortable villas mostly put up in the 19th century. In the 1840s William Kitson had selected this hill area as suitable for villa development and had marked out three drives, each of which ran across the southern slopes of the hill, to provide access. In all about ninety sites, of between two and three acres, were made available and very soon building began. These villas were regarded as pukka residences and were much sought after by wealthy retired people. They were home, too, to a number of bachelors of all ages who normally lived on an allowance provided by indulgent parents or on private means. In Torquay before the First World War a remarkable number of well-educated young men pursued no occupation at all. They lived at home, were apt to dabble in the arts, to play tennis and croquet and were sometimes in peril on the tee. Their main occupation, however, seemed to be that of looking after and entertaining their mothers, or amateur dramatics.

The young Beverley Nichols lived with his father, a retired Bristol solicitor, in, so he states, 'the shabby grandeur of Cleave Court', one of the more than five hundred large Victorian villas constructed on the slopes of the Warberry and Lincombe hills. Cleave Court (now Riviera Court), built in 1839 but later added to, was in Lower Warberry Road. The family first arrived in Torquay in 1905 so that the young Beverley could become a pupil at Wellswood Preparatory School for the Sons of Gentlemen, a suitably pukka prep school for his son, Mr Nichols concluded. His father bought Cleave Court in 1913 and lived there until his death in 1924. In his autobiography, *Father Figure*, Beverley Nichols describes his attempt to murder (if this can be believed) his father, whom he loathed for his drunkenness and cruelty to his wife, Nichols' mother. He writes that once he deliberately propelled his wheelchair-bound father down a steep slope, hoping this would finish him off for good. His father, a resilient fellow, survived this bumpy downhill journey, to die at last in bed, but not by his son's hand.

Murder was rare in 19th-century England and it was not frequent in South Devon, but two cases are worth commenting on, for they throw light on social conditions at the time. These are the murder of a farmer called Jonathan May in 1835 and, at a later date, the murder of Emily Keyse, an elderly spinster, by John Lee at Babbacombe in 1884.

In 1835 Devonshire roads were not routinely patrolled by mounted or unmounted constables. When a crime on a country road or highway came to the knowledge of the authorities their normal reaction was to send a constable or two to gather information about the crime and the victim. At night robbers and footpads felt reasonably safe lying in wait for someone to rob on the unilluminated roads of those days. Moreover, country roads were infrequently used by travellers at night. In the 18th and early 19th centuries highwaymen did operate at times on the highways, mainly on the Exeter to London and the Exeter to Plymouth routes. But in South Devon there were few good pickings to be had for the gentleman of the road. A few highway robberies did, however, occur. The murder of Jonathan May was one and it was to have a curious aftermath and to become a celebrated *cause célèbre*, a case much discussed and mulled over in the House of Commons and the House of Lords.

On the night of 16 July 1835 a well known local farmer, Jonathan May, was riding home after a visit to Moretonhampstead Fair when he was attacked and robbed by two men at Jacob's Well on the Exeter Road. Beaten to the ground by repeated blows from a cudgel he died the next day from his injuries. There was a great hue and cry in the district and eventually two men were brought to trial for the crime, the 22-year-old Thomas Oliver (known as Buckingham Joe), a highwayman, and Edmund Galley, a wanderer who lived by small acts of roguery. Oliver, who confessed his guilt, was hanged at the gates of Exeter Gaol; but as real doubts existed about Galley's guilt he was respited and eventually transported to Australia. Thomas Latimer, editor and proprietor of the Liberal and Radical *Western Times*, published at Exeter, took up Galley's case and succeeded after many years in establishing his innocence. In 1881, Galley, now an ageing colonial shepherd, was pardoned and given £1,000 in compensation. Highway robbery steadily declined after Jonathan May's murder but this was mainly due to the rising prosperity of mid-Victorian England, brought about, it is argued, by the repeal of the Corn Laws. Other factors, such as the great Evangelical Revival, must also have had a civilising effect on those who would normally turn to crime. F.M.L. Thompson's social history of Victorian Britain is aptly titled *The Rise of Respectable Society*.

On the morning of 15 November 1884 the body of a 68-year-old spinster, Miss Emma Keyse, was found battered to death at 'The Glen', a house situated near the *Cary Arms* at the bottom of the steep road that runs down to Babbacombe beach from Babbacombe Downs. It was obvious that someone had attempted to disguise the cause of death by setting fire to her body. John Lee, aged 20, Miss Keyse's servant, one of four employed by her – the other three were women – was soon under suspicion. He was arrested and soon after charged with her brutal murder. It was an open and shut case.

Miss Keyse was one of the large number of Victorian spinsters attracted to Torquay by its reputation for warm summers, mild climate, and lovely scenery. At one time she had been a maid of honour to Queen Victoria. Though not short of money, she was a strict and parsimonious mistress to work for. Lee himself was born at Abbotskerswell, near Newton Abbot. His father worked in the clay mines near his home and also farmed a small plot of land. On his 15th birthday Lee was employed by Miss Keyse to look after her pony, which had belonged to her mother and to which she was greatly attached. Not long after, feeling restless and bored by his job, he joined the navy but was discharged on account of poor health. Returning to South Devon, now aged 19, he got a job as boots at the *Yacht Club Hotel* at Kingswear from which he was discharged for dishonesty. Then he wangled a job as footman to a Colonel Brownlow at Torquay. This position he did not hold for long for, when the family went abroad, he pawned the family plate, was caught, and sentenced to six months' imprisonment at Exeter Prison. On release, Miss Keyse, who had shown much interest in his career, took him back as footman – a fatal move. He appeared to be contrite and swore to go straight. Instead he battered her to death one night and set fire to her and the house. Why he did this is not clear since nothing was stolen from the house. It is argued that he murdered her in a fit of pique for having been dressed down for some dereliction of duty.

After his release in 1907 he returned to his mother's cottage at Abbotskerswell and soon after *Lloyd's Weekly News* signed him up to write his memoirs; later they were republished as *The Man They Could Not Hang* (1907). In this book he recounts how Berry at Exeter Prison tried three times to execute him and failed. It is now believed that the trap stuck because recent heavy rains had swollen the scaffold's woodwork. It seems unlikely, as some local people continue to believe, that the Almighty intervened in the matter: He, surely, had better things to do. Lee was a thief and liar, and violent, to boot. But John Lee remains Devon's most celebrated criminal. Miss Keyse's old home is no more and the site was used later as a car-park.

Miss Keyse's house was not in any way a commodious residence and for such a small house she certainly had a large staff to attend to her needs: three women and Lee, whose duties were to attend at meals and do odd jobs. He had to sleep in the pantry on a folding bed. But to members of her class her staffing situation did not seem extravagant.

Agatha Christie, who spent her early life in Torquay with her parents and later lived at Greenway on the Dart, has some pertinent comments on the servant situation before 1914. In her autobiography she writes:

> Servants, of course, were not a particular luxury; it was not a case of only the rich having them; the only difference was that the rich had more … As you descended the scale you would arrive eventually at what is so well described in those delightful books of Barry Pain, *Eliza* and *Eliza's Husband*, as 'the girl'.

Victorians were well aware of the dangers they sometimes courted from introducing strangers – male servants above all – into their homes and their private lives. Female servants were not, on the whole, a great worry; but a handful were: in 1879 a 30-year-old Irish woman, Kale Webster, progressed from committing robberies in the lodging houses in which she often stayed to murdering her employer, a Mrs Thomas, who lived alone in a cottage in Richmond. But one must not exaggerate: the servant class was mostly docile, for good references from an employer eased their journey through life as servants.

Valets and flunkeys sometimes had access to dangerous secrets or surreptitiously obtained compromising letters, papers, or documents; sometimes they used such knowledge to blackmail their employer. Many such cases are enshrined in the grave columns of *The Times* and other newspapers and in court reports. Miss Keyse had no secrets to hide; her life was blameless; but she courted trouble in employing the violent and aggressive John Lee, a young man who came to her with a bad record for delinquent behaviour. Crimes of this type are rarer today for few people now have live-in servants and not many can afford the expense. Miss Keyse's staff of four servants to run a small house would seem extraordinarily bizarre today.

Devonshire villages and small towns did not need a strong police presence because crime in general was not a great problem; these were really self-policing communities. Everyone was known to others and his conduct daily monitored and commented on by local gossips: this must have inhibited many on the brink of engaging in unlawful or immoral conduct. The local poachers and bad hats, drunkards and petty criminals were known by reputation to many, and well known certainly to the authorities. They did not present any real threat to those among whom they lived and Justices of the Peace had sufficient powers and resources to deal with these social nuisances. In the early 19th century a sprinkling of parish constables were to be found in the three Torbay towns but little is known about their appointment or duties for records have disappeared. It is clear, though, that they were sufficient to maintain law and order most of the time, except in turbulent or euphoric times. On the whole, throughout the 19th century the county was a peaceful place in which to live, and very much on the margin of change.

When rioting occurred on a large scale the militia or army was generally called in and special constables appointed. This happened in 1846 when the harvest failed and the poor were extremely distressed. Bread riots broke out in many Devon towns. Torquay also had its riot. Special constables, mostly tradesmen, were speedily sworn in and the army and the coastguard also sent small contingents of men. It is interesting to note that a body of navvies, employed on the railways works above Torre, went to the aid of the rioters but were repulsed after a slight skirmish. Authority in the person of March Phillips, the chief magistrate, stood firm and more than seventeen prisoners were taken into custody. No lives were lost; there were no bloody incidents to report.

However, riots were infrequent in these parts; and well known radical agitators rarely, if ever, came to Devon, for there was no true proletariat in Devon to stir up, no large concentration of disaffected industrial workers to inflame.

In Torquay, the Improvement Act of 1835 included within its provisions the construction of a lock-up and the employment of watchmen and constables for 'the protection of the inhabitants and property within the said parish'. Charles Kilby, formerly a poulterer on Vaughan Parade, was appointed principal constable in 1835 after the Act, but he was given some other duties as well. Kilby and his two constables, as J.T. White states, 'constituted the police force of Torquay'. By 1841 he had become known as the chief constable and by then commanded a body of six men. *The Torquay Directory*, the local newspaper, criticised 'the inefficiency of the present police force with but three night-watchmen to take charge of a town which covers nearly as much space as Exeter, is obvious to all'. A spate of burglaries had occurred which had much alarmed householders, although no one had been injured by the malefactors. It was simply that a string of burglaries was a most unusual event in Torquay and much commented upon.

In 1857 the County Constabulary Act came into force and following its enactment a chief constable for the county of Devon was sworn in. He was Captain Gerald De Courcy Hamilton, for it was usual in those days to put ex-army officers in command of police units, another body of men in uniform. At the same time, eight constables were appointed to the district of Torquay and in 1871 a new police station was opened in Market Street, Torquay. This is the origin of the town's modern police force. For 25 years Torquay had had a force under its own control, but the Torquay constabulary was absorbed into the Devon Constabulary as a result of the reform of the English police system.

Both Paignton and Brixham had their parish constables but little is known about their responsibilities. When the Devon County Constabulary was created by Royal Warrant in 1856 five constables were dispatched to Torquay in May 1857. The sergeant appointed to head this sub-division was expected to reside at Torquay but, at the same time, he was made responsible for the policing of Paignton, St Marychurch, and Kingskerswell. So two members of the Torquay force were dispatched to oversee Paignton. In 1864, 12 constables were stationed at Torquay but little is known about the staffing position at Paignton at that time, though it is thought that two constables were resident there during this period and they also had to look after the village of Cockington and its neighbourhood as well. As late as 1912 the force at Paignton consisted only of a sergeant and six constables and yet Paignton by then was fully established as a flourishing seaside resort with a resident population of over 11,000. The summer season was always jam-packed with holidaymakers and trippers and sometimes rowdy visitors, especially so when the annual summer fair and carnival was held, during which a great deal of drinking took place and drunks would be found sleeping it off on the sands or on benches in Victoria Park.

Justices of the Peace, who formed the magistracy in South Devon, played a key role, as they did in the rest of England, in law enforcement. They were to a man selected and appointed from the propertied class. No one could be a JP unless he had an estate valued at £100 per annum over and above his disbursements or was entitled to an estate leased for £300 per annum. This restriction considerably narrowed the field to those who were staunch supporters of the status quo. In 1832 the magistrates for the Paignton Division, an area which then included Brixham and the nascent Torquay, were Henry Cary of Torre Abbey, Robert Shedden, a kinsman of the last, and George Templer, the lord of the manor of Paignton. The others were J.B. Yarde Buller of Lupton House and Churston Court, Henry Studdy of Waddeton Court at Greenway on the Dart, Edward Elton, J. Parlby, and two local clergymen: the Revd William Kitson, vicar of Kingskerswell, and the Revd Robert Holdsworth, vicar of Upper Brixham. These could all be called upper-class pillars of the local establishment, all were accepted as gentlemen, and their names familiar to the inhabitants of the Torbay district.

The assizes, held in spring and summer, took place at Exeter with a great deal of pomp and ceremony; so too were held the quarter sessions. These courts dealt with the more serious offences and capital crimes. Magistrates adjudicated less serious crimes, were then termed misdemeanours. In those early Victorian years magistrates for the Torbay area (the Paignton Division) held court in Paignton at the *Crown and Anchor Inn*, for as yet no courthouse had been built at any of the three Torbay towns. When the magistracy sat at Paignton it was always a convivial occasion, the local élite meeting the local élite. Until well into the next century the same class of person dominated the magistracy and to some degree still does. Magistrates were unpaid and the position was an honorary one, much sought after by men of birth, wealth, or those with social pretensions.

Offenders in Devon sentenced to a term of imprisonment were incarcerated in Exeter Prison, the county's main gaol. It also housed the county's gallows, though not many were to suffer within its confines the extreme penalty of the law. In the early years of the 19th century there were prison hulks at Plymouth which held prisoners awaiting transportation. Each Torbay town had its small lock up or police cells to hold suspected offenders, the refractory or drunk but they did not stay in such places for long, usually overnight. Most of its inmates were petty offenders, thieves of one sort or another, or recidivists – life's failures – not masterminds of crime.

Seven

THE CREATION OF PAIGNTON

ARTHUR Hyde Dendy's tomb in Torquay cemetery is in juxtaposition to the Singer family's mausoleum, where Isaac Singer, his wife and children are all interred, together with his aesthetic and fastidious Proustian son-in-law, Prince Edmond de Polignac. These contiguous resting places are a fitting shrine for the entrepreneurs who were largely responsible for Paignton's transformation into a popular seaside resort.

Dendy brings to mind Edward Machin (familiarly known as Denry), the main character of *The Card*, Arnold Bennett's novel about a young man who rises from the lowly position of solicitor's clerk finally to become mayor of Bursley and one of the richest men in the Five Towns. Dendy and Denry, in fact and in fiction, had sanguine temperaments and displayed an amusing insouciance. Each believed the world was his oyster. Both were quick witted, and very sharp. They were cards. But Dendy was born into an affluent middle-class Birmingham family, took up law as a profession, and as a barrister was clearly of a superior social class to Bennett's low-born fictional Denry. But the resemblances are there.

The American millionaire Isaac Merritt Singer, apart from building the grandiose Oldway Mansion – his 'Wigwam' as he called it – was himself not much involved in developing Paignton; but his sons were, and in particular Paris Singer. In early life Paris had acquired a passion for architecture and for putting up buildings and since he inherited a large slice of his father's fortune he could richly indulge his hobby (with support from his brothers) at Paignton. The growth of Preston, as a suburb or residential extension of Paignton, is largely due to Singer enterprise, in particular the Marine Drive and the laid-out seafront area there. A third person also involved in the town's urban expansion was W.R. Fletcher, a wealthy businessman from Birmingham.

These entrepreneurs all came from outside the West Country; but a number of local people, mostly connected with the professions – architects, solicitors, estate agents, accountants – supported their endeavours, and by so doing did themselves much good. Those who participated in all this developmental work found their collaboration richly rewarded, and, for some, it established the foundations for their future success. One may cite the Bridgmans and Couldreys, architects, Eastleys the solicitors and Waycotts the house agents.

42 *Print of Paignton by J.W. Tucker. The tallest building visible is the parish church of St John, flanked by the decrepit Miles Coverdale Tower.*

Urban growth came to Paignton comparatively late. The town, especially the area that lies behind the seafront, looks like a lateVictorian and Edwardian creation. We can roughly date its formation as a resort from the mid-1860s. Torquay by then had already established itself as a flourishing winter resort which for several decades had been attracting many visitors (summer was the off-season) as well as permanent residents of substance, such as wealthy annuitants and members of the professions. Thus Torquay by mid-century was mostly occupied by a wealthy rentier class, who as a group have left their impress on the town. Paignton, on the other hand, followed a different path: it did not appeal much to the very rich nor even to the middling rich, since it lacked the amenities and appurtenances of a smart residential town. Paignton was referred to dismissively as Torquay's poor relation, for in those days it looked a trifle dowdy with its slatternly old town centre, poor streets and roads, and its appalling sanitation, with clogged-up cesspools and its many rubbish dumps. It was an unstylish and plebeian town compared with its much smarter, cleaner, patrician rival, Torquay, whose hills were starred with Italianate villas and its harbour district noted for its several elegant terraces.

The above print of Paignton by J.W. Tucker depicts it as it looked around 1865, and it provides a nice picture for the imagination to work on. The railway had reached the town in August 1859, so one is not surprised to see a small puffing train, with three passenger carriages attached, about to pull into Paignton station, which then resembled a small barn or shed. The tracks from Torquay to the station are clearly visible and are crossed at one point, near the station, by a narrow wooden passenger bridge. The rails lie across open ground, mostly grassland. The hills are lush green, fringed at their tops with copses and spinneys, or isolated clumps of trees. The tallest building visible (naturally!) is the parish church of St John, flanked by the decrepit Miles Coverdale Tower within the ruins of a one-time palace of the Bishops of Exeter; but almost competing with it in height (in this print at least) is the isolated private house named Redcliffe Tower, a bizarre Anglo-Indian edifice started in 1854 by a minor nabob, a Colonel Robert Smith, on the site of a former Martello tower, which he incorporated into the finished building. Smith's intention was to build a replica of an Indian palace. 'Smith's Folly', as locals once termed it, is near the Preston end of Paignton beach.

Of course, there had been some developments since the turn of the century, but the main body of the town remained inland from the sea. A few villas had been built nearer the shore, and Roundham, the hill above the harbour, had begun to attract the attentions of builders. On the whole, though, Paignton in the early 1860s had not greatly changed since the 18th century; nor had the quiet hamlets of Collaton, Polsham, and Preston, with their mud-walled thatched cottages. There had thus been no appreciable growth in housing. The mid-century years epitomised the triumph of British enterprise

43 *Palace Tower or Coverdale Tower, all that remains of the medieval Paignton Palace.*

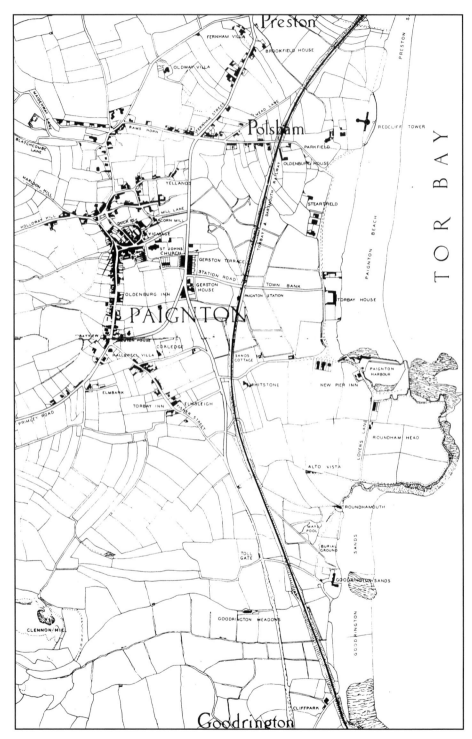

44 *Paignton 1863. The solidly constructed Torbay House had withstood over the years many a siege by the sea, including the great storm of 1824.*

and industry, commerce and trade, but Paignton had been left largely unaffected by these important events.

The only building standing on the fringes of the foreshore was still Torbay House, which had now declined into a boarding house under the management of a Mary Tompsett; earlier in the century it had been a summer residence for Colonel Seale of Mount Boone, Dartmouth, and for his son, later Sir Henry Seale, famed in South Devon as a dedicated and furious foxhunter, the Master of the South Devon Foxhounds. This isolated house could still only be approached across a waste of sand dunes by way of either Polsham Lane to the north or by Marsh Lane (now Sands Road) to the south. The solidly constructed Torbay House had been erected on the only piece of firm ground along the shore and had withstood over the years many a siege by the sea, even surviving the great storm of 1824 when the whole shore area and much land lying behind it had been inundated and the beach itself left littered with the flotsam and jetsam from many wrecked ships.

One of the earlier descriptions of Paignton is to be found in Powhele's *Devonshire* and derives (it seems) from Swete's manuscript account of the district in 1792:

> The parish consists of one village – Payton, and five or six hamlets with many farmhouses interspersed in various parts. The greater part of the houses are built of mud walls and covered with thatch, but not noted for neatness or commodiousness. A great quantity of orchard land.

In 1850 Paignton was now described as a 'neat and improving village and *bathing place*'. The Ward, Lock *Guidebook to Paignton* for 1900 laconically states: 'Thirty years ago a mere village, quite unknown to the world at large.' In 1801 the census had given the town's population as 1,575; in 1851 it had reached 2,746; in the last forty years of the century the population was to treble, to reach 8,385 in 1901.

The only change of great significance before 1860 (apart from the coming of the railway in 1859) had been made in 1837, when the prospectus of the Paignton Harbour Company was issued. This was followed by the passing of the Paington (*sic*) Harbour Act of 1838, an Act that sanctioned the construction of a new harbour in place of the former decayed one. The principal improvements brought about by the Act were the construction of two solid stone piers which now allowed vessels of 150 tons to berth, to load and unload heavy cargo. The private Harbour Company which sponsored the Act desired to give Paignton a small commercial port. It did not fully succeed in this aim and Paignton harbour never rivalled that of Torquay commercially, let alone Brixham or Dartmouth in this respect, both of which had extensive facilities for shipbuilding, ship-repairing and ancillary marine services.

This private commercial company administered harbour affairs until 1936, when the company was finally taken over by Paignton Council, whose main object in making the purchase was to turn it into a tourist attraction. The Council tidied up much of the neighbouring area and in 1938 acquired the foreshore abutting the Paignton Club. By extending the Promenade along the shore and around several cottages, disposed on a low cliff flanking the harbour, they were able to link the promenade at last with the harbour by cutting through a warehouse on one of the quays that blocked access. This work was mostly completed after the War. Today there is an almost uninterrupted promenade, apart from a small section at Redcliffe, from Hollacombe to the harbour quays.

When the railway reached Paignton it eventually stimulated a series of booms in the building trade, for the railway opened up the town to invasion from most parts of the British Isles. When building booms occurred in later years, local developers found the town already provided with a good-enough harbour for their needs, an essential condition since much heavy material – timber, stone, bricks, and such like – had to be imported and the cheapest form of transportation was by ship. Passenger services from London by sea had started up in the 1830s but demand steadily declined once the railway, by stages, was extended from Exeter to Paignton. By the 1860s, then, the foundations for future expansion had been laid. Paignton now had excellent communications both by sea and rail, and the road network had also been greatly improved, in particular the important coastal road from Torquay, from which several roads radiated, leading to Brixham, Totnes, and Newton Abbot, and to other Devonshire towns.

The 1860s, it follows, is the period when Paignton started to take off. There is a letter from the newly formed Paington (*sic*) Local Board of Health to the Principal Secretary of State which describes the parish in not entirely complimentary terms, nor in felicitous prose:

> Paington is a large parish containing five thousand and ninety-two acres of land, and the population it is said of about 3,000 mostly depending on agriculture. The town consists of houses surrounding the church, scarcely deserving the name of streets extending in one direction about a quarter of a mile, and on the other three sides, three quarters of a mile or more, it has also six villages from one to three miles distant, mostly farm houses and cottages occupied by labourers who find employment on the farms.

* * *

The decisive date for Paignton's transformation is 1866, when a Mr McLean sold by auction the 200 acres he owned, land mostly adjacent to Polsham sands. In May of the same year he conveyed Polsham Green – a tract of sandy dunes often inundated by the sea – to the town on condition that the Local Board should in future check all sea encroachments on the land he had given up. The Board was the regulatory body – a local government body –

that concerned itself with Paignton's affairs, though its powers at that time were not extensive; that was to come.

A year before, in 1865, W.R. Fletcher had bought 60 acres of land, east of the railway, including the somewhat neglected Torbay House. He was a successful Birmingham businessman who had made his fortune in the industrial Midlands and now sought a profitable outlet for his amassed funds. On this ground he intended to erect villas for the wealthier classes. Torbay House together with its grounds occupied about five acres, but Fletcher had no intention of preserving this old property.

This developer from Birmingham predicted there would be an increasing demand in the future for villa residences in Paignton and that they would attract retired folk from northern counties and even from Scotland (and he was proved right). The middle classes as a proportion of the total population had grown markedly in Victorian England; they had also greatly increased in number, coincident with the steep rise in the general population, a rise which became visible in the later stages of the Industrial Revolution. People from the Midlands and the North, especially those who had retired enriched from their business activities, were beginning to migrate in increasing numbers to more congenial areas than the Black Country or other industrial districts and usually chose the less-populated southern counties with their reputed salubrious coastal regions. And the coming of the railway was a key factor in this movement.

Fletcher engaged a bright young Torquay architect, George Soudon Bridgman, who was only 27 at the time, to draw up a plan for the development of the land he had just acquired, an area of flat ground lying between the railway and the sea. This was a choice, almost ideal, site for an architect to lay out. There wasn't much that needed to be demolished, but much to be built.

This was to be the first major extension of Paignton seawards, away from its historic centre. Bridgman came up with basically a grid-plan, with inter-secting streets at regular intervals, as in an American city, and with the whole development fronted by an esplanade and with a stout promenade along the shore to keep the sea at bay. Many of the new buildings were three-storied terraced houses, but the plan allowed for considerable variation in size and type of house. His plan was accepted. Building started. Fletcher died in 1877 but his trustees continued with the plan. Bridgman's design was practical, sensible and simple, and must have pleased the developer. One has to say it is not very exciting architecture but it probably looked better when it was first put up, for Bridgman insisted that all the houses should be painted white or rendered white in contrast to the red sandstone so common to this stretch of coast.

By June 1870 much progress had been made: one half of Polsham Green had been flattened and seeded and the roads completed. The first and most necessary task – the construction of a sea wall – had been completed in 1868 so that the building sites would now be protected against winter flooding. Torbay House was finally demolished about 1878. The lineaments of modern Paignton – the Paignton we observe today – then came partially into focus.

It was a clever move for McLean to donate the maze of dunes and wasteland, now Polsham Green, to the town. The sea frequently invaded this low-lying area, especially in winter, and washed into Polsham Road and even lapped on occasion the lower reaches of Torbay Road, infiltrating the extensive marsh lands that lay east of the railway. Before laying out his seafront estate, Fletcher, for example, had been forced to culvert a leat constructed sometime in the past to drain this area; but the expense, in the long run, of protecting his newly acquired estate against the sea's inroads would have cost him much. Without a solid barrier kept under constant repair his houses would have become difficult to sell, at least at the prices he was asking for them. The Local Board built a stout bank against the sea and later a concrete and stone promenade along the shoreline. There was less fear now of the sea.

After his death Fletcher's trustees donated to the town this unutilised tract of sand dunes and sea marsh, which was then converted into the pleasant recreational space known as Paignton Green. The people of Paignton benefited from both these philanthropic gestures; and, indirectly, so too did the entrepreneurs, McLean and Fletcher and their families. Their estates were now protected by a ring of concrete and stone blocks. White's *Directory of Devon*, commenting on some of these improvements, claimed that they 'greatly enhanced the value of the contiguous building land, most of which had by then (1878) been mapped and laid out by the same architect'.

After 1865, the pace of development accelerated and there were several booms in the local building industry, linked with the upturns and downturns of the Victorian economy. But periods of stagnation and depression caused much unemployment among local building workers, for whom work as a rule was either casual or seasonal; and few builders maintained a permanent work force. They recruited labour when needed, which could be 'stood off' at short notice. It is perhaps unnecessary to state that expanding resort towns are apt to attract developers, builders (and a host of jobbing builders), and labourers. Paignton at the end of the 19th century had a large number of small building firms, whose fortunes tended to fluctuate with periods of prosperity and depression. On the whole, though, it seems labourers did relatively better in Paignton than in most other places since urban development, despite a few slow-downs, was fairly constant over this period, 1865 to 1914. In the four years to 1888, as John Pike states, plans for 287 new houses were approved by the Local Board. At the turn of the century the pace of building had in no way abated: 90 houses were put up in 1901 and 78 the following year.

45 *Paignton Promenade and Sands and Preston Beach and Promenade. The Local Board built a stout bank against the sea and, later, a concrete and stone promenade along the shoreline.*

Paignton was now recognised as a coming seaside resort and reputed for its long stretches of sands. These could be traversed at low tide from Holla-combe cliffs to the harbour; but at high tide a stroller would find Redcliffe Tower, built on a small protuberance, lapped by the scampering sea, a slight obstacle to his further progress. The great storm of 1901 did breach the Redcliffe's high sea wall – the effects of which are visible today – but left the edifice intact, still brooding over the sands. The resort was obviously a marvellous holiday home for families: the large expanse of beach provided children with an enormous playground. Their parents could lie on the sand or sit on the promenade and keep a guardian eye on offspring. In the summer season there were donkeys for hire on the beach, sideshows, stalls, and a Punch and Judy man. The Green in the summer was mostly used for playing games or sitting down. The pier, begun in 1878, was a great attraction for old and young and drew large crowds of loungers in the season.

The establishment in 1881 of the Paignton Club on the Esplanade adjacent to the harbour marks Paignton's coming of age. It is a building in the classical style, relieved in front by a colonnade of six Ionic columns supporting a balcony, with a flagstaff in front. It opened as 'The Gentlemen's Club' and only the local élite, then comprising doctors, solicitors, former colonial officials, ex-naval or army officers, were at first admitted to membership. The club's patrons were thus middle- or upper-middle-class, but would in time include lesser fry such as bank managers, accountants, and estate agents, members of the new quasi-professions. At first the vulgarly or ostentatiously wealthy normally were banned, but acceptable if they had been to a good school or were obviously gentlemen. Those in trade were not looked at. The Club was a snobbish and restricted enclave, reminiscent of the *cercles* found in French provincial towns, those exclusive coteries of bourgeois notables that Simenon likes to describe in his novels. Paignton's very 'superior' club was given over to bridge and gossip, gentlemanly soaking and snoozing: it was a place where the town's affairs were mulled over by those in the know. It is significant, then, that by the early 1880s the town had acquired a large and affluent enough élite to support such an establishment. This was a sure sign of material progress.

* * *

It was Arthur Hyde Dendy who coined the phrase that 'Torquay was built for Paignton to look at'. Dendy was born in 1821 and came from a Birmingham family. He practised as a barrister in the Midlands, specialising in equity law, the province of the Chancery Courts, but gave it up after a few years. When R.S.S. Cary came of age in 1849 – he was only 12 when his father, Henry Cary, died in 1840 – he offered Dendy and his brother joint appointment as stewards of the Torre Abbey estate, and they were also asked to act as trustees for the entire property, together with their father, also a lawyer. Cary's solicitors were

Dendy and Lee, probably the younger Dendy's firm. The brothers held this position until sometime in the late 1850s. By then Dendy had acquired Rock House on the Cary-owned Walden Hill as a residence; but when in the 1850s the Harvey brothers built the *Torbay Hotel* below his big verandahed villa he instituted proceedings against them for damaging his property, alleging that the hotel's 40 chimneys rendered his own house uninhabitable. Litigation was protracted and finally the fed-up Dendy removed himself to Paignton.

His flight was also encouraged by the irritating discovery that it was quite impossible to purchase freehold property at Torquay, and as a lawyer he had a great aversion to leaseholds. Both Palk and Cary, between them the land-owners of Torquay, would rarely grant a freehold to anyone. Dendy was thus stumped. Instead, he bought up a considerable amount of freehold property at Paignton and Preston in a parish where there was no autocratic landowner or oligarchy of prominent citizens who could set the rules. Dendy by this time was a wealthy man and was to become more so as the years passed, when he diversified his business operations.

George Templer of Stover House, who died in 1843, was once lord of the manor of Paignton. He was a magistrate for the Paignton division, Master of the South Devon Foxhounds, and owned Compton Castle, once the home of the Gilberts. Templer was a public figure, one of the most important person-ages in the Paignton district and extremely active in local affairs until around the mid-1820s, when as a result of unsound investments he suffered crippling financial losses; and soon after was forced to sell Stover House and other properties in South Devon to stave off bankruptcy. Most of his estate was

46 Torbay Hotel. *When the Harvey brothers built the* Torbay Hotel *below Arthur Hyde Dendy's villa, he alleged that the hotel's 40 chimneys rendered his own house uninhabitable and removed himself to Paignton.*

purchased by the 11th Duke of Somerset in 1828. What precisely happened after that date is difficult to ascertain. The Templer family nominally retained their manorial title until the Law of Property Act, 1922. With its enactment the old copyhold system came to an end in England and with it disappeared that antiquated feudal designation: Lord of the Manor.

Probably most of the Templer land was sold in parcels to comfortably-off and capable local farmers, for Paignton's soil was extremely fertile and the district for centuries had been noted for its high productivity. Agricultural land here was much coveted. The Torbay district had been famed for years for the quality of its cider, which was exported in great quantities to other parts of England; so too was the renowned outsize Paignton early cabbage. Black's *Guide to Devonshire* for 1878 suggests: 'Paignton should be visited in the apple-blossoming season for the cider apple is largely cultivated in the neighbourhood, and acre upon acre groan with luxuriant orchards.' When Dendy came on the scene in the late 1850s there was apparently no shortage of freehold land to purchase in Paignton, land that was not given over to agriculture, such as the foreshore area, and that was its chief attraction in the eyes of the blossoming entrepreneur.

Dendy was the man who made Paignton a 'fun place' for late Victorian, mostly lower-middle-class holiday-makers and trippers; but after the First World War, it should be added, it began to attract black-coated workers, such as shop assistants and clerks, as well as the skilled worker in good employ (those called the 'aristocracy of labour'), that is, the thrifty working class, composed of families who were able to save enough for an annual week's holiday by the sea. Now we should examine Dendy's building activities, for he complemented the work begun by W.R. Fletcher.

In the 1860s Paignton had no hotels. Travellers either had to put up at one of the inns in Winner Street or Church Street or stay with friends and relations. They could of course have chosen to take a room at one of a number of

47 *By the turn of the century Paignton was recognised as a coming seaside resort.*

48 *Paignton from the south, with the new pier in the background. When the urbanisation of Paignton speeded up there was a need for more accommodation; there were some boarding houses and a few people took in visitors.*

hotels in Torquay, the *Royal* still the most popular until the *Torbay* opened its doors. When the urbanisation of Paignton speeded up there was obviously a need for much more accommodation for visitors: Dendy stepped into the breach. To meet the expanding demand he opened the residential *Esplanade Hotel*, one of the first buildings on the Front, and followed that up with the construction of the *Gerston Hotel*, also residential, in Station Square. For some years they were the only decent hotels in the resort and the *Gerston*, in particular, catered for the commercial classes. There were of course a number of boarding- and lodging-houses of varied quality and a few people took in the occasional visitor. Later Dendy was to acquire Parkfield and Steartfield, both large houses, near the seafront, and he made the first his Paignton residence.

The Station Square area soon become the hub of the new town and the terminus for public transport. Previously Winner Street and Church Street had been the chief retail areas where people mostly shopped; but as the town developed both Palace Avenue and Victoria Street displaced these. By the 1880s the smarter shops were all located in these streets, later supplemented by Torbay Road which led from Station Square down to the seafront. In Torbay Road was later built in 1914 Deller's Café with special bricks imported from Holland. Deller's was once the finest modern building in Paignton, but pulled down in the 1970s and replaced by a trumpery, nondescript block which defies description. The Festival Theatre is yet another example of what should not be built. Dendy's name is commemorated in Hyde Road and Dendy Road. There is, I believe, no Arthur Road.

49 *Deller's Café. This was built in 1914 with special bricks imported from Holland. It was once the finest modern building in Paignton and the most fashionable venue for all of South Devon.*

Dendy's great contribution to the new seaside resort was a pier. In late Victorian and Edwardian England piers were enormously popular, as popular as the *palais de danse* and the cinema between the wars. He thought of buying Teignmouth Pier which was for sale, dismantling and erecting it on the foreshore at Paignton, but this in the end proved to be impracticable. Instead he commissioned Bridgman to design a new pier incorporating a pavilion, and this the architect did. Construction started in 1878 and the Paignton Pavilion Pier, as it was then called, was opened the following year for the summer season. It was 750 feet long and included a billiard hall and theatre. It offered popular musical concerts, dances, and other entertainments, such as a roller skating rink. From it ran a service of steam passenger launches to Torquay. It was at once a great attraction and a great success, though Dendy himself did not make much money from this particular enterprise, but he had many other irons in the fire and these certainly paid off.

An intelligent and educated, hyperactive and enthusiastic man, Dendy on occasion was irritated by Paignton's Toytown Local Board and its small corps of part-time administrators, whose watchword, it seemed to him, was caution and whose main characteristic was an extraordinary reluctance to accept innovations. At times the Local Board and its minions interfered with the profitable running of his enterprises by pointing out, for example, that he was in breach of some bye-law or other. Dendy was the owner of a number of horse-drawn bathing machines nicely positioned on Paignton beach, which were pushed into the sea when occupied by bathers. They could only be used by 'ladies', as those with some pretensions to gentility were then called, for a local bye-law prohibited men from bathing south of Redcliffe Tower. Preston beach to the north was reserved for male bathing and the boundary was set at Redcliffe Tower. The separation of the sexes on bathing beaches was common in those days, mandatory in a decent resort. At Torquay, Beacon Cove was reserved solely for female bathers and men had to slog up Beacon Hill and then down to Meadfoot beach before they could disrobe and go swimming.

The perception of the female body, even if clad voluminously in bathing attire, was also linked with Victorian conceptions of social class and the idea of respectability. It was then presumed that no decent woman would wish to be gaped at lewdly. The labouring classes had fewer inhibitions about casual

50 *Paignton and the Pier from the Esplanade. One of Dendy's many contributions to the new seaside resort was a pier. He commissioned Bridgman to design a pier incorporating a pavilion.*

or disordered dress: they were under no compulsion to be fussy in such
matters: people who lived higgledy-piggledy in the warrens of the poor could
hardly be expected to attain the demure standard of modesty demanded by
the respectable classes. Decorum on the beach was a *sine qua non* of respectability; and so this extraordinary (in some ways) system of etiquette, of what
is proper and what is not, served as a social marker in Torquay and Paignton,
as elsewhere in Victorian England.

In August 1871 a man was prosecuted at Paignton for bathing too near the
bathing machines, and fined in the Magistrate's Court. Because of this bye-
law Dendy could not obtain any male customers for his machines and was
starting to lose money on his venture. There had been a previous rumpus
when Local Board officials had inspected his machines and found that copies
of the current bye-laws were not properly displayed on them. The public, as
usual, backed Dendy and when he put up for election to the Board he was
returned top of the poll and within a year became chairman of the Local
Board, a position he occupied from 1873 to 1877. That was the way Dendy
did things: he dashed straight at an obstacle and knocked it down.

Dendy's resignation from the same Board in 1877 is perplexing. In 1877,
as Penwill states, this body resolved 'That the thanks of the Board be tendered
to Mrs Singer [Isabella Singer] for the improvement at Preston Sands by
erecting a sea wall and making a path thereon.' Dendy was the only member
of the Board who churlishly voted against the resolution, and the following
month he resigned his chairmanship and with it his seat. A possible inter-
pretation of his act is that he disliked the Singers for having come to a town
where he saw himself as its most important citizen, Paignton's overlord by
virtue of his wealth, his landholding, and the scale of his enterprises. It is also
possible that he had disliked Isaac Singer (for Singer himself was now dead)
as a brash American, one who had offered higher-than-average wages to his
workers at Oldway, as a result of which other employers had been forced to
pay higher rates. Singer's generosity to the working classes was not applauded
by all people since some wished to keep wages down, or at least stable. Even
the Local Board was now obliged to pay higher wages to its own labourers.

Dendy, if thwarted, could be a difficult customer to handle. A former
lawyer, he had been expertly trained to argue a case and he was prepared at
all times to act as his own counsel. And of course he was a snob. Very few
in these Victorian sunset years were not: England was a very class-conscious
nation, with an elaborate system of class relations and subtle nuances of
behaviour clinging to social positions. Singer, once a jobbing artisan and an
American mountebank, might well have been regarded by Dendy as only
every other inch a gentleman, despite Singer's obvious wealth, his lavish style
of living, and his great generosity. This American in Paignton, so the legend
runs, was snubbed and cold-shouldered by the local gentry (of whom Dendy

would have seen himself as one) and as a result the people he invited to his entertainments were never the *crème de la crème* of Torbay society but usually the families of local tradespeople or the better-off, with a sprinkling of the professional classes. However, Singer was always regarded by the generality as a *grand seigneur*, as the real Squire of Paignton.

Dendy, very much a live wire, had multiple interests. He operated two hotels, as well as the Paignton Pier Company and the Bathing Machine Company, and he even built a theatre mainly for his own diversion, called the Bijou, at the *Gerston Hotel*, and in December 1879 the first performance of 'The Pirates of Penzance' was given on its small stage. This was for copyright reasons. Oddly, in the circumstances, both Dendy and Singer shared a passion for the theatre. In 1872 he started an omnibus service to Torquay and, parallel with that, ran a steam passenger service from Paignton pier to Torquay. These were not really in competition – they served different needs – and both proved to be lucrative. In 1883 he opened a cycling track behind the *Esplanade Hotel* for enthusiasts, for those caught up in the great cycling craze, the craze for being on wheels (Shaw was one and also H.G. Wells) of the later 19th century. Lastly, he owned his own local newspaper. This list does not exhaust all his interests, which were versatile. It is obvious that he was a man of much restless energy.

Dendy played the violin and owned a Stradivarius. He was no Paganini but a good amateur musician. Stradivari were rare and comparatively costly even

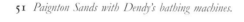

51 *Paignton Sands with Dendy's bathing machines.*

52 *Bathing machines, 1896. Dendy was the owner of a number of horse-drawn bathing machines nicely positioned on Paignton Beach. They could only be used by women.*

then. They acted as status symbols, for only the well-off could afford them. The ownership of a Cézanne or a Francis Bacon serves the same function today. Such objects of value tended to mark a man as a person not only of wealth but of taste. Dendy also maintained a schooner yacht and a yawl, and he liked to go cruising in the former. What turned out to be his last cruise took him to the North Sea, where he struck a rock and the boat foundered in shallow water. During this incident he broke a leg and, what perhaps was worse, lost his precious Stradivarius which went down with the yacht. Distressed by his loss, he employed divers to recover his effects and, he hoped, his violin, which they did. After long immersion in salt water the violin had come apart. The fragments were sent to a London expert who put them together. Afterwards, Dendy declared his Stradivarius played better than ever. Luck was ever on his side: but Dendy went no more a-cruising.

He died suddenly of a heart attack in August 1886. The local newspaper, the *Torquay Directory*, published an effusive obituary, of which these lines form part:

> Mr Dendy was a man of much wealth – it has been said, with what truth it is impossible to say, that he paid income tax on £20,000 annually; at all events, the many enterprises he entered into proves that he possessed great financial resources … he has conferred very great advantages on Paignton by undertaking enterprises which no one else would possibly attempt, but which by means of the resources at his command he was enabled to carry on whether they happened to be successful financially or not.

Dendy was married and had one child, Mary Henrietta, who married Sir John Seale of Dartmouth in 1879, and their eldest son was to become the fourth baronet. Dendy himself had no son and therefore no heir to take over his enterprises. After his death, the Dendys soon vanished from Paignton life and from memory. His daughter Mary had predeceased him in August 1882. Today only a few street-names commemorate the Dendy family and few people now recognise the name. In 1894 the tract of land that includes the Victoria Park area – about nine and a half acres – was compulsorily purchased from the Dendy trustees and turned into a park, Victoria Park, and very soon it became Paignton's best known, most popular and pleasant recreational area, a great boon to the town.

Times, however, were beginning to change. In December 1894 the Paignton Local Board, with whom Dendy had at times wrestled, met for the last time, and a few days later the Urban District Council was instituted, with far wider powers. This Council in time was very much managed by the 'shopocracy', who became the most powerful interest group in the town.

* * *

In 1870 Isaac Singer and his family arrived in Torquay from London where they had been staying at *Brown's Hotel*, Dover Street. They had recently escaped from Paris, from the impending horrors of the Franco-Prussian War, the Siege and the Commune. Isabella, Singer's wife, was in poor health after the difficult birth in Paris of her sixth and last child, Franklin. Her London physicians recommended the West Country as an excellent place for invalids, and Torquay, the premier resort in those parts, as ideal for recuperation; and so they came to Devon and took rooms in the *Victoria and Albert Hotel* in Belgrave Road,

53 *Paignton Beach. A local bye-law prohibited men from bathing south of Redcliffe Tower. Preston beach to the north was reserved for male bathing.*

54 *Dendy also ran a steam passenger service from Paignton pier to Torquay.*

Torquay. Torquay's mild climate soon raised their spirits and much improved Isabella's health. They made up their minds to settle in the district. But, like Dendy before him, Singer soon found it impossible to purchase freehold land on which to build his dream house. He had tried to buy Isambard Brunel's estate at Watcombe, Torquay, but found that, although the famous engineer had died in 1859, his property was not on the market (Brunel Manor, the French chateau-style house built on the estate after his death has no connection with the Brunel family). Lounging about one day at the hotel, he came upon the young George Soudon Bridgman, who had been engaged by the proprietor to design an extension and other improvements. Singer was at once impressed by the architect, a courteous, charming, and obviously clever young man, and concluded on the spot that he was the right man to build the great house he had for so long envisaged. Bridgman jumped at the offer and agreed

55 Victoria and Albert Hotel. *In 1870 Isaac Singer and his family arrived in Torquay and took rooms at this hotel in Belgrave Road.*

to prepare draft plans, according to Singer's specifications. He soon set to work on provisional drawings for his preposterously rich client – an American millionaire! Manna from Heaven! Singer instructed him: 'I want a big wigwam, and I shall name it "The Wigwam".'

In 1871 Singer purchased at Paignton the Fernham Estate, about 100 acres, then mostly parkland and orchards. Later, after Isaac died, the Singers were to acquire more land. The estate in 1871 included Oldway House (renamed 'Little Oldway' by Singer), a villa built by Major Thomas Studdy around mid-century, and Fernham, another commodious villa. There were several old cottages close by and an inn, *The Rising Sun*. The cottages and inn were soon pulled down. Now Singer had a fine uncluttered site for the imposing house Bridgman was to design for him. On

56 *George Soudon Bridgman. The architect, a courteous, charming and obviously very clever young man, here photographed when he was Master of the Torbay Lodge of Freemasons in 1877-8, impressed Singer.*

it was eventually erected Oldway House (Oldway Mansion or plain Oldway), but Singer always referred to it as the 'Wigwam'. Singer had a penchant for Indian names and ways, which had their origin in the many years he spent as an itinerant mechanic and strolling player in the small towns and settlements of rural and frontier America.

The earliest known Singer ancestor was a Reisinger of Frankfurt am Oder, who was probably a Hungarian Jew. Around the year 1700 one of Reisinger's sons married a Protestant, in all likelihood a Lutheran. Their youngest son Adam, an adventurous young man, emigrated to America in 1769 at the age of 16, with his father's help. Once there, he shortened his name to Singer and married a girl of Dutch origin. Both husband and wife were Protestants and the family continued in that tradition. Isaac Merritt Singer was born of this union in 1811 in the State of New York. He left home at the age of 12 and took up the craft of wood-carving and was also an adroit self-trained mechanic, for which he showed great talent and inventiveness. But he was torn between pursuing two disparate professions, that of a mechanic, inventor and improver, and a career as an actor. As a stage-name he adopted that of Merritt and called his troupe the Merritt Players. In 1844, when he was 33, he disbanded

57 *The Masonic Hall has been in continual use since 1891. George Soudon Bridgman, who gave the land to the Masons, can be seen standing on the far right.*

58 *George Soudon Bridgman in Victoria Park in the 1890s with his house, Courtland House, in the background.*

his company and retired from the stage after spending 14 years in the vain attempt to become a great thespian.

During these years another of his talents was startlingly revealed: he was a master of the art (or craft) of seduction. A married man, he always kept a string of mistresses by whom he was to have numerous children. He maintained this habit until late in life. The remarkable thing about all his womanising was that he rarely threw aside an old mistress and always provided for his illegitimate children, in one way or another. He liked his children, whether born in or out of wedlock, whether male or female. Singer was unique in that he always acknowledged his numerous children and was proud of them; he rarely concealed their existence from his circle of friends. In this respect, he was a decent man. By 1860 Singer's tally was 18 children, of whom 16 were still living. At that time, he was

59 *The Wigwam. Singer instructed his architect, George Soudon Bridgman, 'I want a big wigwam, and I shall name it "The Wigwam".' The final cost was £100,000.*

keeping three families in New York together with a fourth, the legitimate one. By his last marriage to Isabella Boyer he had a further six children, and possibly other children by occasional mistresses.

It is usually believed, even in Torbay, that Singer invented the sewing-machine which carries his name: he did not. What he did was to introduce improvements into its design so that it ran more smoothly and broke down less frequently. He simplified the basic mechanics and made it small enough to fit into the average home. The improved sewing-machine could be mass-produced under factory conditions, and in mass-production Americans were the pioneers. Vast numbers of Singer sewing-machines were sold in America, more than 110,000 by 1869, and they became extremely popular in homes all over the world. By 1860 Singer's firm was the foremost producer of sewing-machines in America and Europe, and soon in the world. You could even acquire one on hire purchase, a popular innovation for those on low incomes. Singer and his partner, the attorney Edward Clark, became millionaires and their sewing-machines a household name. In 1863 the Singer Manufacturing Company was incorporated.

Singer's last wife, Isabella Boyer, was 30 years younger than her 50-year-old husband. She was half-French, and had married in her teens. She was still married when Singer came on the scene in Paris in the summer of 1862 and by autumn she had become his mistress. She was soon divorced from her first husband and in June 1863 they were married, Isabella then being in an advanced state of pregnancy. A son was born soon afterwards and named Adam Mortimer Singer, the first of the six children they were to have.

Singer's scandalous and notorious love life had become common knowledge in America. When he beat up one of his mistresses because she protested at his taking another, the crude facts were duly reported in *Leslie's Weekly*, which had a circulation of over 150,000, and were taken up by other newspapers and magazines. Things were getting too hot for both of them in New York where they were not received in polite society and rejected by the 'Four Hundred' (so named, it seems, after Mrs William B. Astor's ballroom which could only accommodate 400 guests, the supposed cream of New York society). Singer retired from active direction of the company in 1863 and sold his shares in the business. Four years later he left for Europe, urged on by his wife who missed her homeland. Never again did they return to America, to the country where Singer had made his millions. They settled in Paris in a house on the boulevard Malesherbes and a further three children were born there. The Singer ménage fled from Paris in the autumn of 1870 and went straight to London where they took rooms at *Brown's Hotel*, the starting point for their Devon saga.

Singer's reception in Paignton throws light on Victorian attitudes to blood and breeding: he was not recognised by the local gentry, or what then passed for it in South Devon, because he had once been 'in trade', a manufacturer of domestic sewing-machines. Such attitudes persisted in some circles well into recent times, until the aristocracy itself went into business by commercialising country houses and estates and opening enterprises like tea rooms and safari parks.

These comments are further confirmed by a somewhat exaggerated report in a local newspaper after Singer's death: 'He tried to get into society by giving a grand ball, to which all the aristocracy of the neighbourhood were invited but they mercilessly snubbed him, and in revenge he asked all the tradesmen of the place, and gave them an entertainment the like of which for magnificence has hardly ever been seen in England.' His sons were more successful in achieving social acceptance, possibly because their manners and mannerisms, their interests and hobbies, were obviously English and conventionally upper-class, and, perhaps of more importance, they were not in trade at all. The 'blackballing' of Singer in Torbay can hardly be explained by his scandalous reputation in America, for there is no reason to suppose that local people knew anything about his past life; he behaved well and generously in Devon and caused no scandal, unless of course great wealth is in itself a source of scandal.

The house that Bridgman built for Singer in 1873 was in brick with stone dressings. We can see from early photographs that the chimneys were excessively tall and the dormers prominent. The foundation stone was laid in 1873 and the final cost came to around £100,000. The original mansion, though impressively large (the largest house in Paignton), did not necessarily delight all eyes, only Isaac Singer's. Oldway's original approach was to the north, along a driveway which roughly followed the lines of the grounds. This route skirted the Torquay Road to Little Oldway, and from there to the main door of the Mansion. This gave a visitor the illusion that the grounds were far more extensive than they were. Today the main entrance to Oldway lies to the east, straight up from the Torquay Road, and this change came about in 1929, when Oldway was transformed into a country club. The Riding and Exercising Pavilion, the Arena, was the first building to be put up and during its construction the Singers made Little Oldway their temporary home.

Singer's Wigwam was not quite finished when one of his daughters married a New Yorker at St John's parish church, Paignton, in early July 1875. She was Alice Merritt and her mother was one of Singer's American mistresses. It was, indeed, a very expensive and lavish affair: her wedding outfit cost more than £2,000 and Singer's wedding present, a set of diamonds, more than that. There was much banqueting, several balls, and other celebratory festivities. Local people were impressed and dazzled by the splendour of the occasion, the entertainments, and display of wealth. In Paignton Singer was a very popular figure. Every year he observed three special days: Christmas, when he had meat and other provisions distributed to the poor; the Fourth of July, on which day the patriotic Yankee gave a grand party, and his own birthday which he honoured by entertaining a large party of children at Oldway and supplied each with gifts. It is typical of his generosity that when the circus came to town he bought tickets and invited a host of children to attend, each of whom was further regaled with gifts of sweets.

He could not be present at his daughter's wedding because he had been taken ill some time before and could only lie upstairs listening to the revelry. On 23 July 1875 he died, leaving an estate valued at between $13 and $15 million, a vast sum in those days. He was never to see his Wigwam in its final state. The family wanted to bury him at Paignton Cemetery, but so much space was required for the large family mausoleum they planned to construct that the authorities felt unable to comply; instead his resting place became Torquay Cemetery, at Hele, which occupies an extensive area. The Singer mausoleum at Torquay was broken into in 1974 for rumours had circulated for many years that the tomb was a treasure house of jewellery and other precious things. Apparently, none was found by the grave robbers, who were caught and punished.

After Singer's death, his widow and the six legitimate children continued to make Oldway their home. Isabella Singer was a handsome woman though we would regard her today as too fleshy, but she certainly agreed with the taste of her time: the slim boyish flapper look had yet to become fashionable. She was the model specially chosen by the sculptor Frederic Bartholdi for his giant statue of 'Liberty enlightening the World', which was presented by France to the United States in 1886 and which greets one at the approaches to New York harbour.

Since its completion in 1875 Oldway had not been altered apart from the addition of a large octagonal palm house near the Arena. It was Paris Singer who acquired from his brothers and sisters the family interests in Paignton and who planned to rebuild Oldway. By profession a trained architect, he knew what he was about when he took on the task of redesigning the large mansion built by Bridgman. Paris was not inhibited by the conventional view of a gentleman's home, as that of a country mansion restrained in style; neither did he suffer from 'ghastly good taste'. He approved of Continental rather than English styles: he wanted a magnificent house – a palace, yet not a copy of some vulgar plutocrat's edifice. Versailles was chosen as the model for the new Oldway. One imagines that Sir Robert Palk would have understood his choice, for had not Sir Robert patterned his rebuilt Haldon House on Buckingham House (later Palace)?

Oldway was substantially altered in the years 1904-7 and the only elevation left unchanged is the west one. The east front was given a nine-column loggia or raised terrace, inspired by the Place de la Concorde; the north, a projecting pedimented portico; and the south is 18th century in style, based on a small music pavilion in the grounds of the Petit Trianon at Versailles. Paris demolished his father's private theatre on the first floor and inserted in its place a magnificent imperial stairway and gallery, all in marble with bronze balusters, based on Lebrun's designs for a staircase at Versailles. Facing the stair was positioned David's 'The Crowning of Josephine by Napoleon', David's best and most famous work, a very large oil-painting, and this was acquired by the French Government in 1946 when the sale of the house and its contents took place. It now hangs in the Palace of Versailles.

The Singers had employed Achille Duchesne, the leading French formal landscape architect, an exponent of the traditional French classical style, to lay out the grounds. A number of French workmen were also brought over from France not only for specialist work on the house but to help with the new gardens. When Duchesne finished his work, Oldway could boast of a lake and pools, a grotto garden, an extremely large tropical hot-house, and a fine Italian garden to the east. Some stone sphinxes in 18th-century style were also placed to the south of the house, and these Bridget Cherry nicely calls 'delightfully haughty'. Before Oldway was purchased in 1946 by Paignton Council for

60 *Singer Mansion. Paris Singer extensively remodelled Oldway in 1904-7. He was not inhibited by the conventional view of a gentleman's home and Versailles was chosen as the model for the new Oldway.*

£45,000, the grounds were mysterious, romantic – numinous almost when evening twilight filtered through the tall trees. There was much overhanging foliage, clumps of tall bamboo and fronds, dense masses of vegetation, pathways that led to secret places. Since then many large trees have been felled, the grounds tidied up, tamed, and mystery has departed. Paignton Council certainly saved Oldway from the developer, but then made it into a tourist attraction, with the usual litter of litter bins and signs, tennis courts and bowling green, and public lavatories.

Pevsner in his monograph on the buildings of South Devon expresses no admiration for Oldway. Influenced by the austere rationalism of the Bauhaus, a group which focused on the functional element in architecture and in other things, Pevsner likewise did not care much for the flamboyant or decorative, the purely aesthetic. Paris Singer, needless to say, did not believe that a house was merely a machine for living in. Nowadays, Pevsner's idea of excellence is suspect and, it seems, is already slipping into history's dustbin. The so-called Modern Movement in design and architecture appears to have had its day. Of Oldway Pevsner writes:

> a house like an American millionaire's at, say, Newport Rhode Island: front with giant Corinthian pilasters and a centre with clusters of giant Corinthian columns, sea front with giant Ionic columns, mansard roof, a vast marble staircase with skylight and ceiling paintings in the centre and a marble gallery.

Built by Paris Singer to his own Versailles-inspired designs. Mr Singer was indeed the son of an American magnate, Isaac Merritt Singer.

The second edition of Pevsner's once influential book, largely rewritten and much expanded in 1989 by Bridget Cherry, reveals appreciation for Oldway's special qualities. It speaks now of 'two stunningly bombastic fronts' to the north and east, and of the 'fine formal grounds'. The tone is quite different. There are no dismissive references to American millionaires, as though they are the chief repository for bad taste and vulgarity in building. Oldway is an attractive house, in parts flamboyant and florid, but very much in tune with 'advanced' modern taste for decoration. It is certainly among the most interesting buildings in South Devon and certainly the best in Paignton (though that is not saying much!). It is extraordinary to find such a splendid house in the town.

61 *Singer Mansion. Paris Singer built a magnificent imperial stairway and gallery all in marble with bronze balusters.*

As a young man Paris Singer spent some time at Cambridge but left without taking a degree. Then, accompanied by a tutor, he set off to see the world and in Tasmania met Lillie Graham from Western Australia and married her. Both were under age. Consequently, Paris had to seek permission from the Courts of England before he could return to Devon. From this first marriage Paris had five children; but he was already separated from his wife when he met Isadora Duncan in 1909 and fell in love in her. She had formerly been the mistress of Ellen Terry's son, Gordon Craig the stage designer, and had borne him a child. Paris and Isadora lived together only intermittently, for she was often away on engagements and, what is more, their temperaments clashed, leading at times to passionate quarrels and separations. Their two children, Deirdre and Patrick, also born out of wedlock – Paris's divorce had yet to come through – were tragically drowned at Neuilly in 1913 when the stationary car in which they sat with their nurse slipped its brakes and plunged into the Seine. Paris brought Isadora back to the quiet of Paignton, to Oldway.

Barefooted she danced in the ballroom or outside on the trim lawns in a loosely flowing tunic, supposedly copied from a Greek vase; but even much Dionysian leaping up and down and to and fro on the greensward could not quite quell her troubled spirit: she grew bored with the placid delights of Oldway and the bucolic pleasures of Devon. It is said that Paris built the Villa Marina, adjacent to the Redcliffe and sitting almost on the beach, for her, but there is no evidence that she ever occupied it. Very soon she returned to France. Later she was a welcome guest of the Soviet Government and married the Russian Imagist poet Sergei Esenin in 1922 and together they visited the United States. He finally went mad and in 1925 committed suicide, writing his last poem in his own blood. Two years later, driving at high speed along the Cote d'Azur, she was strangled when the flowing scarf she was wearing caught in the spokes of a wheel.

Paris by that time was remarried and living in great style in Palm Beach. Together with Addison Mizner, who was famous for designing rococo palaces for American millionaires, he had created a luxurious residential club called the Everglades. A writer has suggested that he built the new Palm Beach Resort as a substitute for his lost love, Isadora. Perhaps. The fame of Everglades even reached Europe. Run on curious lines, membership was not permanent and not automatically renewed and Singer could make or break an aspirant to social status in Palm Beach society. Over six feet tall and distinguished in appearance, with copper blond hair and a small beard, he was both intelligent and charming and became a celebrity in America, something he had never achieved in England. He invested heavily in real-estate in nearby Miami, and although he lost part of his fortune in the Great Crash of 1929 he remained a rich man.

Paris became a naturalised American citizen, claiming it was the Inland Revenue that had driven him from England, as they had taken 80 per cent of his income. He lived with his second wife, Joan, at his villa at Cape Ferrat and rarely visited Paignton because of increasingly bad health. He suffered dreadfully from insomnia and, finding he could only sleep well on a ship, he chartered a steamer in 1931 and spent much time cruising up and down the Nile in search of sleep. He died the following year, suddenly, in a London hotel and was interred in the family vault at Torquay Cemetery. *The Times* obituary described the importance of his schemes in the development of Paignton but it was Paris who was also largely responsible for the expansion of Preston as a residential suburb of Paignton.

In 1876 the trustees for Isaac Singer's estate erected a sea wall at Preston; and in 1902 the road from Seaway Corner, Torquay Road, to the Redcliffe Road (now the Marine Drive) was widened by 40 feet and linked with the one that ran along Paignton Green. Now there was a continuous seafront thoroughfare from Hollacombe to Paignton Harbour. On the whole, though, Preston beach, backed by its seawall, promenade, and a level expanse of green, was

62 *Paris Singer was never lordly. Tall, smiling and distinguished looking, he expressed in his person and conduct Paignton's more democratic ideals. He is seen here with his second wife, Joan.*

regarded by local residents as more exclusive than that at Paignton. The Council did not provide tents for renting at Preston, only rows of white-painted huts on the promenade or green, the majority owned by retired people, shopkeepers, and members of the professional classes, who paid an annual fee for the privilege. Trippers much preferred commercialised Paignton beach with its pier, stalls, and donkeys, and its longer stretch of sands. Paris also owned much land to the west of Oldway, reaching up to Marldon, and much of Preston, which was divided up into building lots. At the outbreak of the First World War, the patriotic Paris converted Oldway at his own expense into a hospital and it became the American Women's War Hospital. After the war it was never again used as a residence by the Singer family, though Paris retained a few rooms for personal use. One must say that it was the building of Oldway, not its use, that Paris had most delighted in, like a painter who loses interest in a work once it is finished.

Paris Singer was never lordly. Tall, smiling, and distinguished looking, he expressed in his person and conduct Paignton's more democratic ideals. He behaved as though class distinctions were not at all important. He was a man before his time.

63 *The Villa Marina, now painted pink, was built by Paris for Isadora.*

Eight

THE FALL OF THE HOUSE OF PALK

anity Fair has a cartoon of Sir Lawrence Palk, 1st Lord Haldon, in its
March 1882 issue, one in its series devoted to statesmen. The artist is
'Spy' (Leslie Ward) who depicts Lord Haldon standing, slightly stooped,
holding his top hat behind him. This cartoon of the recently ennobled Sir
Lawrence reminds one of a kindly but perplexed headmaster who has just
come across some awful dereliction.
Spy's cartoon, which one feels is not
meant to be a true caricature, is subscribed 'Torquay'. It may, then, be
accepted as a good likeness of Sir
Lawrence at the end of his career and
his life, for he died almost precisely a
year later, on 23 March 1883.

The 4th baronet almost succeeded
in rehabilitating the family's reputation, but it was really too late. He could
never substantially reduce the mountain of debt inherited from his disreputable father; and, furthermore, he
was to add to it by his various costly
improvement schemes. All Sir Lawrence Palk could do was to hang on,
to conceal his chagrin, and to present
a brave face to the world.

Sir Lawrence was a friend and loyal
supporter of the dazzling Disraeli.
They met not only in the House of
Commons but often at Torquay, a
town which Disraeli had discovered
through his platonic friendship with
Mrs Sarah Brydges Willyams who had
retired there, a friendship that began
in 1851 when Disraeli first came to

64 *Sir Lawrence Palk, 1st Lord Haldon, as depicted in a*
Vanity Fair *'Spy' cartoon by Leslie Ward after J.J. Edwin
Mayall.*

65 *1st Baron Haldon by Joseph Brown. He almost succeeded in rehabilitating his family's reputation but could never substantially reduce the mountain of debt inherited from his disreputable father.*

the town to meet the elderly widow and it was to continue until her death in 1861, when she left Disraeli her villa and her fortune. She sent him roses from Torquay and he replied with violets from Hughenden. Both Disraeli and his wife found they liked Torbay and continued to frequent it over the years. It was a pleasant retreat when Disraeli felt jaded from political life and Parliamentary labours.

Sir Lawrence had built a baronial mansion on Lincombe Hill. It was known as the New Manor House to distinguish it from Torwood Grange, the old manor house, which belonged to the Palks but now was used as a workshop by the Harvey brothers, Jacob and William, builders and entrepreneurs. The New Manor House was begun in 1862 and completed by January 1864, in which month Sir Lawrence and his wife moved in. They were to entertain within its walls many distinguished visitors and also members of prominent local families. Previously Sir Lawrence had lived at Meadfoot in the elegant central house of the family-owned Hesketh Crescent. However, in 1860, the year when he inherited the baronetcy at the age of 42, he decided to build a fine mansion in Torquay so as to entertain guests on a more extensive and lavish a scale than was possible at Hesketh Crescent. The New Manor House was also a useful base for carrying on his various activities, such as the promotion and improvement of Torquay and work pertaining to constituency matters.

It had become a tradition for the Palks to send their sons to Eton and there Lawrence duly had gone. After Eton he purchased a commission in the Ist Dragoons in 1835 and soldiered on with his regiment until 1840, having obtained the rank of lieutenant. These were quiet years for the military. Lawrence Palk therefore spent most of his career in drills, manoeuvres, parades, and having his horses groomed, or on garrison duty. What he acquired from the peacetime army was a command of horses and men, a knowledge of horsemanship, and an interest in fox-hunting, which the great Cockney grocer Jorrocks described as 'the sport of kings, the image of war without its guilt, and only five and twenty per cent of its danger'.

In 1845 he married Maria Harriet Hesketh, only daughter of Sir Thomas Henry Hesketh of Rufford Hall, Lancashire, after whom was named Hesketh

66 *Hatley St George, Lincombe Drive. The classic simplicity of the first villa to be built on Lincombe Hill in 1846 was to be challenged in 1862-4 by the new 'Gothic' baronial mansion, The New Manor House, built for Sir Lawrence Palk.*

Crescent, designed by the Harvey brothers and completed in 1848. By his marriage to Maria Hesketh Sir Lawrence had four sons and a daughter. His heir was Lawrence Hesketh Palk, born in 1846. The second son, Robert, a soldier, died of malaria in 1878 while on garrison duty at Gibraltar; the third died of fever at Umballa, South Africa, in 1876; and the fourth and youngest, Edward Arthur, survived to become in 1938, by several twists of fate, the 5th and final baron. Part of the price paid for colonial wars and imperial expansion was the decimation of the aristocracy's offspring, especially younger sons. The majority died not in battle in foreign parts but from disease. Neither of Sir Lawrence's surviving sons – Lawrence Hesketh and Edward Arthur – was in any way brilliant; his first-born, on whom the family's fortunes depended, soon showed himself to be an ass and totally inept in business affairs. He was to become another drone, a member of the lounging classes like his grandfather.

Now we should examine Sir Lawrence's role as Torquay's great improver and leading urban developer. Robert Cary was also active in these fields and his activities complemented those of Sir Lawrence, for Cary as well appointed land agents in the 1850s to develop commercially his Torre Abbey estate and other properties: their results are to be seen in Belgravia, adjacent to the Abbey grounds, and on Waldon Hill, St Marychurch, and Babbacombe. But so far nothing much had been done by either landlord to house the working

Lady Palk

Pretty Eva & Eddie Palk

Sir L. Palk.

67 *Three Palk family photographs. Sir Lawrence married Maria Harriet Hesketh, after whom he named Hesketh Crescent; they had four sons and a daughter, three of whom are shown in the centre photograph.*

classes. The homes of the poor were tucked away in interstices, for much of the hillier, loftier ground was now occupied by substantial villas or reserved as plots for the rich and aristocratic. The poorer classes lived mostly in congested Swan Lane and George Street, narrow passages between rows of shacks; in the down-at-heels district of Pimlico, and in derelict cottages and hovels on the fringes of the town. In the early 1860s around 2,000 men, women and children of the poorer classes were accommodated in six common lodging houses situated in the notorious Swan Lane and George Street and in the Pimlico and Madrepore areas. Sanitation was appalling, the stench abominable, for Kitson as Chairman of the Local Board had vetoed a proposal to build a public wash-house for the denizens of the lower depths. This proposal came from the humane Edward Vivian, a Liberal, who raised the question annually and each time was rebuffed by Kitson. This went on for nearly twenty years until the penny-pinching Chairman withdrew his veto.

The servant class mainly lived in the attics, basements, and outhouses of villa properties or in rooms above stables and mews. Many of the remainder of the working classes lived with friends and neighbours or in cheap lodging-houses, or rented space for a few shillings a week from a householder, himself probably in need. Very few people owned their own homes. A few were of no fixed abode and found shelter where they could, or they simply lived rough. There were always vagrants in the Torbay district, most of whom slept on the beaches in summer or under upturned boats, in barns, or in rough shelters put up on waste land. There was also a marked number of distracted alcoholics. They haunted the cheap cider-houses, common in South Devon. Rough cider – scrumpy – was the potent tipple of the poor and addiction to it usually spelt ruin, for in the end it unfitted a man for any sort of persistent work.

In 1859 the ageing Sir L.V. Palk, activated by his son and by William Kitson, agreed that Ellacombe Valley would provide a suitable tract of land for the erection of cheap working-class homes. This project became practicable once Market Street was constructed in 1853, a roadway that opened up the Ellacombe Valley for habitation. Rows of tenement houses were quickly built in Ellacombe and were eagerly sought after by workers and artisans since rents were within their reach. These dwellings were a great boon to the town because at that time no suburban development had taken place in Torquay; there were no outlying built-up areas which could siphon off surplus population from central Torquay. One effect of this attempt to house the poor was a decline, over time, in ruffianism, vagrancy and alcoholism, although of course other factors were much at work, such as improvements in wages, increases in the percentage of those employed, and the spread of the Victorian notion of respectability. On 6 September 1867 Sir Lawrence and his son (who had come of age on that very day) donated Ellacombe Green to the town as a recreation ground, the place where the captured Russian gun was sequestrated for 16 years among the plebs before being returned to its former glory on Cary Green, adjacent to the harbour, where it now could be viewed by all classes.

Another beneficial scheme was the widening of Fleet Street, between the bottom of Union Street and the Strand. This was Torquay's main thoroughfare but by mid-century it had become a shambles, fringed by a medley of shops and cottages, meanly built of lath and plaster, some with small gardens in front. There were even small two-storey houses abutting the road and these could only be entered by going down several steps from the street. This had mainly come about because the Palks and Carys, often at loggerheads, could never agree on what should be done to improve the area, an area where Palk and Cary estates were contiguous: and so nothing was ever done.

In 1865 Sir Lawrence surrendered his rights in the road and allowed the Local Board to go ahead with their plan to construct a broad highway through the main town, from the Strand up to Castle Circus. From the latter a road ran to Chapel Hill, near Torre station, and then onward to Newton Abbot and thence to Exeter and other parts. Fleet Street was widened from 23 to 45 feet and decent shops and houses were put up in place of the old ramshackle, gimcrack dwellings and business premises. Sir Lawrence had gone along with the scheme; indeed, he had strongly supported the project.

By the late 1860s the lower part of the town had been transformed into an extremely attractive shopping and walking district, where people delighted to saunter and to take the sea air, and it was to remain largely unchanged, in design, until long after the last war. The better shops, gown shops and jewellers, tended to cluster along Fleet Street or on the Strand and both places became busy shopping areas where the middle classes took coffee in the morning and tea in the afternoon. Torquay could never boast of any celebrated restaurant – the best meals were always served in the great hotels, such as the *Imperial*, where foreign chefs were employed – but it had a number of pleasant cafés, coffee shops and patisseries. The habit of dining out never really caught on with local residents, only with visitors. Today all has changed.

Another great project Sir Lawrence concerned himself with was the creation of a large outer harbour. In the early years of the century Sir Robert Palk's son and grandson, advised by Dr Henry Beeke, had substantially improved the inner harbour, but over the years it had become too small for the needs of the growing town, and other problems had arisen. To begin with, the volume of traffic using the Strand had grown immeasurably in the season, which of course meant winter; the harbour was not easily accessible for large vessels and impossible at low tide; and in summer there was no accommodation whatsoever for yachts, which had to lie to outside the harbour, a dangerous practice in bad weather. In November 1862 Sir Lawrence submitted proposals to the Local Board of Health for its improvement. After much public discussion, Sir Lawrence applied to the Board of Trade for permission to make and maintain additional piers, wharfs, and other works, and an order was granted. 'This was', as J.T. White confirms, 'a comprehensive and well devised scheme, but it was never carried out.' In 1866 a further Provisional Order was obtained from the Board of Trade, under the General Pier and Harbour Act of 1861, for a smaller and less comprehensive project, and this was the one finally adopted. Work commenced in 1867 and was completed in August 1870.

Some years before, the sea face of Beacon Hill had been cut away to make space for the construction of the Baths above Beacon Cove, on which work started in 1853 and finished in 1857. In 1867 the remainder of the hill was cut away and levelled to provide a site for the new Saloon (the combined amenities became known as the Bath Saloons, later the Marine Spa). The hill was further cut into to provide necessary level land for the erection of sheds and supply stores. Great quantities of stone and debris were excavated and used in the construction of quays and wharfs. J.P. Margery was the experienced engineer used for all the harbour works and the contractor James Mountstephen, a Plymouth builder of repute.

The total cost of the construction of the Haldon Pier, as the great breakwater was named, and its ancillary works came to nearly £70,000, and it

68 *Cary Parade. By the late 1860s the lower part of the town was an attractive shopping and walking district and would remain largely unchanged until long after the end of the Second World War.*

all came out of Sir Lawrence's pocket. Torquay had an inner harbour of six acres, and now an outer harbour of ten acres, where large vessels could enter and berth at all tides. It was a fine achievement. On 24 August 1871 Sir Lawrence and members of his family were given a banquet at the Bath Saloon and a picture of the baronet, painted by the well known Victorian portrait-painter, Sydney Hodges (who had also painted Bishop Phillpotts), was presented to him. The speech was delivered by William Harvey, one of the Harvey brothers, long established builders and entrepreneurs in Torquay. Fittingly, William Harvey was also one of Sir Lawrence's oldest tenants and the largest owner of property on his estate. Harvey's words were to the point:

> With this picture I am desired to convey to you our best wishes and thanks for the enterprise and public spirit which you have shewn in developing the resources of the town by the erection of the harbour; and it is gratifying to

69 *The Strand, Torquay in the 1920s. By the late 1860s the better shops tended to cluster along Fleet Street or the Strand and it was here that the middle classes took coffee in the morning and tea in the afternoon.*

know that in doing what you have, you have not looked so much for an immediate return as to the benefit it will confer on the town at large.

The importance to the town of the new outer harbour cannot be under-estimated. Torbay, already popular with West Country sailors, very quickly developed into a fashionable yachting station, not quite the equal of Cowes but fairly close. Sailing as a sport by mid-century had already found favour with the upper classes and the *nouveaux riches*. It was a rich man's avocation and hobby. At a later date two of its best known devotees were the Prince of Wales and his friend Sir Thomas Lipton, the Scottish businessman who had made a fortune from a chain of grocers' shops and the sale of Lipton's special brand of tea. The Prince accepted the position of Commodore of the Royal Thames Yacht Club in 1874 and was elected Commodore of the Royal Yacht Squadron in 1882. And so sailing and yachting had become by the end of the century the sport of kings, like horse-racing, and that fact commended it to social climbers. Sir Lawrence Palk, Torquay's most prominent and distinguished citizen, was likewise appointed the first commodore of the Torbay Yacht Club, founded in 1863, a club which was honoured with a royal warrant in 1871.

Hence, by the 1870s, Torquay had acquired a 'summer season' to comp-lement its winter one. In high summer parties of yachtsmen, sailors, and well-wishers from all over the British Isles forgathered at Torbay to participate in

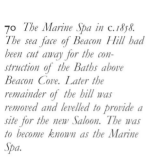

70 *The Marine Spa in c.1858. The sea face of Beacon Hill had been cut away for the construction of the Baths above Beacon Cove. Later the remainder of the hill was removed and levelled to provide a site for the new Saloon. The was to become known as the Marine Spa.*

sailing events, to race and to have fun; and the Regatta, first held as early as 1811, became the summer's high point. It always generated a festival atmosphere in the town, which became crowded with sightseers and visitors; tradesmen and hoteliers did extremely well. For children there were special sporting contests and much fun.

Although respected and honoured for his contributions to the town's welfare, Sir Lawrence did not gain financially from his harbour enterprise; indeed, it must have contributed further to his long-standing financial embarrassments, for he had now locked up a great deal of capital in a venture that paid no dividends. Moreover, the sums raised all came from mortgages on his estates and other properties. But, at that time, Sir Lawrence saw things differently. He had other schemes in mind which he thought would eventually benefit his family as well as the town.

His father, under Kitson's inspiration, had sought to persuade the people of Torquay that an extension of the railway from Torre station to the Strand would be beneficial to commerce and trade and increase the town's revenue. An alternative route from Torquay station to the Strand, following the shore, had been explored but was, on several grounds, ruled impracticable. The general problem was that the élite and the better-off liked the town as it was, as a quiet haven for the better classes. They deplored the prospect of a railway bringing dirt, smoke, and clatter into the heart of the town. Since they were carriage folk and therefore had easy and comfortable access to both railway stations, each situated on the town's fringes, they saw no need for a terminus to be built close to the harbour. A number of property owners had even urged that the station should be located far outside the town at Aller, halfway between Torquay and Newton Abbot, and further argued that no railway line should be allowed to desecrate any part of Torquay for that would alter its character as an upper-class watering-place; but this was too extreme a view even for most diehards. But the majority of those concerned put their thumbs down to the proposal of a line, an extension, to the harbour. Sir Lawrence continued to argue his case.

Those who directed the Palk estate office had already shown a marked interest both in the Stover Canal, which had been begun by James Templer in 1792 to shift the clay from the mines he owned along the Teign valley, and the Teign Valley Railway, built at a later date, in the 1860s. These enterprises had been promoted to bring clay, granite, and minerals from the Haytor quarries and the surrounding countryside to the Teign estuary, whence they could be shipped in bulk to other parts of Britain. Palk's agents had speculated that the estate would greatly benefit if heavy materials were loaded at their privately owned harbour: but in order to do so a railway had to be constructed, a branch line running from Torre and terminating at the harbour or close by; but this plan, as we know, was blocked. Sir Lawrence purchased 175 shares in the Teign Valley Railway Company and also invested £15,000 of his own money in its debenture stock.

When the Palk family settlement was undone, in 1885, with the enactment of Lord Haldon's Estate Bill it was found that these stocks and shares in the Palk portfolio – shares which had been purchased at two pounds – were worthless. This had been an unwise investment and he received no return from it: it was simply another debit item, among many, recorded in the estate account books. Why Sir Lawrence pursued this expensive chimera for so long is difficult to ascertain; but in 1874 he had dropped his pilot, Kitson; or rather the pilot had dropped him, for Kitson resigned from his office and all his

71 Belgrave Hotel, *Torquay. For many years the* Royal Hotel *together with the* Torbay *and* Belgrave *hotels on the seafront had sufficed to accommodate visitors, but with the coming of the railway in the 1850s demand for rooms expanded.*

duties and ceased to have anything to do with Sir Lawrence's affairs. So, too, did Kitson's son, John, and his brother, Charles, all of whom had acted in various capacities for Sir Lawrence. Thus the guiding hand had gone. But in any case Kitson was growing old; he was 74 that year and latterly, it seems, had not given as much time and thought to the estate as before. A very shrewd man indeed, he well knew that financially Sir Lawrence's affairs were in a parlous state and he had no wish to damage his reputation by any involvement in, as he foresaw, the coming débâcle, the final crash. Sir Lawrence had never enjoyed an easy relationship with his chief agent and advisor; he always had very mixed feelings about Kitson, Torquay's most prominent solicitor and banker; and these sentiments, as we know, dated back to the 1840s, to the time when he and his wife bitterly resented having to live on a comparatively small annuity, an annuity moreover which had been arranged by the solicitors Kennaway and Kitson, then managing the estate for the absent debtor, Sir L.V. Palk.

For many years, the *Royal Hotel* and a few other establishments, together with the *Torbay* and *Belgrave* hotels on the sea front, built in later years, had sufficed to accommodate travellers and visitors; but the coming in the 1850s of the railway made Torbay easy to reach from most parts and the demand for rooms expanded commensurately with its growing popularity as a resort. It was no longer a far-off place, a winter retreat for the few: it had become a famous watering-place. Percy Russell estimates that 'the total number of rooms available in 1850 could hardly have exceeded 150, with 70 lodging

72 *Map of the railways. The arrival of the railway made Torbay easy to reach from most parts.*

73 *The* Royal Hotel c.*1852.*
His father had rebuilt the
Royal Hotel *but in Sir*
Lawrence Palk's eyes it was still
not grand enough for a town to
which royalty and the nobility
were coming.

house keepers, who may have provided another 350 rooms, say 500 in all'. Sir
Lawrence gave his mind to the promotion of the hotel trade. This was a Palk
tradition, for his father had rebuilt the *Royal* on the Strand and had transformed
it into the town's leading hostelry, into an elegant hotel with a ballroom big
enough to contain many dancers and large enough to host public lectures and
other entertainments. But in Palk's eyes it was still not grand enough for a
town to which royalty and the nobility were coming in increasing numbers.

Sir Lawrence was chairman and a leading shareholder in the Torquay
Hotels Company, set up in 1863 with a capital of £70,000, whose main purpose
was the building of a great hotel on the hill above Beacon Cove. The auditor
was Charles Kitson, William's younger brother. The contemplated site was
already occupied by two villas – the Cove and the Cliff – but both were
purchased and demolished to make way for the new building. Apart from
constructing a new hotel the company also acquired the *Royal* (the old *Royal
Hotel* Posting House) and its adjacent stables, properties which it intended for
further development. The foundation stone of the new hotel to be called the
Imperial Hotel, a suitably grandiose designation, was laid in March 1864 by
Lady Palk. It was a seafront hotel, an imposing four-storey block only separated
from a steep cliff by a terrace and a narrow strip of garden, so that from its
sea-facing windows one looked right across to Brixham and the coastline
leading westward to Elberry Cove and Churston Point. The *Imperial*, in its first
state, had about fifty bedrooms but it was enlarged in 1871 and again in 1922
when it absorbed the Marina, a sizeable villa just eastward of the cove, on the
bank above. In the 20th century, the *Imperial Hotel* became the finest of
Torquay's great triumvirate of hotels, the others being the *Grand* at Livermead
and the *Palace* at Babbacombe.

74 Imperial Hotel, *Torquay and the* Grand Hotel, *Torquay. In the 20th century the former became the finest of Torquay's triumvirate of hotels, the third being the* Palace *at Babbacombe.*

It was a *sine qua non* that a smart resort should boast an imposing and commodious hotel serviced by an army of liveried flunkeys, footmen, bell-boys and porters, and a smoothly efficient and obsequious managerial staff. Scarborough had its *Grand Hotel*, Brighton the *Metropole*, and Bournemouth the *Royal Bath Hotel*. The *Imperial* followed this pattern of greatness and unostentatious splendour. The truly ostentatious hotels were more a product of the Edwardian age and catered especially for American millionaires and other opulent foreigners.

Between the wars the *Imperial*'s tea dances, a type of entertainment which first became fashionable in the 1920s, were celebrated, much patronised by Torbay's *jeunesse dorée*, by the occasional gigolo with lustrous brilliantined hair, tapping ash from his long cigarette holder and appraising the older women, and by cads displaying two inches of white cuff and Ronald Colman moustaches. Mothers warned unmarried daughters about *them*. 'Berry' Pleydell or his brother, 'Boy' (Harrow and Oxford), Dornford Yates' handsome upper-crust heroes, would have felt perfectly at ease in the place, a hotel that had plenty of class and the right sort of guests in residence. It may be likened to *Barribault's Hotel* in Wodehouse's *Full Moon*:

> The personnel of its staff are selected primarily for their ability to curl the upper lip and raise the eyebrows just that extra quarter of an inch which makes all the difference.

A number of Sir Lawrence's benefactions and donations to the town have already been referred to. He was unquestionably more public-spirited than the reclusive Robert Cary, though even he was not ungenerous in providing sites for public buildings, parks and churches. It matters little whether Sir Lawrence's munificence was or was not primarily inspired by his agent Kitson: the point is, that Sir Lawrence followed his suggestions, without demur, and even initiated charitable schemes of his own devising.

Sir Lawrence's parliamentary career began in 1854 when he was returned unopposed for the South Devon Division, a seat he held as a Conservative until 1868. The 1867 Reform Act divided the county into three divisions and he and Lord Courtenay were elected as the members for East Devon, which included Torquay. They continued to represent the constituency until the collapse in 1880 of Disraeli's last ministry, when the Liberals swept into power. Sir Lawrence defended the agricultural interest, the land-owning class, yet was mildly reformist in his views: he reminded his colleagues in the budget debate of 1874 that 'if cottages were not built in which labourers could live in decency and comfort, it was natural they would become members of Agricultural Labourers Unions and listen to agitators'. This was a direct reference to Joseph Arch, who attempted to improve the condition of agricultural labourers by creating the National Agricultural Labourers' Union in 1872.

The redoubtable Sir Massey Lopes, parliamentary leader in the Commons for South Devon, was much opposed to any local imposition of rates for he believed this would be ruinous to the landed interest. Both he and Sir Lawrence were against the idea of local taxation contained in certain provisions of the 1872 Public Health Act. Palk argued (his words are taken from Hansard) that he was 'convinced that before many years had passed the Board in London would put their hands deeply into the pockets of the ratepayers in rural districts, and compel them to carry out fancy regulations quite unsuitable to the circumstances of the labouring classes'. Sir Lawrence took seriously the responsibilities and duties attached to being a Member of Parliament. He was in no way a lethargic backwoodsman from the shires but a very public-spirited politician, quite the opposite of his father. At heart he was a traditionalist and sincerely believed that the landed classes represented all that was best in the country and that paternalistic landlordism worked in the best interests of all the classes.

In 1880 Sir Lawrence was elevated to the peerage as Baron Haldon, soon after Disraeli ceased to be Prime Minister. The peerage, of which Lord Haldon was now a member, had became by the 1880s the most important active political element among all landowners. Disraeli after losing the election did his best for his party and his friends: Sir Lawrence Palk was rewarded for having been a loyal party man and a good friend in the Commons.

And so in 1880 Lord Haldon forsook the hurly-burly of the House of Commons for the deep tranquillity of the House of Lords. Relieved of onerous parliamentary duties in the Commons, he was able now to spend more time in Devon, at Haldon or at Torquay. A year after leaving the Commons he narrowly escaped death in Exeter. He was seated in a carriage driven by his son Edward when a runaway frightened horse smashed into it. Both men were pinned under the overturned vehicle; though badly shaken, neither was seriously injured. Lord Haldon could now lead the life of a country gentleman and a fox-hunter as well as experiencing the pleasures of serene Torbay.

Lord Haldon died at Haldon House in March 1883 (the same year that Kitson died), but was survived for many years by his widow, the Dowager Lady Haldon, who lived on a jointure of £1,500 under the family settlement. She continued to reside at Torquay, in the New Manor House, until 1889, when the start of the sales of the Palk settled estates caused her to move to Whitchurch, Oxfordshire, where she died in 1905. If the 1st Lord Haldon left behind any monument, it is Torquay itself. His name is commemorated in Haldon Road, one of the roads on the crest of Lincombe Hill.

* * *

Like his father, the 2nd Lord Haldon was honoured in *Vanity Fair* by a Spy cartoon, ironically subscribed 'A Legislator'. This was, and was probably intended to be, a sneaky reference to the private Act which made possible the sale of his estates to all and sundry, an event that was to spell 'finis' for the family as landowners. Spy's portrait suggests that a degree of physical degeneration had occurred in the family since the days of Sir Robert Palk, who was a beefy, sanguine and tough fellow, a true countryman, a simulacrum of the legendary John Bull. Lawrence Hesketh, with his long Pixie ears, weak chin, and dancing-master's narrow waist, and with a monocle screwed into his eye, in his person reveals little of Sir Robert, the founder of the family who always enjoyed rude, good health. Instead Lawrence Hesketh is depicted as foppish, as a popinjay or stage-door Johnny. And dimwitted he certainly proved himself to be in his life.

Lawrence Hesketh Palk was born in 1846, educated at Eton and Christ Church, Oxford, and, following the pattern of his class, purchased a commission in the army. He served first as a lieutenant in the Royal First Devons and then, until 1879, in the Scottish Fusiliers, when he transferred to the Royal Berkshire Yeomanry. As was usual, on succeeding his father in 1883 he resigned his commission. His wife, whom he married in 1868, was Constance Mary, eldest daughter of the 7th Viscount Barrington, by whom he had four children. Those are the bare facts of his biography. Burke lists his London clubs as the Marlborough, South Devon, and the Turf. The last gives a clue to his ruling passion: an addiction to gambling. The Turf, founded in 1868, was situated in Grafton Street, Mayfair, and was the haunt of those devoted to horse racing and allied sports. But the 2nd Lord Haldon was also a devotee of 'spider racing' and lost large sums by his miscalculation of the insect's route across a plate, which beforehand had been divided into segments, on which those gambling placed bets. It could be likened to roulette, with the spider taking the role of the ball. Lawrence Hesketh was not good at the game; he was extremely unlucky; and his enthusiasm helped to lose him his estates.

His foolishness may be illustrated by his venture into fox-hunting. In 1878 the territory of the South Devon Hunt was divided into two, the Haldon and the Newton sides, and Sir Lawrence Palk with Sir John Duntze jointly took over the Haldon Hounds. Their kennels were kept at Haldon House. In 1882 both masters retired and a new Master, Edward Stud, took over. When Lord Haldon died in 1883 and his eldest son expressed a wish to take on the pack, Stud courteously stepped down and presented the pack to him. As soon as he took office, Lawrence Hesketh relegated the First Huntsman, the much-liked Dan North, to the position of Chief Whipper-In, and declared his intention to hunt the hounds himself. He also obtained drafts, which he paid for, from the Belvoir and other famous packs. He was neither regarded as a great huntsman nor was he popular with the hunt and, worse, he greatly over estimated his abilities as a Master of Foxhounds. Soon he found the cost of running a pack too great to bear and in September 1886 was compelled to give up the Mastership. Fox-hunting was an expensive business and must have cost Lawrence Hesketh about £3,000 to £4,000 a year. The celebrated sporting writer Nimrod (the sobriquet adopted by Charles Apperley) had declared: 'Money is the *sine qua non* of hunting'. Although he must have known his estates were heavily burdened with debt (that surely must have been evident once he came into his inheritance), yet he persisted for over two years in running a hunt and paying for everything. What in fact he achieved was to turn a subscription pack into a fashionable one, a practice which the knowledgeable Surtees much abhorred. His conduct is nicely summed up by Raymond Carr: 'The South Devon went through a trying time with Lord Haldon. He took over the pack in 1884, paid all expenses, insisted on hunting "his" hounds and then found it all too expensive and gave it up in 1886 after ruining the pack.' You cannot outrun the constable. Lawrence Hesketh certainly was not fleet enough. It was now time for a reckoning.

The Palk estate at Haldon had been badly neglected in late years. It was reported at the time of his father's death in 1883 that the farms and other buildings at Haldon were in a very bad state of repair, 'insufficient for modern requirements' and that in order to maintain their rental 'a very large sum should forthwith be expended on repairs of existing buildings and on new farm buildings, drainage, and other improvements'. The Palks had never been known as improving landlords, yet they had managed reasonably well until the great depression of the 1870s and 1880s, a period of universal catastrophe for farming in Britain and Europe, a depression mainly induced by the flood of cheap food imports (much of it grain) from America and other parts of the world.

Something had to be done. His legal advisors concluded that the only way out was by the sale of land and leases. On paper Lord Haldon owned an estate of 10,109 acres, returning a gross income of £109,275 a year in rentals and other returns, and these facts were advertised in the New Domesday Book of 1878 and thereafter included in various genealogies. In the eyes of the world he was a landed magnate, a term commonly used to denote any landowner with an estate exceeding 10,000 acres. Much prestige in those days accrued to a person owning land and in Devonshire the Palks were looked upon as one of the county's leading and richest families: the truth that they were almost paupers (by their standards) was not widely known.

Lawrence Hesketh, consequently, found his estate heavily encumbered with debt; there were also his personal debts, of no mean extent, to be dealt with. Between 1850 and 1885 the Palks, as we know, had laid out £100,000 on such projects as the new harbour and the Teign Valley Railway Company and all this money was raised by effecting mortgages on the estate; in 1868, for example, the manor of Ilsham, comprising 424 acres, had been mortgaged. It follows that such loans had to be serviced annually, which further reduced net income. Lawrence Hesketh, by nature improvident, was therefore forced to borrow in order to maintain an expensive way of life. He had also insured his life to the tune of £171,300 and the yearly premiums on these policies came to over £5,300. By 1885 his personal debts came to over £35,000. On paper his Torquay estates produced an annual rental or income of £22,500 and the Haldon estates, leaseholds, and investments another £15,000, that is, a total gross income of £37,000; but the net income accruing to him was only about £5,000, so far as can be ascertained. About 90 per cent of his income now

75 *The Princess Pier and Princess Gardens. When the 2nd Lord Haldon's estates were liquidated, the local authority, using powers awarded by its borough charter in 1892, was at last free to develop its plans to attract more visitors. In 1894 the Princess Garden was opened, together with the Princess Pier and its small pavilion, and named after Queen Victoria's daughter, Louise, who had laid the foundation stone for the pier.*

went in servicing this vast debt. Lastly, in the past jointures or annuities had been effected for brothers, sisters and widows so that they all could live in decent respectability. Widows, in particular, had to be provided for, like the Dowager Lady Haldon, but they absorbed tidy sums of money by living so long. The Dowager Lady Haldon's jointure produced a yearly income of £1,500 and she also had the right to reside at the Manor House until her death. Widowed ladies, in the main, were apt to live an unconscionably long time, at the expense of a family, and that the Palks knew full well. Well-born wives normally brought some money or property into a family but with the Palks much of it was used to shore up the family finances and it simply disappeared once the crash came.

All this made the 2nd Lord Haldon's financial position untenable. He was on the brink of insolvency. When the sums were done, it was found that mortgage debts had reached £400,000. One creditor, for £100,000, was the West of England Insurance Company. This company put pressure on him to sell his estate so as to pay off his creditors, of which it was the largest. Lawrence Hesketh's solicitors thought it prudent to comply and sales of parts of the estate soon followed. Thus fell the House of Palk.

That is not the end of the story: Lawrence Hesketh was declared a bankrupt in January 1891. Later in the year the estate was disentailed by Lawrence William, the heir, with the consent of his father. As a consequence, Lord Haldon was compelled to sell his interest in the estate subject to the payment of his existing debts. Nearly all his properties were now sold, with a proviso contained in the condition of sale that no new buildings or additions to existing buildings could be put up without the planning permission of the surveyor to the Torquay Local Sanitary Authority. In June 1894 a sale by the Liquidation Estates Purchase Company took place at the Bath Saloons when further properties were put up for auction: 'the remaining uncovered portions'.

The following year Haldon House, the old family seat, was sold: that signalled the demise of the family's influence in South Devon. It certainly went unlamented in local government circles, where the authorities had striven over the years to enhance their statutory powers with regard to the planning and control of Torquay, attempts which had at times been baulked by the major landowners, the Palks in particular. Of late years these officials had often found themselves at odds with the family. In the early 1880s, for example, one bone of contention was the question of the tolls levied by the market company the Palk's owned (Torquay market had been built on their land), tolls levied on produce entering the town. On the death of the 1st Lord Haldon in late January 1883, *The Torquay Times* stated that in recent years 'the Town and its chief landlord had not been able to reconcile interests' so that there had been a 'decline in Lord Haldon's personal popularity'. The 2nd Lord did not in any way endear himself to the town because of his known character and lack of real interest in local affairs; and once he started liquidating his estate his reputation plummeted. Few admire a loser.

Lord Haldon's bankruptcy was reported in *The Times* and then recorded in genealogical compilations such as *Burke* and *Debrett*. He was only able to effect his discharge from bankruptcy in 1898, five years before his death. But he was not alone. Lord Haldon found himself in excellent aristocratic company.

76 *Rock Walk. Whilst Princess Pier and Princess Gardens were under construction a raised walk was built which followed the contours of Walden Cliff. It was planted with sub-tropical plants and palms and became a hidden delight for romantics.*

Sir Edward Courtenay, the 12th Earl of Devon, whose seat was Powderham Castle, near Exeter, owned over 20,000 acres in Devon and 33,000 acres in Ireland but he still went bankrupt in April 1872, owing about £100,000, and yet again in 1878, this time for £20,000. In nearly all such cases financial embarrassment had arisen from personal extravagance and too great a devotion to the pleasures of the turf and other sporting activities. 'Fast women and slow horses', as the Victorians expressed it, were the predominant factors in their ruin. They refused to retrench. And all this happened at a time when agricultural prices were tumbling and the value of arable land was declining.

Lawrence Hesketh ended his life in London – he died in 1903 – after some years of residence in Berkshire, where he had been appointed JP. He lived with his unmarried second daughter, Mary Evelyn, at Onslow Gardens, South Kensington. His mother also resided there, in Pimlico. And so by the end of the century no member of the immediate family was to be found living in Devon. In 1914 the last remnants of Palk property in Torquay – a field in Lincombe Hill and allotments at Ellacombe – were sold. At the same time the mortgagee put up for sale the titles of the manor of Tormohun, which was purchased by a Frank Clark, and that of Ilsham by the Revd George Whidbourne. Both titles were valueless for no land was attached to either; they were purely honorific. The Palks now had no claim to any part of Torquay. The great estates put together in Devon by Sir Robert Palk, the nabob, and

77 *Torre Abbey Gardens, showing the designs and famous palms that pleased so many visitors. In 1933-4 a new promenade was built joining Torre Abbey Sands and the Princess Pier.*

owned by his descendants for nearly 150 years had finally been dismantled and scattered. Torquay's *ancien régime* had passed into local history.

The Palks were not in any way literary. Only a few items are listed under the family name in the British Library Catalogue; one is a sale catalogue of the contents of Haldon House, another is a 20-page pamphlet, published in London in 1886, entitled *The Evils of Party Government*, a most curious effusion; for what impelled Lawence Hesketh to authorship is not easy to determine, but he clearly had no talent for writing. His essay is a plea for an end to faction and the amalgamation of parties under a strong-minded leader like Pitt in the national interest. The question is posed but how it can be achieved is not answered. Another example of Lawrence Hesketh's impracticality, it is mere rhetoric.

The 3rd Lord Haldon's life was ill-starred from birth. For many years Lawrence William Palk lived on a small annuity and his army pay and he did not marry into wealth. When in 1903 he succeeded to the barony he inherited little. He had followed his father and grandfather to Eton and then was commissioned into the army. He became a captain in the Royal Fusiliers in 1892, and from 1893 to 1901 was occupied in engineering and mining enterprises in Australia, China, and America. During the Boer War he served with the Imperial Yeomanry and in the Great War with the Northumberland Fusiliers and the Hampshire Regiment, being mentioned in despatches.

+ PROGRAMME. +

Monday, February 27th, 1905, & Every Evening

Reduced Prices to Saturday Matinees
Fautetils 3s.   Other Seats 2s., 1s., and 6d.

1 Overture .. "The Catch of the Season"
Halters & Raker
*During the Overture a new ad novel and interesting Pictures will be
shown by the World's Advertising Co., of 14 & 15 High Holborn, W.C.*
2 Mr. Ben Albert ... ... Comedian
3 Miss Ray Wal'ace ... ... Mimic
4 Mr. Wilson Hallett .. Mimic and Sitleur
5 Miss Dorothy Kenton .. The Girl with
the Banjo
6 Ovide & Ludine .. In a Charming Illusion
7 The Two Kings ... Comedy Musical Act
8 Miss Amy Clevere .. Comedienne
9 Mr. Harry Ford ... ... Comedian
10 Mr. Fred Karno's Troupe of Comedians
in "MUMMING BIRDS"
11 The Harry Alaskas ... Comedy Act
12 The Musical Twin-formed Bohemian
Sisters
13 The Lady Haldon in a Comedy Interlude,
by Arthur Branscombe, entitled:
"THE SPORTING DUCHESS"
The Duke of Bayswater ... Mr. EDMUND GURNEY
"Battersea Bob" ... ... Mr. ALLEE WESTWOOD
Toby ... ... Mr. GEORGE TAYLOR
The Duchess of Weldingborough . The LADY HALDON
14 Mr. George D'Albert ... Comedian
15 Mr. Arthur Roberts & Co. in the highly
successful Olia Podrida, entitled:
"WHERE'S THE COUNT ?"
Joe Muggins nicknamed "The Count"
... ... Mr. ARTHUR ROBERTS
Pr'fessor Clarke ... ... Mr. STANLEY DAMERAL
Lucy, his Niece ... ... Miss LUCY WEBLING
Lieut. Ashers v., in love with Lucy Mr. JULES WRIGHT
Count Tycoff, a Hun inn .. Mr. EDWIN PALMER
Mary Hiosenmaid in love with Joe Miss RUBY CLENATE
16 Miss May Moore Duprez .. Comedienne
17 Mr 'George Drawee and his Dog

*The above Programme is subject to alteration, and the
Management disclaim responsibility for the unavoidable
absence of any Article announced to appear.*

RONISCH Grand Piano used on stage supplied by Messrs.
METZLER, 41 & 43, Great Marlboro Street, W.

SPECIAL NOTICE.—To meet the requirements of the London
County Council—The Public can leave the premises at the
end of the performance by all exits and entrances, all doors,
gangways and passages must be kept clear.

The fire-proof screen to the proscenium opening will be
lowered at least once during every performance to ensure its
being in proper working order.

MATINEE EVERY SATURDAY AT 2.15.

JAS. HOWELL & ARTHUR YATES, Joint Acting Managers

78 The Sporting Duchess. *The final appearance of Lily Miska (Lady Haldon).*

In 1893 he married Lidiana Amalia Crezencia, daughter of Jacob Maichle, sometime a colonel in the Russian army. When they first met she was working as an actress on the London stage, under the name Lily Miska. She was 37 in 1893, her husband 24 years old, and they were to have but one child: the Hon. Lawrence Bloomfield Palk, born in 1896, who became the 4th Baron Haldon in 1933. The propensity of peers to marry actresses is difficult to comprehend. It had no economic foundation, unlike marrying rich American heiresses whose fortunes came from trade and manufacturing. In Lawrence William's case it cannot be explained by a degree of bohemianism or a desire for social emancipation but, perhaps, rather from sheer infatuation with a much older and more experienced woman. She was limited in the roles she could play by the traces of a foreign accent and when Sir Lawrence met her in the 1890s her career had not advanced: she remained a minor actress; and as she was not fortuned did not bring any money to the Palk family. It was a bad move on Lawrence William's part.

After 1903, he became the bane of the prissy Edmund Gosse, Librarian to the House of Lords. Lawrence William, now the 3rd baron, did not take his seat in the Lords but nevertheless insisted upon using its facilities. He had the habit of coming into Gosse's sanctum and taking wads of House of Lords' notepaper, an act which much irritated the librarian, especially as he had to put up with a bankrupt peer, for Lawrence William had also been declared bankrupt in 1903, just ten months before his father's death. His bankruptcy had been deferred for some time, on patriotic grounds, while he continued to serve in South Africa. Lily Miska – Lady Haldon – left the stage on marrying; but in 1905 she did return once more (under her married name, the Lady Haldon) in *The Sporting Duchess* at the Tivoli Theatre, London, where she took the rôle of the Duchess of Weldingborough. She was not seen on the boards again and in any case she was beginning to age. Over the years their lives were to have many ups and downs, and to end sadly. Their major problem was always a shortage of cash.

Nine

THE LAST RESORT

Torquay's halcyon years were the '60s and '70s of the 19th century; Paignton's the inter-war period when a boom in cheap seaside holidays took place and more of the working class went on annual holiday, usually by train. In the previous century taking a holiday had been almost exclusively a middle-class habit. The upper classes, in search of winter sunshine and of interesting places, much favoured the Mediterranean, and the cultivated classes especially Italy and Greece. Monte Carlo, for example, was then noted for its rich clientele, its gamblers and adventuresses, its milords and Russian nobles, and above all for its plutocrats. Smart and raffish, luxurious and lavish, by 1914 it came to symbolise capitalism at its apogee. E. Phillips Oppenheim, who relished the elegance and pleasure of high life on the Côte d'Azur, liked to set his mysteries there, and his novels were extremely popular with the English public in the 1920s.

Holidaying implies expense and obviously is only possible when a surplus from income is available, over and above subsistence. Those at the lowest level can never travel, except as vagrants or soldiers. But for the majority of the population real wages started to rise slowly in the second half of the 19th century. We may date this long-term trend in living standards, associated with a steep rise in Britain's gross national product (GNP), from the last half of the 19th century, although economic historians continue to debate the forms and effects of the trade cycle. This meant that by the 1930s much larger numbers could afford to go on holiday. Another factor associated with this trend – holiday-making and the holiday trades – is technological: improvements in transportation, of which steam power and then the internal combustion were the most conspicuous. Thus the Marxist historian, E.J. Hobsbawm, comments:

> Industrial capitalism produced two novel forms of pleasure travel: tourism and summer holidays for the bourgeoisie and mechanised day trips for the masses in some countries such as Britain. Both were the direct results of the application of steam to transport …

With the introduction of the Holidays with Pay Act of 1939 eleven million British workers secured the right to paid holidays; before that around 4½ and 7½ million (estimates greatly vary) were said to enjoy paid vacations. Since the great majority of insured workers were male, of whom a high proportion were married, the actual number of persons who travelled to seaside towns or to other places was significantly higher than the figures given. The social effects of such a large movement of people – men, women and children – were great, especially during the height of the summer. Many towns and resorts, particularly the smaller ones, came to depend upon a tourist and transient population for their livelihood. Few came to Paignton in the winter; they came mostly in the summer season, in July and August, when visitors overflowed the town and middle-class residents bitterly complained they were forced to queue for local buses and that the best produce – meat, vegetables and fruit – was bought up by the legion of hoteliers and boarding-house keepers in their midst. It was estimated in 1912 that Paignton's resident population of 11,240 had been swollen to over 19,000 that summer. This trend continued unabated after the war and was not markedly affected by the great depression of the early 1930s.

Torquay for a long time had been chary of advertising itself and until 1919 the so-called Baths Committee had been solely responsible for all official advertising; then in 1924 a Baths and Publicity Committee was appointed and given the task of attracting a different class of visitor to the town (for that is what it came to). Torquay Corporation wanted to attract more visitors in the summer season, for Torquay had early acquired a reputation as a town in which the rich wintered and that reputation lingered. Times had changed: the upper classes had been decimated by the war and most were less affluent than before. Death duties had become an oppressive burden; large numbers of the officer class had died in the war (the Cary family provides a good example); others were forced to sell their ancestral estates. Farming, moreover, continued to be depressed and had not recovered from the steep fall in prices of land and of its products that had occurred in the late 1870s. Those who survived the war, and the equally devastating influenza epidemic that followed, which killed more than the great conflict itself, were inclined to prefer the Continent, which so many had first visited in wartime. It was also the dawn of the motoring age. It was now possible to traverse the Continent by car, and in comfort. But these social changes hardly affected Paignton, which had never aspired to be a fashionable, a posh resort. The pleasures it offered were simple: the sea, the sun, and sunbathing, for in the 1920s the last had become a veritable cult with youth and even the not-so-young. Exercise of all kinds had become a national fetish and at Deller's Café in Paignton the Women's League of Health and Beauty, founded by Mrs Bagot-Stack in 1930 and after her death in 1935 taken over by her daughter Prunella Stack at the age of 20, held its weekly 'keep fit' classes. Its members, clad in white sleeveless blouses and black silk shorts, performed rhythmic exercises to music. Women no longer wished to affect an interesting pallor, a Pre-Raphaelite whiteness of

79 *The Strand in Torquay in the 1920s. In 1850* White's Directory of Devon *noted that* Hearder Family Hotel *contributed to Torquay's social life with 'a spacious Subscription Room and News Room'. Torquay had a reputation as a town in which the rich wintered.*

skin, but aspired to the bronzed look of the great open spaces. At Torquay and at Paignton people lay in rows on the beaches and soaked in the sun. The parasol, once a normal accompaniment of the Victorian or Edwardian lady at the seaside, was old hat; sun-glasses and suntan oil the rage. It was Germany that led the way in the 1920s, other countries followed, and in Britain hiking and cycling also became extremely popular.

This, then, was the great era of the boarding-house and hotel in South Devon resorts, such as Torquay and, in particular, Paignton. Numerous private homes near the sea and sands, detached or semi-detached, were utilised to take in visitors, and a significant proportion of the resident population came to depend on the holiday trade for its livelihood. John Walton's book on the Blackpool landlady is an excellent study of conditions in the North of England. In Blackpool, he writes:

> Many lodging-houses were run by single women, whether spinsters, widows, deserted wives or women separating from their husbands ... unattached women played a very important part in the accommodation industry.

But Torbay reveals slightly different trends. Keeping a boarding-house was essentially a fall-back occupation. Anyone with a house, owned or rented, could adapt it as a boarding-house or, more pretentiously, as a 'private hotel'. There was usually no need to employ extra staff for the labour of a wife or husband, supplemented perhaps by children, or in a larger house a maid or two, would suffice.

Opening a boarding-house was a reasonably attractive proposition, especially if the husband had a small pension or some other source of income to tide over hard times. A possible alternative was shopkeeping, but this was a riskier pursuit since the occupation demanded some commercial skills, such as a flair for selling, a good head for figures, or a manner that pleased. For the untrained it was obviously a chancy business to enter and many small businesses and shops did in fact go bankrupt in seaside towns in the 1930s and their stocks were sold off at auction for very little. Those who succeeded in trade, or gained a modest living from their enterprise, were mostly people with some past experience of their occupation, such as milliners, haberdashers, confectioners, and bakers. Yet many seeking independence, and those equipped with a small competence, did take the plunge. Even in Victorian times the middle-class Miss Matty in *Cranford* was forced to sell tea when she lost her fortune and thus gained a modest living.

It became a practice for boarding-house keepers to build an annexe, or, more commonly, a small room or wooden shed in the back garden where the owners could sleep at night during the busy summer season, so that all available rooms could be let as bedrooms, and hence maximise profit on the house. It was, however, also at times a precarious occupation, for so much depended on the state of the weather and the upturns and downturns of the trade cycle: a string of bad summers or a severe recession could reduce to penury proprietors without money put by. Yet despite having to face these vicissitudes, or vagaries of other sorts, people continued to take up the occupation. Why some were successful and others not, is difficult to determine: location, size of establishment, quality of management, all must have determined the outcome. At the lower level, it was common for those who lived in terraced houses, even persons who occupied poky houses, or bungalows and chalets, to provide bed and breakfast accommodation – a hand-written card placed in a front window was sufficient advertisement – or to offer a room or two to let. An astonishing number of people took in visitors, discreetly.

Landladies have been much caricatured, as in *Punch* and a flood of comic seaside postcards, as rapacious harpies, charging extra for HP or brown sauce and the cruet. But so much depended on goodwill that most landladies who did well and were normally booked out for the season tended to curry favour with their guests, who after all were their best advertisers.

Many servicemen had returned from the war shell-shocked, gassed, wounded or mutilated, and many more were still suffering from neurasthenia, first induced by battle or the prospect of battle. Others had acquired tuberculosis, one of the commonest diseases in those days. There were ex-soldiers, apparently still healthy, who never worked again and declined into invalidism, so of necessity their wives were forced to become the chief bread-winner. Keeping a boarding-house was typically a woman's business, the husband normally a mere auxiliary or handyman, unless employed full-time outside the home or engaged in seasonal work, for the demand for labour in seaside towns expanded greatly in the summer season. Other ex-soldiers, made disillusioned by the failure of the utopian slogan that England would become 'a home fit for heroes to live in', sank into apathy when faced with reality outside the trenches. But other men, sanguine of temperament, would sink their small capital or savings into a house which they then opened as a boarding establishment or guest-house.

There is a passage in John Presland's *Torgu* which is worth quoting because it describes some of the peculiarities of a typical resort town:

> There is a large population who … except for selling each other the ordinary commodities and 'taking in each other's washing', seem to have no occupation; the greater number of them are not engaged either in growing anything or making anything, nor in a profession. In the summer, it is clear, the influx of seasonal visitors from large towns gives occupation and an income to very many of its inhabitants, but for eight months of the year they apparently have 'no visible means of support'. I suppose that the existence of so many of these seaside towns, which are neither fishing, nor agricultural, nor manufacturing, nor trading, betokens a large body of middle-class people living on small but unearned incomes who find a greater amenity of social life at Folkestone or Swansea or Ilfracombe [or Torquay and Paignton] than they would in a large town. This class seems destined to disappear in the near future under pressure of modern economic conditions.

This was written of Paignton in 1920. His prediction has not been realised, but we should add that many middle-class people themselves went into the hotel trade as fixed incomes declined. It was also quite common for proprietors not to own their boarding-house or hotel but to rent the property from a landlord on a long-term lease. Presland also refers to another curious feature of such towns: Paignton, for example, was comparatively deserted in winter, when penetrating east winds from the sea whistled and howled along deserted streets and sea fogs descended on the town.

It was the habit between the wars for some better-off families to rent a house for all or part of the summer season and sometimes for much longer periods. Roundham with its large villas and the Preston district were particularly favoured for this purpose. Presland does not mention the importance to the town's economy that derived from the building trade. A majority of the young men were employed in it as bricklayers and masons, plasterers and painters, others as electricians and plumbers. There was a post-war boom in building, both in the public and private sectors, when, for example, much of Preston was developed. The Paignton Urban District Council first ventured into this field in 1919/20, to make up for housing arrears caused by the war. This great expansion of council housing owed everything to the policies of Dr

80 *The last tram ran to Paignton in 1934.*

Christopher Addison, Britain's first Minister of Health. Before that, the Council
had owned only four small cottages, for in pre-war years private enterprise
was expected to provide most of the new housing and houses to rent. Stanley
Gardens, opened in 1920, was the first Council estate, others followed, even
at Preston, and the process continued until it was once again interrupted by
the exigencies of war. In 1937/8 there was another great boom in private
housing and large parts of Marldon, Preston, and Goodrington were built
over. This happened, too, at Torquay, where its suburbs and outlying districts
like Chelston, Shiphay, and Hele, were attracting speculative builders. There
was also a great deal of ribbon development in these years and the main
routes into the town were much favoured for detached or semi-detached
houses, to which the Torquay to Newton Abbot Road is a notable witness.
There was no need to provide access roads and land was relatively cheap
along main roads.

Although 1.6 million were recorded as unemployed in 1937 in Great Britain,
conditions were much more favourable in Torbay, where the housing boom
gave much employment and private builders were extremely active. In Torbay
there was almost full employment, though wages were not high, largely provided
not only by the building industry and its ancillary services but by the holiday
trades. Elizabeth Brunner in her study of the holiday industry states that as
late as 1941 there were '4,084 insured workers in the distributive trades and
2,957 in the hotel trades out of a total insured population of 16,193'.
Conditions, however, were not so good in Brixham, for its fishing industry
had gone into decline and there was no special demand for housing, despite

the fact that much accommodation in the town was old or of inferior quality. We do not have figures for the host of farmers' wives and daughters in the surrounding rural districts who took in guests during the season. They doubled-up as boarding-house keepers in the summer.

The evolution of the hotel industry is a subject in itself but must be dealt with summarily in this final chapter. A successful boarding-house keeper tended to upgrade his establishment and to change its name from that of plain boarding-house to guest-house, from private hotel to the grander 'Hotel', each step forward in status normally associated with the purchase of adjoining property, enlargement of the premises, or other such improvements, such as gentrification of the property. Others would open a restaurant within the hotel, open not only for guests but to anyone. A hotel gained much kudos with the establishment of a cocktail or public bar, frequented by locals. This is what happened to numerous seafront hotels at Paignton and other nearby locations, to which beach-goers would wander at noon for a beer and in the early evening for a sundowner, a gin-and-It or a gin-and-French then being the fashionable drinks in the better hotels.

Although Flaubert ironically claimed that hotels 'ne sont bon qu'en Suisse', Torquay in fact had a number of excellent ones, including the *Imperial* and the *Grand*. The latter, erected adjacent to Torquay station, opened in 1881 as the *Great Western Hotel* and was owned by the railway company of that name. It became the *Grand Hotel* just twenty years later, under new management. There was also Bishop Phillpotts' Italianate villa, Bishopstowe, with its 20 acres of grounds. After the Bishop's death in 1869 it was occupied for 37 years by the Hanburys, brewers from Birmingham, now active in local affairs at Torquay, and then by Sir Arthur and Lady Havelock; but it was really too commodious and too expensive a house to maintain as a private residence in the stringent years that followed the Great War and so was converted into a hotel, two large wings being added. *The Palace Hotel*, as it was renamed, officially opened in August 1921. Between the wars these hotels became widely respected for their excellence, especially the *Imperial* which also had a reputation for exclusiveness and *bon ton*. But Brunner cautions us that pay was low except for head waiters and chefs and living conditions for staff spartan. In the late 1930s she reports that 'one lounge waiter at a big Torquay hotel works 84 hours a week for a wage of 30s. exclusive of tips' and she also mentions a housekeeper working 71 hours a week for the same wage. There was consequently a large change-over of staff at hotels; few remained permanently at a hotel, except for managerial staff. Many relied on itinerant Irish labour for its waiters and chambermaids.

Paignton had no establishment that could compare with any one of the great Torquay hotels, except perhaps the *Redcliffe* at Preston, which was, however, in comparison small in scale (it has, however, been much extended since then). The old Redcliffe House had been acquired by Paris Singer early

81 Hotel Redcliffe, *Paignton. The old Redcliffe House had been acquired by Paris Singer and converted into an attractive residential hotel with direct access to the sea.*

in the century and converted into an attractive residential hotel, with direct access to the sea. It was where William James stayed in 1908 when, as we know, he and his family visited the Findlater sisters. Many of the town's larger hotels, such as the *Esplanade*, the *Palace*, and the *Hydro*, were located along the seafront or in adjacent areas. The two towns did not really compete in the matter of accommodation since, in the main, each tended to attract a different class of patron. We may caricature their differences (grossly exaggerated of course) in Hilaire Belloc's lines: at Torquay 'the Rich arrived in pairs and also in Rolls Royces. They talked of their affairs in loud and strident voices.' At Paignton, however: 'the Poor arrived in Fords, whose features they resembled.'

Between the wars, Paignton tended to be run by a small oligarchy of shopkeepers, tradesmen, and businessmen – what has been referred to by social historians infelicitously as a 'shopocracy' – a tendency that was also emerging at Torquay. There was, of course, always the odd gentleman in retirement who devoted his stifled energies to Council or Borough affairs; at times, councillors espoused some particular cause, such as drainage, the provision of more parks or public conveniences, the state of the roads, or law and order. It was their monomania that drove them into local politics. Percy Russell, writing about Torquay Corporation's attempt to erect a Pavilion, a building where entertainments could be staged for visitors, comments:

Controversy continued, and provided a classical example of the acute and permanent division of opinion between the mass of the residents on the one hand and the traders and hotel and boarding-house owners on the other … seaside residents are mainly elderly people, usually living on fixed incomes, and therefore reluctant to see the rates go up because of provision made for seasonal visitors.

As at Torquay, so too in Paignton, there were conflicts between local residents and a Council bent on attracting more visitors to the resort. Thus the town, in the main, had two powerful interest groups and a considerable amount of tension and conflict was at times generated between them. Residents, for example, were not happy about trippers brought to the town by charabancs, especially Welsh miners and their families, who were apt to become a nuisance by their proletarian behaviour and excessive boozing, or noisy parties from the industrial Midlands: the tone in Torquay was genteel, at Paignton more lower-middle-class. Some traders and shopkeepers did not mind at all, notably publicans, the owners of cheap cafés or amusement arcades, cinema managers, and proprietors of fish-and-chip shops. We may sum this up by saying that the majority of retired people wanted to conserve the town as it was, whereas the business community sought to improve the town in the interests of commerce, of which they were the beneficiaries. Both groups were self-serving, self-seeking. The latter wanted more provision for car-parks, amusements, and leisure facilities; the former thought the town already had enough. The 'shopocracy' usually got what it wanted, though not always when a particularly ferocious campaign was waged in the press; at times councillors were forced to cave in or compromise: the voice of 'democracy' was heard in the land. It is alleged – it always is – that there was much jiggery-pokery and backstairs influence employed to buy up land scheduled by the council for urban development or other improvements. This might have given rise to bribery and corruption, for we have been alerted to such dangers by the notorious Poulson affair of the 1970s.

Paignton was run by those engaged in business and commerce, often not well educated, certainly not over educated, and in the main philistine in outlook. Their philistinism is evident in the type of buildings they have allowed to be put up or pulled down, actions which must dismay those sensitive to the architecture of their surroundings, to the Betjemanites in our midst. Tradesmen and shopkeepers, publicans and hoteliers, have tended to monopolise the majority of public and official roles. On the whole, though, they have done a reasonably good job to advertise the town and to bring in visitors and increase prosperity. The Paignton Club, formerly the Gentleman's Club, and once the habitat of those who really mattered, lost its lustre over time as Paignton's sole repository of gentlemen, and now other classes of people are responsible for the town's destiny, and this has happened all over the land.

There are no agreed-upon criteria to establish whether this is a good or a bad thing: but it is one of the myths of the 20th century that change is always for the better. What we can say with certainty is that we must live with history's failures, for not everything is rectifiable, and buildings once destroyed are lost for ever. We cannot revive a past landscape.

* * *

Beverley Nichols called Torquay 'a citadel of Philistinism' and by implication he included Paignton in his anathema. It is a trite accusation. Nichols was comparing provincial towns with London, home to the ballet and the theatre, the opera and the picture gallery. But this would be true of most countries where the contrast between a capital city and its provincial towns, in cultural terms, is always marked: one has but to think of Paris. Only Germany, perhaps, is different with its ancient university towns and former courts. The philosopher Kant spent his entire life in Konigsberg. It did not stifle his intelligence.

The Torbay region had no university, only Schools of Arts and Crafts at Torquay and at Paignton, and a Commercial College and Technical College at Torquay. One could not expect a vibrant intellectual or aesthetic life to flourish in either town. There were, to start with, no good bookshops. W.H. Smiths had to suffice for purchasers of the latest novel or biography. There were, again, no good antiquarian or second-hand bookshops in either town, though Torquay in the 1930s acquired two small establishments on Victoria Parade. One innovation did help readers in rural Torbay, that was the existence of a travelling library, a van stuffed with books which came to villages such as Marldon and from which books could be borrowed for a few pence a week.

Torbay between the wars was mainly a residential district, with an unusually large proportion of elderly or retired people, and with a preponderance of women. Its younger and middle-aged middle-class inhabitants were wont to pursue golf, tennis, or sailing: the quest for knowledge did not greatly excite these comfortably-off people. Beverley Nichols' search for novelty, for the latest thing in the arts and literature – a gayer world in every sense – was not for them: they were quite content to read Buchan and Sapper and Dornford Yates; and in art they were inclined to admire pictures of stags at bay on Exmoor or paintings of Dartmoor ponies. It is doubtful if anyone in the district, apart from the inhabitants of Dartington Hall, owned a John Nash, a Ben Nicholson or a Graham Sutherland. And they were not at all dismayed, one thinks, to find that Stanley Baldwin's favourite novelist was Mary Webb. There was cold comfort in that for Torbay's minute literati and even smaller intelligentsia. The tastes and values of middle-class Torbay families reflected those of the Brown family in Richmal Crompton's series of *Just William* stories. Philistines they may well have been; average, decent people they certainly were.

* * *

By the 1930s the great private landowners had departed. The Palks had been gone for some years, the last fragments of their once great estates having been sold in 1914. Then in 1930 Commander Henry Cary sold Torre Abbey to Torquay Corporation for £40,000, but he still derived an income from the large unsold portion of the estate, mostly situated at Babbacombe and St Marychurch, and a Cary Estate Office was maintained near the harbour; Richard Mallock followed suit by selling Cockington in 1932 to the same body for £50,000. Neither landowner remained in the town; both left Devon. By the early 1930s, then, Torquay Corporation had become the town's leading landlord. This trend – the replacement of aristocratic landlords by municipal authorities – was to occur at all resorts and watering-places during the inter-war period, mainly due to the expanding role of local authorities and of their powers: this was the culmination of a long process of economic and social change, changes that had started to speed up around the mid-19th century. It testified, as well, to the growth of democratic reforms within Britain and to the decline in the influence of the gentry and aristocracy on local affairs.

We left the 3rd Lord Haldon on the brink of the First World War, in which he served with distinction, being mentioned in despatches. They were then living in Pimlico, London, in much reduced circumstances. Lady Haldon died in November 1928. Soon after, in January 1929, he remarried. His second wife, Edith Castle, was a widow (Lord Haldon seemed to have a penchant for widows) but this second marriage lasted a bare 18 months. Her body was found at the foot of the Black Rock, Brighton, in May 1930. The Coroner brought in an open verdict, but the facts would certainly suggest suicide. She had left their Brixton flat or lodgings without informing her husband and had taken the train to Brighton. Lord Haldon broke into tears at the inquest and exclaimed pathetically: 'We were like Darby and Joan'. In all likelihood she had become depressed by their lack of money and the fact that they were forced to live in a cheap boarding-house, where they went under the name of 'Mr and Mrs Haldon'. *The Times* reported her death, correctly, in the headline 'Lady Haldon's Death'. Lawrence William Palk, the 3rd Lord Haldon, died alone at Stratton, near Bude, Cornwall. It was an unfashionable boarding-house area. *The Times* obituary declared of him:

> In 1885 the family estates included the greater part of Torquay and St Marychurch. In 1885 the late peer's father obtained a special act of Parliament giving him the right to deal with the settled estates, and the late peer sold his interest in 1891, subject to the payment of his then existing debts. His affairs afterwards became involved.

It was indeed a cautionary tale: for his affairs had become more than involved, opaque. These events were to cast a darkening shadow over his only child, Lawrence Edward Bloomfield Palk, born in Sydney, Australia. In the years 1893 to 1901 Lord Haldon had been seeking his fortune in foreign parts, Australia, China, and America. He was mainly engaged in engineering and mining enterprises. It seems, though, that he was not successful and bankruptcy finally caught up with him. It was customary for the Palks to send their sons to Eton but Lawrence Edward went instead to Beaumont College, also located at Windsor, then a leading Catholic public school, which suggests his mother was either born a Catholic or became a convert to that religion. He was just 18 when war broke out and volunteered for the army. Like his father, his war record was exemplary and he was mentioned in despatches. He served in Gallipoli, Egypt, and Mesopotamia, where he was on the staff of Sir Stanley Maude's Tigris Army.

Then peace broke out; the years that followed were for him a more trying time than the war years. He was unable to continue with his military career for there were so many ex-officers in the country and cutbacks in the armed forces were taking place. He had been trained for no profession, had entered no university. Like many young men of his type he went out to the colonies. He was in turn a farmer in Kenya, a film actor, a furniture salesman, a sea-cook on a cargo steamer – his biography reads like a Hollywood actor's – and had ended up in the late 1930s jobless, driftless and destitute in London. In his last days, he had no means apart from public assistance and a job as a packer at a West End store. Not perhaps too astounding a decline and fall for a Lord Haldon, for the past two generations of Palks had revealed grave faults of character. They had failed to live up to the standards set by the founder of the dynasty, Sir Robert Palk. Lawrence Edward had been in poor health for some time and died at his lodgings on 17 August 1938, aged only 42. What follows reads like the plot of a Victorian melodrama such as *Lady Audley's Secret*. On 15 March 1939 *The Times* reported the news: 'Lady Palk, birth of a son'. This was odd since it was widely believed that Lawrence Edward had never married and the report excited much interest in the family. Now an heir had mysteriously surfaced, seven months after Lawrence Edward's death, following upon which Edward Palk, the fourth son of the 1st Lord Haldon, had assumed the barony.

At the trial of Lizzie Ireland and Isabella Blackett at the Chester Assizes in November 1940 the story of the mysterious heir was unravelled. Both women were charged with conspiracy, and Blackett was described as a 'nurse-secretary' to Mrs Ireland. The main conspirator, Mrs Ireland – who went under the alias of Marcia Lady Haldon – had married a Canadian doctor, a Dr Ireland, in 1917. It was not denied by the prosecution that Lizzie had met Lord Haldon in London and had been good to him but that they had become lovers seems unlikely. She claimed that she had married Lord Haldon in June 1938 at Edinburgh and that her 'marriage certificate' was written on paper franked with the House of Lords crest.

The facts revealed at the trial were these: Mrs Ireland adopted a newly-born baby from a woman at Middlewich. She then took the child to her country residence at Toft, near Knutsford. Blackett went to the Registry Office to register the birth of a son to Lady Haldon. The vicar of Toft was called to her country residence – a cottage – and baptised the child Lawrence Edward Bloomfield Haldon, the son of the widowed Lady Haldon, born seven months after his father's death. The village policeman affirmed he also visited the cottage and had been invited in to see Lady Haldon, who lay in bed in a darkened room, bewigged and heavily made up, one supposes, to counterfeit a more juvenile look. Lizzie Ireland pointed to a cot in which a baby lay and declared: 'This is the future Lord Haldon'. This seemed an unlikely claim since she was 61 at the time of the supposed birth. But Dr Ireland, whom she had remarried since the event, said he had also gone to the cottage on the day the child was born and had 'no doubt that it was his wife whom he attended', a curious statement from a medical practitioner since he must have been aware of her real age.

Lizzie Ireland (as she was known before her elevation) was sentenced to three years' penal servitude and Isabella Blackett to 12 months' imprisonment. Then her husband, Dr Arthur John Ireland, went on trial at the Chester Assizes in February 1941, charged with giving false information concerning a birth and with making a false statement that a birth had taken place. Dr Ireland's plea of 'not guilty' was accepted by the prosecution. His defence counsel argued he acted under the influence of his wife. Mr Justice Croom-Johnson passing sentence said: 'I think that public interest will best be served by allowing you to go back and continue your duty. I had in mind to sentence you to a term of imprisonment, but I have been struck by your military record.' It was wartime; there was a shortage of trained personnel; and Dr Ireland was now serving with the RAMC. There are several things one would still like to know about the deception but Britain was at war and newsprint scarce and *The Times* did not report the case at length. The real heir presumptive to the barony, Colonel Edward Palk, died on 11 January 1939, aged eighty-four. With the death of Colonel Palk the Haldon peerage became extinct. The heir presumptive to the baronetcy was Wilmot Lawrence Palk, great-grandson of the 2nd baronet. When he died in 1945 leaving behind no heir both the barony and baronetcy were now extinct.

Today Lizzie Ireland would be diagnosed as a disturbed personality, her conduct as lunatic. That she knew Lord Haldon is not in doubt, but whether she ever went to bed with him is. At her trial she was described as of independent means and a witness, a police officer, deposed that she owned a number of houses, a motor car (not so common in those days), and employed a chauffeur. Where had her wealth come from? Isabella Blackett had been a school teacher and previously bore an exemplary character, according to the

82 *Little Oldway. Paris Singer's daughter, Lady Leeds, stayed on at Little Oldway, the oldest part of the Singer estate, until she died in 1980.*

the same witness. Was this a case of *folie à deux*? The only plausible explanation is that Ireland was besotted with the aristocracy, with titled people, and wanted to pose in public as the Dowager Lady Haldon, a grand enough designation. This makes sense since Lord Haldon had no money to pass on: all he could leave for a wife was a title.

* * *

The Palks, the Carys and the Mallocks were no longer living in Torbay, nor were the Singers at Paignton, apart from Paris Singer's daughter, Lady Leeds, who stayed on at Little Oldway until she died in 1980. The Champernownes, we know, had sold their 400-year-old Dartington estate to Leonard and Dorothy Elmhirst in 1925. Most of the Carew estates were sold in the 1920s to cover death duties and other liabilities. Haccombe, an estate of 1,700 acres, including the mansion house, was finally put on the market in 1942 and bought by a London businessman who wanted to farm. The Carews stayed on the estate until the end of the war, before moving to a manor house near Dorchester, but 18 months later they left England altogether and went to the Bahamas. Other landowners were to depart soon after the Second World War. Lord Churston retired to Fort George, Guernsey, and Lupton House, his former seat, was transformed firstly into a hotel and is now a school. Churston Court, once the seat of the Yardes, has become a popular hotel and hostelry. The Seales of Mount Boone, Dartmouth, settled in Monmouth. Their old home, which had become much dilapidated over the years, was pulled down. Follaton House, just outside Totnes, once owned by a collateral branch of the Carys of Torre Abbey, became council offices; so, too, Forde House at Newton Abbot. Members of the Courtenay family lived there until 1762; thereafter it was let to others. The house was never the Courtenay family seat. The Teignbridge District Council acquired the property in 1978 and now it forms part of the Council's complex of administrative buildings. The Dukes of Sutherland deserted Torquay many years ago when Annie, the Duchess, died. The 4th Duke got through most of his inheritance, selling estates in Scotland and elsewhere, by the time he died in 1963. His attitude was one of *après moi, le déluge*.

Only the Cliffords of Chudleigh, an old Catholic family whose ancestry goes back to the Conquest, returned to their mansion, Ugbrooke, situated on the Exeter to Plymouth Road. They came back in 1957 to reclaim it as a family home. Rebuilt for the 4th Lord Clifford by Robert Adam (who also designed the castellation) and with grounds laid out by Capability Brown, it was then in a bad state of repair, for grain had been stored by farmers in its panelled rooms. The Cliffords restored the main house to its former glory. Oldway was sold for £45,000 in May 1946 to Paignton Council and its contents auctioned. Some time later David's vast painting of 'The Crowning of Josephine' went back to France and is now in the Louvre. This is what the Singers always wanted. Today the mansion is the headquarters for Paignton Urban District Council. Its gardens have been thrown open to the public and visitors allowed to use its tennis courts, bowling green, and other facilities.

And so all of Torbay's grandees and those in surrounding districts virtually disappeared by the 1950s and no longer play any significant political or social role in the lives of Devonshire people. The large landowners had been been forced to sell their estates as a result of economic pressures, of penal rates of taxation, of high death duties, and the gathering forces of social change. The war was followed by a period of extreme austerity in Britain, for Attlee's Labour Government had set its sights on creating a more egalitarian country. It used its available resources principally for rebuilding industry and re-establishing the export trade, and for the creation of a welfare state. For the better-off it was not a good time to be in Britain, except for middle-class socialist ideologues. Travelling abroad in any degree of comfort became impossible since the government had imposed stringent currency regulations. In South Devon this was the end of an era, almost the end of the traditional civilisation people there were habituated to. There would be no going back.

The social transformation of Torquay was final: its fine shops in Fleet and Union Streets and around the Strand closed down one by one by the early

1960s and re-opened to suit the tastes of a new type of visitor. The old Marine Spa was demolished and in its place a leisure centre erected; high-rise blocks of flats started to sprout on hills above the harbour. Holiday camps were already popular before the war but now they proliferated; so too did caravan sites. Often they were sited close to the sea, on cliff-tops. The old boarding-house is still popular but many have been transformed into self-catering establishments, flatlets and holiday homes. The traditional landlady is an extinct race.

Torquay was the last resort on the south coast to be developed for the privileged classes, to be fashioned to please the upper classes. It was the westernmost watering-place beyond Exmouth and Teignmouth. It soon eclipsed both. It was famous abroad and in its heyday attracted the nobility and aristocracy of the Continent and a sizeable number of Americans, Southerners and Northerners. There was no comparable place on Devon's northern coast.

Torquay's decline as a fashionable watering-place coincided with the Victorian sunset; its fall with the end of empire. Torquay and Paignton have been fused as a result of rapid urbanisation, of developments which have obliterated traditional landmarks. If, like Rip Van Winkle on the Catskill Mountains, a sleeper awoke in Torbay he would be amazed to find that the separate identities once enjoyed by its towns and villages have almost disappeared: instead, he would witness a mass of housing almost totally encircling the bay in every direction and its once green hills covered with bungalows and chalets, detached and semi-detached houses. It is as though Torquay's few remaining Colonel Blimps, muttering octogenarians, were contemplating the Simla they once knew, a hill town, a resort, its sahibs and memsahibs now all vanished. The 'natives', to use their vernacular, have taken over.

Ten

THE LAST FORTY YEARS

T HE old social world of Torbay may have disappeared by the end of the
1930s but it was still traditionally regarded as a respectable and rather
proper place where the pace of life was measured by the sedate activities
of an ageing population and expectations kept within an established social
boundary. With the war years, all this was to change and new qualities were to
emerge of resourcefulness and endurance and, in 1943, an unexpectedly strong
spirit of raffishness that had hitherto been far from Torbay's perception of
itself and which was never to be quite eradicated.

With the fall of France in June 1940, the few months of the 'phoney war'
came to an abrupt end but Torbay had already experienced the first of two
large, though temporary, shifts in its population. In anticipation of bombing
to come, the London County Council sent a large contingent of evacuees to
the area (many of whom were bemused by the red cliffs of Devon having
known only the white cliffs of Dover). They were soon to be joined by
evacuees from the blitzed cities in the Midlands and South Wales. The ladies
of the WVS, working with the billeting officers, administered the placing of
the evacuees robustly and efficiently. Any house deemed to have a spare room
had to take in an evacuee, and nursing homes and small hotels were not
exempt from this strict ruling. Torquay, making a patriotic war effort, was
described as 'full to bursting'. This was probably, for many people, the defining
moment of the war when their lives changed with the loss of privacy.

People soon became aware of the big changes in their lives with the
introduction of a vigorously enforced blackout. There was no street lighting,
all cars had dipped headlights and, in the country, signposts were taken down,
though not removed. All these changes immediately affected social life and
were closely supervised by the new ARP Wardens. At the same time people
were faced with the rationing of all the essentials that made life so comfortable:
food, petrol and clothing. In fact, many people found they could supplement
their rations from their own back gardens and the nearness of the countryside
gave easy access to the black market: there were accounts of people who
never needed to claim their ration. Petrol was soon rationed and quickly
curtailed all social life after dark that was not within walking distance although,
in time, ingenious ways were found to acquire the pink fluid.

The RAF arrived in September 1940 for a year of training before being sent to Canada, and preparations to deal with the impending dangers started with the building of the gun emplacements, at Daddy Hole Plain and Elberry Cove. There is a Torbay and South Devon Air Gunners Association to this day. Morrison and Anderson shelters were distributed to supplement the street shelters, three of which were built in the Strand. With the menacing air-raid siren that could go off at any time, barrage balloons suspended over the harbour, and every citizen charged with carrying a gas mask in a square brown box, Torquay's life was certainly not the same. And not the same either at Paignton Zoo which now housed evacuees of its own from Chessington Zoo near the London bombing. For those too old for the call-up, the newly named National Fire Service Unit welcomed volunteers to arm their fire trucks, an unexpected realisation, for some, of a childhood ambition. In 1940 after the retreat from Dunkirk, when the threat of invasion was at its greatest, the Home Guard was established, giving all Torbay's Great War veterans, from colonels to corporals, the opportunity to feel that they, too, could make a contribution.

The beaches were still accessible but daylight air attacks and barbed wire fortifications and mined areas, such as those at Anstey's Cove, discouraged people from trying to recall carefree pre-war days. Anyone walking along the sea front ran the risk of being machine-gunned and many were, including Torquay's Chief Education Officer who was killed protecting his children from the bullets of a low flying plane. But there was still the cinema (open on Sundays) and the pubs where people could hear Lord Haw Haw on the radio, broadcasting from Germany and threatening that the streets of their county town, Exeter, the 'Golden City of the West ... would run with blood'. People, reading about the presence of Fifth Columnists, became very aware of anyone whose antecedents were not totally rooted in England.

Torbay was on the flight path for all the bombing raids on south Wales, the Midlands and Plymouth but never on the receiving end of such massive bombing. There were direct hits on shops and houses at Castle Circus and, during one school holiday, Lauriston Hall School had a direct hit. The *Imperial Hotel* and the *Palace Hotel* were both bombed. But where Torbay suffered was from 142 tip and run raids. These were very frightening because unexpected, with no warning siren as the planes flying over from Cherbourg were able to fly under the radar screen. In 1942 Mrs M. Lawrence, picnicking between Bishop's Walk and Marine Drive, saw three planes fly so low above her that she could see the pilots' heads. She heard three explosions and then saw the fighters return to machine-gun two or three little rowing boats floating off the coast. One man was killed and the others wounded. They were patients from the *Palace Hotel* RAF Hospital. The explosions had killed the occupants of a row of houses on Warbro Road. Mrs E. Patterson, one quiet Brixham

Sunday morning in May 1943, was looking out towards Berry Head when she saw six planes flying low towards Torquay. One of the bombs she heard falling landed on St Marychurch, Torquay killing 21 children and their teachers in Sunday school. A friend of the author remembers picking apples in her garden near Castle Circus, hearing the siren, being immediately strafed by a low flying plane and seeing the bullets knock the apples from the trees. It is not surprising that when a plane was shot down on Torre Sands no one attempted to rescue the men from the burning plane: the horror of this impressed several small boys who, 50 years later, recalled the scene in their reminiscences.

By far the largest increase in the population came in 1943 when hundreds of thousands of Americans and Canadians arrived in Torquay by train from Liverpool. Their real destination was several miles down the coast at Slapton Sands where the conditions were considered ideal for practising the D-Day landings, but they were billeted in Torbay and Newton Abbot and everyone made for Torquay for a night out. The arrival of the Americans and Canadians in Torbay at this stage in the war must have created a feeling of optimism in the population, that, at last, something was being done. It cheered up the girls and the release of a lot American food through the civilian employees in the canteens certainly cheered up their families. Down in Slapton Sands, where a radius of 25 miles had been cleared, there was much understandable anger among the civilian population whose livelihoods had been drastically affected. But Torquay became the centre for fun. The doyens of Torquay's social world in the 1930s would have been appalled. The rendezvous for the locals to meet the GIs was not one of the pre-war grand hotels but the YMCA at Castle Circus and the Torquay pubs. It was a world of silk stockings and Lucky Strike and jeeps racing about town. The big band era was at its peak with new dances, swing and jitterbug, and Glenn Miller broadcasting from London or from his base in Bedford. It was also a brief interlude, a chance to recapture some sense of normality for these young men, especially the Canadians, who had already seen a great deal of fighting. At the same time, they would have known that Operation Tiger at Slapton Sands was not going well and that hundreds of troops had already been killed in the exercises, though this information was not to be released for many years. At Torcross, at the southern end of the beach, a Sherman tank, recovered from off shore a few years ago, stands in silent tribute to those young men who never left the English shore. The year following the invasion saw a large increase in the number of births. Yet many romances did lead to marriage, and there are web sites on the World Wide Web in which American and Canadian octogenarians pay warm tribute to the people of Torbay. The children certainly enjoyed the presence of these young men. In preparation for the invasion the troops, even whilst on leave, regularly used to do six-mile route marches to keep fit and children running

83 *Torquay D-Day, 3 June 1944. The closure of the Torquay waterfront extended some distance back into the town. The soldiers are marching past the three public air-raid shelters that had been built in the Strand.*

alongside chanting 'give us some gum, chum' found them generous with their bubble gum and Hershey bars.

As D-Day approached, Torbay overflowed with boats of all kinds. Aircraft carriers provided the watching Torquinians with views of spectacular take-offs and landings and shocked them when they witnessed at least one tragedy. Liberty boats brought the men ashore to join the Americans and Canadians in those final few days of 16 May to 1 June 1944 when poor weather postponed the invasion. Torquay must have been an extraordinary place to be at that time, generating a feeling of tension and expectation that it would never have had cause to experience before.

It all ended suddenly on 3 June 1944. Before D-Day the coastal road to Paignton was closed together with all the beaches. The closure of the Torquay waterfront extended some distance back into the town. The absence of the Americans and Canadians from the streets alerted locals to the fact that something was up but even so it was a shock when, overnight, the boats in the harbour vanished, together with all the GIs. Special landing craft for the

Normandy Beaches had been built at Brixham and in the River Dart, and the slipways built to launch them are still visible in Torbay harbour today.

Torquay had a part to play in the next stage of the war when, after D-Day, the American 124th Army General Hospital was established at Denbury for casualties straight from the battlefront, and staff and recovering soldiers would come into Torquay to the popular pubs. The Americans had requisitioned the *Palace Hotel* to use as a hospital, and Oldway Mansion had become a hospital for the Royal Air Force and the Commonwealth Air Force, so there was still a military feel to Torquay, albeit one that was not so strong and vigorous.

An unexpected development was the setting up of a camp for Italian prisoners-of-war that was, reputedly, lightly guarded as they worked on the land. This resulted in a fair amount of happy social activity in the neighbourhood, making up in a small way for the missing GIs. An altogether different type of camp was the one near Stover for displaced Poles, which was not to close for 15 long years. The legacy of this camp is that there is now a sizeable Polish population well established in this area.

With the threat of invasion fading and tip and run raids no longer a danger, life in Torbay started to seem more like the old days. Paignton Zoo was open, a circus was held there in 1944, visitors returned to Kent's Cavern and the racing fraternity was back in action at Newton Abbot with greyhound

84 *Brixham embarkation. Special landing craft for the Normandy beaches were built at Brixham.*

racing in Torquay. But social changes had been set in motion following those heady days of 1943-4, and there was now a great enthusiasm for dancing. *The Imperial, Palm Court Hotel* and Spa Ballroom all had nightly dances with popular tea dances twice a week. It all helped to generate a feeling of energy, to challenge the dreariness of war on the home front and dull the fear of what was happening in Europe and the Far East.

By the late summer of 1944 the blackout was phased out and lighted shop windows were back. But the quest for food was ongoing. The YMCA cafeteria over Dunn's Hat Shop in Union Street was open until 9 p.m., providing civilians and service men and women with hot snacks, and in Paignton the British Restaurant, part of a nationwide chain, was open to provide good meals at good prices. Even the Torquay and Paignton Gas Company weighed in with frequent and free 'Cooking Demonstrations for Wartime Catering'. And there were always ads encouraging a further war effort by filling jobs in the NAAFI canteens. A three-day 'Dig for Victory' campaign came to the Town Hall in Torquay at the end of 1944: there was advice from the *Daily Mail* agricultural expert, cooking and gardening demonstrations, and an edition of the widely listened-to Brains Trust.

In the last year of the war the Home Guard was stood down and local energy went into a series of savings campaigns with people being persuaded to invest in Government War Savings. There were numerous Victory Year appeals and fund drives to establish funds for the homecoming soldiers. Dancing was now extended to include a Mayoral Ball and a Torbay Ball, no doubt in the pursuit of funds. Visitors were starting to come in increasing numbers to re-establish the *raison d'être* of Torbay. Responding to their complaints The Devon General Omnibus & Touring Co. listed the 'priority' travel for workers and apologised to visitors for the lack of pre-war standards, especially during the peak hours. The Council, taking note of the visitors, turned its attention to the future and started planning.

Victory in Europe, 8 May 1945, was celebrated but muted by the knowledge that so many were suffering in the Far East. 15 August and VJ Day followed the midnight broadcast that war was over and crowds filled the Torquay streets, singing and dancing. Long-hoarded fireworks made a surprise appearance, and the following morning the town was bedecked with bunting. In Paignton there were large crowds and a bonfire on the Green. Looking ahead to problems with the return of their men, Brixham put up 50 prefabs which were regarded as the latest in domestic design technology. In Paignton, the long line of Preston Green beach huts which had been used by the Council throughout the war as a storage for paper and cardboard was given a fresh coat of green paint. The Mayor of Torquay, getting straight down to business, acknowledged the necessity of finding money for advertising in order to keep the visitors coming.

85 *Torquay Town Hall. Salute the Soldier, fund raising for the returning men.*

Torbay entered the 1950s still involved in the wider world as host to the third round of tariff talks to reduce trade barriers, later to be known as GATT. Previously held in Geneva and Annecy, 13 hotels were requisitioned for the talks that continued into 1951. Later in the year 150 Anglo-American oilmen from ESSO gathered in the *Victoria Hotel* and 300 delegates of the motor trade discussed the future in the *Imperial Hotel*. It was an indication of a possible way ahead for Torbay's own future.

There was a backward glance when The Natural History Society held an exhibition of pictures of old Torquay to remind Torquinians of the past but the Festival of Britain, showing the way forward, was celebrated locally. There was a surprising role reversal with Paignton, not Torquay, being one of only 14 Devon and Cornwall local authorities represented at the official opening. The Queen's Coronation in 1953 was celebrated in traditional style with fêtes and street parties and there was still a general sense of the old days. The fashion conscious crowd still made Bobby's on the Strand their meeting place, enjoying the music and harbour view from the restaurant. Just along the waterfront, Chanel provided court presentation gowns for local debs. All the old preoccupations were back: the Paignton Dog Show in 1951 had 250 entrants, reduced to 145 participants, when long standing pre-war favourite fox terriers were overtaken by cocker spaniels in popularity. Expectations of entertainment were still relatively undemanding. The early 1950s were the days of the popular Hollywood films of Esther Williams with her synchronised swimming to music, and the Torquay Leander Swimming Club performed its famous water ballets to capacity houses at the Spa pool. (As late as 1958, hundreds watched as the Club and the Life Saving Society took the icy Boxing Day dip in the sea.)

The Torquay Operatic Society had a runaway success at the Pavilion in 1951. The show was accompanied by the same Torquay Municipal Orchestra that had played under many distinguished conductors before the war. But within two years, television and apathy and rival night-time attractions brought the closure of this popular orchestra amid much bitterness. The rival attractions catered for the younger generation and followed on from the war years. Nightly dancing was all the rage in the *Victoria* and *Grand* Hotels, the Town Hall, the 400 Ballroom and at the Paignton *Hydro*, and, of course, The Marine Spa claimed to have the best bands. All the famous names of the time were there in Torquay, Ted Heath and Johnny Dankworth and Sammy Herman with singers Eve Boswell and Petula Clark. There were two dancing schools and at Richings there were rock-and-roll practice sessions. Music, too, was moving on. Throughout the 1950s the young were developing an interest in music and fashion and Torbay also saw one of its manifestations. Long-haired Teddy Boys nightly paraded along the Torbay Road in drape cut jackets and drain pipes, with crepe soled shoes and fluorescent socks. The local proprietors of the cafés they frequented were surprisingly tolerant, dismissing them as a 'pseudo variety', not up to the real thing in London. Loud rock-and-roll music may have irritated beach goers but it did not result in arrests, and a Chief Inspector remarked in 1957 that juvenile courts had been quiet for some time.

Bomb damage was repaired: the rebuilding of St Marychurch, destroyed in 1943, was started in 1952 and re-consecrated in 1956. Pre-war plans to improve the sea front in Torquay were reactivated and work began in 1954 on the approach to the Princess Pier. By 1959 the two-tier circular promenade, an extension to Princess Garden, had been completed by the Borough engineers and was later to be listed as an historic parks and gardens. Old Torquay had narrow winding streets and the large summer crowds that now flooded in made residents aware of the increase in traffic congestion and the problem of finding somewhere to park. The hunt was on for sites, and the lower end of Union Street, where there was poor housing, started to be cleared for a multi-storey car park with access from Abbey Road and the sea front. It was a problem that was not going to be resolved for many years. Paignton, too, had identified congestion and parking problems, but with coaches, not cars, and

The Sight of this 'tis strange to say
Made me think of you to-day
at **TORQUAY**

1426

1918

MABEL
LUCIE
ATTWELL

Wish you were here
at **PAIGNTON**

86 *Novelty cards. By the mid-1950s Torbay had very much resumed its role as a holiday resort with full summer bookings and crowded beaches.*

this despite a new fleet of buses launched by Devon General Transport in 1954.

By the mid-1950s Torbay had very much resumed its role as a holiday resort with full summer bookings and crowded beaches. With strict currency restrictions, overseas travel was difficult and families were happy to spend their summer holiday – and in most cases – their only holiday on or near a beach. The prospect of a two-week break from work on a sunny beach with a few drinks and a dance in the evening was the modest expectation. The old hotels and guest houses were still there but no new hotel was being planned to challenge the famous old triumvirate. Rather the reverse, with caravans and camping emerging as an alternative and cheaper form of holiday for people struggling to re-establish their lives. Camp sites in 1953 provided for a tent or small caravan for the better-off and a small camp shop. At the Waterside Holiday Camp in Paignton main drainage did not arrive until 1953; it was all rather spartan. Again, poor housing was demolished to make way for new and better sites as Devon County Council took steps to control the caravanning that was in danger of becoming chaotic. One Council member undertook an aerial survey to demonstrate that saturation point had been reached, but also indignantly reported that the owners of the caravans were not all quite so poor and needy as imagined as a number of caravans were being towed by Rolls Royces and other expensive cars.

Torbay Borough Council had the foresight to make plans to ensure that the beaches stayed crowded and the hotels full, and at the beginning of the 1960s financed a holiday guide brochure in which, for a fee, the hotels could advertise. As funding dried up the already established Hotel Association took on the guide and at the same time set up the Coach Operators Workshop. Operators from the North and Midlands came to see for themselves why Torbay should be promoted as a special destination. The immediate result was that, for a time, 70 per cent of the tourists came by coach: the scheme was also helped by the willingness of three-star and four-star hotels to accept early and late season discounts for these coach parties. The Hotel Association's next step was to become a member of the British Hotels and Restaurants Association. Pre-war Torbay had prided itself on its independence and insularity but now the Hotel Association went round the country actively advertising the resort. And further success came when a wider target was reached at the annual London conference. The training of staff had always been a problem and in an attempt to raise standards of service the Association set up the Torbay Group Training Scheme which, helped by government grants, encouraged staff to go to the South Devon Technical College: the larger hotels and even proprietors of smaller hotels ran their own day-release schemes.

There were few professional hoteliers, apart from the major players. As they had in the 1930s, a gradual stream of people came down to the coast to try their hand at running a small hotel: many were dependent on family for help, with students helping out in the busy summer months. There was not a great deal of money in the background to shore them up in hard times and, when new government regulations were brought in to establish standards, these small hotels, unable to bear the cost, started to struggle and finally close. Altogether 40 of the middle-ranking hotels that had been catering for the new visitors disappeared. On the continent, governments recognising the importance of the growing tourist market, gave subsidies to their hotels. Hoteliers in Torbay knew of this and there was widespread resentment at the lack of government initiative. But other changes were starting to have a more positive effect on the fragile tourist market.

At the end of the 1960s access to the Devon coast had been made easier by faster trains. A decade later saw the completion of the M5 motorway from Exeter to Birmingham where the M6 would later take traffic up to Liverpool and beyond. This development was very good news for the coach parties who were playing such a major role in Torbay's recovery plans. It was also some encouragement for them to brave the Devon roads that were starting to be clogged by the caravans and mobile homes heading for Paignton and Brixham. It was also good news for drivers as there had been a great increase in car ownership during the mid-1960s.

With organised and determined plans in place to keep Torbay as a popular holiday destination, there was a mini-tourist boom in the early 1970s. But any optimistic hopes for a smooth path to increasing success were to be disappointed. A culture of mass tourism was emerging as a result of the changing pattern of working life. This was a change that was to be exploited by the new Leisure Industry and much of it was directed overseas with the opportune lifting of the currency restrictions in 1974. The horizon for foreign holidays immediately expanded and Freddie Laker and Thomas Cook became household names, the one providing cheap fares, the other all-inclusive package holidays at a price that was the same if not cheaper than the going rate in Torbay. And there was no question that the weather abroad would be anything other than sunny and hot. Visitors from the industrial Midlands and the North now drove down the motorways to the airports and even the coach parties headed for the ports. Local business was soon down 30 per cent and the fierce competition between the hotels caused many of those who had survived the privations of the mid-1960s to close. The English seaside resort, with its unreliable weather, was now no longer the obvious choice for a holiday. In Torquay the grand hotels suffered. Vernon Duka, the astute manager of *The Palace Hotel*, was quoted in the local newspaper when he remarked that people no longer came to spend the entire winter in Torquay: 'that lifestyle ended in the 1960s, now they winter in the south of Spain or the Canaries.'

Torbay Borough Council and the Hotel Association continued their efforts to display Torbay's ageing charms but in the early 1980s the hotel slump was not helped by the property recession. Many of those who had survived the cull of the 1970s now collapsed. The changes were to be seen all around. In an interview with the *Herald Express*, John Williams of Williams & Cox, one of the most senior of Torquay's tradesmen, was quoted as saying:

> Most of the style has gone out of Torquay altogether now, these days there are two Torquays, an overcrowded one in summer and a half empty one in winter.

Loss of style was the response to the changing world, the price paid in trying to provide all weather entertainment for the new visitors. Anne Born, writing in 1989, was to point out how inappropriate was the atmosphere of the cheap cafés, souvenir shops and amusement arcades, filled with gaming machines, so close to the elegance of the Pavilion and gardens. And the smart shops that had once beguiled the *beau monde* had all but vanished. But the problem of a half-empty Torquay in winter could be resolved, and in 1982 The English Riviera Tourist Board was established to use a long-term strategic approach to promoting tourism. The Board was helped by the useful fact that real disposable income was just about to increase: between 1981 and 1988 it would go up by 25 per cent. Another factor was the increasing amount of free time enjoyed by the population, with newly flexible working hours, additional bank holidays and paid holidays. People took early retirement and lived longer. Urry Shields in his *Tourism and Society* in 1999 suggested 'tourism is no longer a differentiated set of social practices with its distinct rules, times and spaces. It has merged into other social activities. Many people are tourists most of the time: tourism has simply become cultural.'

The English Riviera Tourist Board had almost immediate encouragement. Torbay was voted the third most popular resort in England in 1982 and in 1986 won a national competition, The Changing Face of Tourism. And this change has been quite radical. Overseas travel has increased in the last 10 years but the volume of domestic tourism has remained level because of second and third holidays that have now become normal. It is this market that The English Riviera Tourist Board has tapped into and will continue to do for the foreseeable future. The need now is to provide for a demanding, knowledge-able and well-travelled public. It has not been easy as this grumble in *The Times* in 1988 from Stephen Nichols, an hotelier in Brixham, points out:

> Tourism in the Torbay area has dropped by 25% in the last 10 years. What the average British holiday maker now wants is an ensuite room overlooking the bay, with colour TV and all facilities, and a garage within 10 yards of the Hotel for £10 a night, bed and breakfast.

The English Riviera Tourist Board has found the answer. The accepted standard for a holiday is no longer those two weeks in the summer. The natural season, June to September, has been extended to the Turkey and Tinsel extravaganza in the winter, and most hotels stay open the whole year. Flexibility has become the target and attractions are not altogether beach-based, though the famous views still play their role. The principal hotels advertise short breaks all the year and accept single night bookings, aiming to cosset and pamper in a luxurious atmosphere not unlike the past. The Marine Spa may have passed into history but many hotels across Torbay are now offering the modern-day equivalents: saunas, solariums, steam rooms and spa baths, gyms and jacuzzis and beauty salons.

Back in 1982 the *Herald Express* revealed the dramatic drop in the number of deck chairs over the previous decade. This trend has continued and those bucket and spade holidays are now a distant memory. Now, family parties, groups of friends and children all have entertainment specifically designed to attract them. Reminiscent of the 1930s are house parties with murder and mystery weekends. With the nation's current interest in health and physical activity there is greater emphasis on sport. At the same time Torbay has been able to exploit itself as a base from which to explore not only the timeless attractions of the area but also the new Eden Project. But not everyone wishes to be on the march, and for many people happy and profitable afternoons and evenings are spent in familiar surroundings at one of the Bingo Clubs: Gala Bingo claims to pay out £18 million every week or a winner every three minutes.

The merging of Torbay's splendid past with the present is a rare occurrence but has been accomplished by Torbay Council. Inspired by the opulence of the Register Office in Singer's Oldway Mansion and 'a setting reminiscent of the Palace of Versailles', the idea of getting married on the English Riviera has attracted many romantics, for Torbay has always been a place for honeymoons. But nuptials today have to survive endurance tests with the newly popular 'stag nights' and 'hen parties'. These short breaks attract people from a wide area who come not only to celebrate a wedding and enjoy the seaside atmosphere, but also to enjoy the good quality nightclubs. But it is regarded also as a reason for heavy drinking and many hotels and self-catering places specify 'no parties of single young people'.

Torbay has been able to take advantage of the new focus for world tourism. There is a rising demand for holidays afloat and new destinations as an alternative to going round the Caribbean, and, with the doubling of fuel prices, operators are looking at economical cruises that do not involve going at full speed from port to port. The English Riviera Tourist Board has been quick to exploit the opportunity and together with the other regional deep-water harbours – Dartmouth, Fowey, Falmouth and Tresco – Destination South West has been formed. Representatives were invited to the Sea Trade Show in Miami, the mecca for the cruise industry, and the outcome was encouraging. In August 2002 Torbay saw 800 Americans come ashore from a cruise ship anchored in the bay and more than 160 cruise ships are expected over the next three years. Dartmouth is already being compared with Italy's Mediterranean port, Portofino, by cruise passengers.

The great hotels from Torbay's ascendancy have accepted the changing expectations but at the same time have succeeded in preserving their intrinsic character. The *Imperial*, once owned by renowned hotelier Michael Chapman, was sold on to Trust House Forte and is now in the hands of the Paramount Group of Hotels. Once visited by members of the Russian Imperial family, it is the only five-star hotel in the South West. It impressed the 2001 edition of the *Rough Guide*, a thoroughly modern critic, as a 'sumptuous 1860s palace – has all the aristocratic trimmings and loads of period atmosphere'. But it is not too grand to follow the preoccupation with health and beauty like its lesser rivals. The *Palace*, a four-star hotel, once the Bishop of Exeter's villa,

Bishopstowe has long established sporting facilities with professional coaching and is a centre for trade exhibitions. That stately old Victorian hotel, the *Grand Hotel*, has been given a face-lift and imposes a challenge on its streamlined 1960s bow fronted neighbour. In Paignton the three-star *Palace Hotel*, once the home of the Singer family, has maintained all its old style, if a trifle heavy-handed, with the Paris Restaurant, Singer coffee lounge and Washington bar. And the *Redcliffe Hotel*, an earth-coloured Indian fantasy, also in Paignton, had a successful new wing added in 1986 and its huge ballroom provides a venue for ballroom and sequence dance groups.

Influenced by the fashion on the Continent, there has been an increase in self-catering. Italianate villas and Victorian houses have been converted and apartments designed to encourage long lets. In Paignton, long the bastion for self-catering, and where in the 1930s families rented a house for the season, life continues as usual in Roundham and Preston districts. But, as a sign of the times, the Council is following the trend that is seen elsewhere in the country. The old maxim, that hotels and residential areas do not mix, is being turned on its head. In recognition of a shrinking hotel industry, restrictions on the use of designated property are being lifted where requested and judged appropriate.

There have inevitably been noticeable changes to the face of Torbay and of Torquay in particular. Starting in the 1960s with the enthusiastic embrace of modernism, the results have received a mixed reception. The 1964 Princess Theatre of glass, steel and concrete slotted into the waterfront area to everyone's approval. The criticisms became louder when it was perceived what a challenge the new buildings were to the charm of the Italian stuccoed villas on the hills, the ones that had been illustrated in so many lithographs and coloured prints. At night the rewired glittering strings of lights illuminate Torquay, magically bringing to life its sobriquet 'Crown of the Riviera', but daytime reveals the ungainly developments on the hills to the east where three blocks of flats were built in 1962 and nicknamed 'The Three Ugly Sisters'. Waldon Hill to the west, and once owned by the Carys, was decorated with a group of buildings with pagoda-like roofs. To this day these buildings dominate the landscape.

Ironically, if there had been a rash of high-rise buildings covering both these hills there could have been some majesty in an imposing skyline as in Monaco or Hong Kong. With the white yachts and smart motor cruisers in the marina, the balmy weather, palm trees and illuminations, the promenaders could almost be in the south of France. Further building was slowed down by the volume of criticism, though two handsome streamlined, bow-fronted blocks of flats were to go up, one cheek by jowl with *The Grand* and the elaborately decorated gates at the entrance to Torre Abbey gardens. There was one last blast from modernism as late as 1987 with the building of The

87 *Torquay and Vaughan Parade at sunset. With the white yachts, balmy weather, palm trees and illuminations, this could be the south of France.*

Riviera Centre, a massive low-slung concrete building with great glass windows reflecting the sea and sun. It was built next to Torre Abbey gardens on a swathe of what had once been Cary land. The Torquay hotelier Clifford Murrell gave *Rosetor Hotel*, and land once owned by Angela Burdett-Coutts, to the Council for the specific purpose of building a conference centre. Conferences had gradually expanded since the war and were seen as a very good source of income but Torquay, despite being an attractive resort, did not have a large enough venue and delegates were just as happy to go inland, and Harrogate and Birmingham cornered the market. By the time the Centre opened in 1987, conferences had become an important part of corporate life and Torquay with above average sunshine and growing attractions has succeeded over the years in increasing the volume of bookings, but the modest capacity of 1,500 in the main hall ensures that the big political party conferences remain tantalisingly along the coast in Brighton and Bournemouth. The English Riviera Centre and Torbay Council run the Centre, with conference fees paying for the upkeep of the much needed all-weather sporting facilities and large pool. And the BBC has put the Centre on the media map, using it to host the 'Antiques Road Show,' 'Songs of Praise' and 'Question Time'.

The Murrell family were to continue the updating of Torquay's new look 10 years later with the building of a large hotel complex on Chestnut Avenue just across from The Riviera Centre. It was based on the fortuitous availability of a sizeable amount of land adjoining their well-established hotels, the *Derwent* and *Victoria*. Guests find themselves in an oasis full of sporting activity, with the TLH Leisure Resort providing all-weather fun and entertainment in a smart and modern atmosphere that transcends the generations. Here, also, are the specialist mini-breaks and weekend 'escapes', bowling and dancing holidays.

The vicissitudes of Torquay's old Marine Spa, once the mainspring of social life, have rumbled on in the background throughout the last forty years. It is a story of elegant tea dances to modern discos. The Marine Spa survived the initial post-war years; there were still visitors for the liver packs, ear nose

88 *Torquay's old Marine Spa, once the centre of social life.*

and throat irrigation, sulphur, bran, oatmeal and soda baths and Swedish massage. But as the costs escalated, patients went elsewhere and the fine old building fell into disarray and was demolished by Torbay Council in 1967. Coral Island was built on the foundations but only the sun terraces were reminiscent of the old Spa; the rest was a lively amusement and leisure area that only really came to life in the summer with the visitors. And so it remained limping along, closed in winter, closed altogether in 1988, but reopened three years later with disco dancing, slot machines, wrestling, bingo and bars and restaurants. The attractions may have been updated but there was still the lack of visitors all year round and Coral Island was becoming dilapidated. With the growing general public interest in health, there were plans in 1993 to revive the old Marine Spa days with renewed health spa facilities and a gym alongside the now inevitable nightclubs and restaurants. The idea had been persuasive: the precedence was the £100 million success of health spas in France where there were already 41 centres and more opening all the time. Torquay visualised becoming the first centre in the country for modern day seawater treatments, but the proposed cost of £8 million failed to find backers after initial interest. The financial package had also included a Torbay Leisure Centre at Paignton and this part of the plan did go ahead.

In 1995 an altogether different future was seen for Coral Island by the Torbay Family Church who proposed that an international Christian conference centre be built there as a beacon for the faithful: this idea also failed, and so things remained until 2001 when another development got under way. Torbay Waterfront Project on Beacon Hill quay, near the site of the old Marine Spa, has been on the Council's drawing board since 1996 and diverse funding includes European and lottery money. The inner harbour is being cilled to keep the tide permanently in but the most ambitious part is a £2 million project in tandem with Beacon Quay. It is part of the zoological living coast and will be run by the very successful Paignton Zoo and is expected to attract 300,000 visitors a year to enjoy, among other attractions, deep underwater viewing of penguins. Visitors to the new aviary shop will find a reminder of the old marine spa. Four Victorian arches have been restored with much difficulty and will be incorporated in the new design.

Not everyone is happy about these changes but there is general agreement that the area, the home of the Royal Torbay Yacht Club, needed to be smartened up and an attempt made to deal with the parking problems. Sailing is an important and traditional part of Torbay's world and all across the bay there are sailing schools. Brixham has a very fine marina and good quay, and like Torquay, The Brixham Yacht Club holds regular events. The August Regatta is an established date in the yachting calendar but there are more international plans. In the past Torbay has hosted Olympic events. There are hopes of bringing the Tall Ships Race to the bay, and in 2002 Torquay was the only stop-over in Europe for the 29,000 miles International Around Alone Yacht Event.

Britain's first town marina was built in 1982-4 and welcomed as a stylish adornment to the harbour area, adding to Torquay's continental image. But a far more painful change finally started in 1988 after much public discussion and campaigning. The Fleet Walk Precinct project, at the southern end of Torquay's once famed shopping area, tore the heart out of the old town. This was where a mishmash of Victorian houses and shops had been built on the old Palk and Cary estates. It had always been a poor area and had been allowed to become depressed and slightly tatty: by contrast, Torre further up the hill traditionally was always considered more salubrious.

It was the old story of a dispute between a council, intent on attracting more visitors, and the local residents and shop owners who were going to bear the brunt of the changes but not necessarily benefit from them. Decisions were made against local advice and it was felt that people who could have been more influential were too busy creating business to sit on the endless committees.

Gavin Stamp, writing in *The Daily Telegraph* in 1985, informed a wider world of the undermining of the old order right in the middle of Torquay. He described how the 'Save Torquay Old Town' group, chaired by Danny da Costa, had commissioned an alternative to the existing plans. The proposal was to rehabilitate the old buildings and historic cobbled alleys that were tucked under the steep and picturesque rock bluffs. They visualised creating arcades and chic shopping areas that would have been just as effective but far less disruptive.

Stephen Gardiner, the architectural correspondent of *The Observer*, wrote: 'if the Conservative run council gets its way a chunk of small shops – much of it with a delightful Betjemanesque character of the best seaside kind – will be replaced by a vast shopping centre.' The Royal Fine Arts Commission was called in, and there was a public enquiry, but compulsory purchase orders went ahead despite the massive opposition. Contemporary press photographs show the scale of the upheaval, with the whole site gutted. More than 30 years on from the perceived design mistakes in the 1960s, architectural ideas are more sympathetic to the local environment. The firm working on the project specialised in the new ideas for urban conservation and care of listed buildings and worked under the new Town Planning Ordinances. The result was a semi-pedestrianised area and an interesting mix of stylish open terraces and tiled walkways with shops amid a profusion of foliage and potted palms in large faux-porcelain pots. And the partial conversion of the road to a walkway has continued up the first part of Union Street.

The entrance to Fleet Walk from the Marina is past the new Winter Garden. It gives a nod to the Pavilion but could happily be a Star Wars set and despite

89 *The Fleet Walk Precinct Project 1988. Contemporary press photographs show the scale of the upheaval, with the whole site gutted.*

90 *St John's and the 'Three Ugly Sisters' survey the devastation.*

91 *The surviving Cary Estate Office amidst the turmoil of rebuilding.*

its name is purely commercial like the Pavilion itself. A 'Friends of the Pavilion Group' saved that charming building from proposed demolition and it was sympathetically remodelled in 1986-7 and is now a listed building. A link with the past was to be established when the Cary Estate submitted an application for the development of the building they owned between the Winter Garden and Vaughan Parade along the Marina. It was viewed as the final piece in the jigsaw by the developers of Vaughan Parade who won a design award in 1991 for their Victorian design. The Cary building is largely unchanged, still with its original ceiling and floor, but is now the Café Sol, a bar and brasserie.

Torquay has become part of the new international world where city and town centres are paved, pedestrianised and festooned with greenery around potentially profitable shopping arcades with parking hopefully tucked away on an upper level. It is all part of realising tourist expectations. The local view is that Torquay was, for a time, a ghost town. Local shops did not survive the high rents and, having banned cars from the town centre, parking was still a problem (currently being reconsidered). With its large ageing population Torquay could have become a smart retirement resort. Much of the opposition to the Fleet Walk plan came from this group and from the old Torquinians, many of whom have now moved to Salcombe and Shaldon or the country. But for the economic progress of a town the hard truth is that not a great deal

92 *Detail of the Pavilion. A 'Friends of the Pavilion Group' saved the building from proposed demolition. It is now a listed building.*

of money was generated or spent locally by this resident population. The Council's emphasis had to be on presenting Torquay as a seaside resort in tune with the new expectations of a younger generation.

Other areas of Torquay have made changes whilst essentially staying the same. 'Salubrious Torre' is now known as the Chelsea of Torquay and its residents share their interesting streets (and Torquay's only recording studio) with a large student population from the Continent, Scandinavia and Japan. Students, especially from France, have long been part of the Torquay scene; back in 1980 it was voted the top host resort. Peter Sager, in *Pallas The West Country*, makes a nice point: '[Torquay] is a popular centre for learning English which is best done while floating in the sea.' A more vibrant and modern club culture has also developed. And it is not only the students who participate in and enjoy the new scene. There is also a youthful and steadily growing home market for clubbing.

Beyond Babbacombe and in an almost unchanged part of Torquay is St Marychurch. Always an historic district of much individuality with arts and crafts, it has long since been pedestianised with Fore Street closed to traffic. The area is part of the tourist trail with the Model Village and the recreated Victorian world of Bygones and, if they venture further down the Babbacombe Road to Ilsham Road, there is Kent's Cavern, the most important stone-age caves in Britain that so fascinated Victorian visitors. Torquay's scenic golf course is just across the road from St Marychurch, Torquay United Football Club within walking distance and, with the expanse of Babbacombe Downs for dog-walking, the area has maintained a good balance of interests for residents and visitors alike.

Paignton, where there is a palm tree in every front garden, has developed along lines in keeping with its character and has done rather well. G.S. Bridgman's well designed late Victorian town centre, admired by Pevsner and Bridget Cherry, has been well served by the Borough Architectural Services Group who have restored the area of narrow and winding streets around Princess Street. In an attempt to control the flow of cars, there are plans to rejuvenate Victoria Street, Winner Street and Church Street in the historic part of Paignton. Palace Avenue, with its row of black and white, well-preserved

93 Paignton, where there is a palm tree in every front garden.

half-timbered houses and the old Palace Theatre overlooking the enclosed garden, is a gem.

There have been casualties. The splendid Dellers Café, with its art deco frontage and long history of being the most fashionable venue for all of south Devon, was demolished in 1965 because, one presumes, it was unable to keep up with the times. This had not been the case in the past when it had been the first premises to install electric lights. The Paignton Picture House, built just before the First World War and now the oldest surviving original cinema in western Europe, was closed in 1999 but not demolished. Now called the Torbay Picture House, it is owned by the Paignton and Dartmouth Steam Railway and is in a good state of preservation with the old comfortable velvet seats and screen intact. Given the cinema's place in history, the moguls of the British film industry have been keeping an eye on how things develop. The popular replacement is very much in tune with the 21st century: stylish and brilliantly lit, the multiplex Apollo cinema is almost a throwback to 1930s modernism. It has been welded on to Paignton's own 1960s contribution to architectural change, the Paignton Festival Hall, built in the area on the seafront where old Torbay House withstood the great storm of 1824.

Paignton's reputation is based on its beaches and two of the best in the region are here (plus The Seaside Award). The climate may not be as balmy as Torquay because there are no hills to protect the beaches but it is still a busy family resort and the new attractions are designed to enhance a beach holiday. The innovative Quaywest was the only outdoor waterpark in the country and is now part of what is called Quaywest Resort on Goodrington Sands; it even has a stop on the Paignton and Dartmouth Steam Railway. Open for most of

94 *Palace Avenue Gardens, Paignton, in 1907. In the 21st century this is still a pleasant discovery.*

the year, the associated beach facilities are straight from the south of France. There are no longer donkey rides but Professor Mark Poulton's Punch and Judy plays to a traditional audience. And still there, in true seaside tradition, is the Victorian pier, open all year including Christmas Day and offering the same range of amusements, though many of the games are now controlled by microchips. Not all the attractions depend on a beach. Paignton again uses rail links to its advantage, just as it did when it was linked to Torquay by rail. This time around it is the enduring interest in old steam trains that has made such a success of the Paignton and Dartmouth Steam Railway that chugs along a seven-mile stretch of the old Great Western Railway: there are occasions when it is carrying a conference or hosting a dinner dance. The town is also fortunate in having the 75 acres world famous Paignton Zoo, with its reptile and tropical house and imaginatively designed micro-environments which satisfy those seeking to examine the wonder of nature. It is now even better known in the UK since the popular BBC series 'The Zoo Keepers'.

Visitors to Paignton have a choice of good hotels including the famous *Redcliffe Hotel* that would seem more at home on the plains of India. Self-catering is still the thing in Roundham and Preston but most of the old-style caravan and camping parks have changed beyond recognition following the growth in the 1990s of the more sophisticated holiday villages like Center Parcs and the more recent Oasis Villages, and they have become quite international with many visitors coming from Scandinavia, Holland and Germany.

Brixham is still a traditional working port but Torbay Council, working with the Brixham authorities, has the twin problem of making provision for the demands of EC directives and regulations (mainly to stop over-fishing) whilst maintaining the harbour and quays that are a magnet for visitors. Many of these are local day-trippers who come on the ferry from Paignton and Torquay. Because of the town's natural landscape there is not a great deal of space for manoeuvrability although it is this very absence of a town public beach and promenade that has helped Brixham maintain its original character. But there have been a number of important developments around the harbour including a new fishing quay with ice plant and refrigeration unit that still supplies London restaurants.

At the same time the town has had to accommodate a steady flow of new people, many of them retired, and there have been a number of residential developments on the steep hills; the search for suitable sites for housing is not easy. It has also been accepted that there is a need to provide a new town centre: a major scheme is currently being considered, backed by European money. Brixham is a favourite destination, by car, for those in the surrounding countryside and, as in the rest of Torbay (and the rest of the country), congestion is a problem with no easy solution.

All these problems in Torbay stem from the fact that Devon's population has increased at one of the highest rates in the country, 19 per cent over 30 years, much of it concentrated in the south and east of the county. In 2001 Torbay had a basic population of 64,600 that reached 76,400 in summer. Historically, it has always been a depressed area with local wages below the national average and, conversely, the unemployment rate above the national average. Nevertheless, there has been a steady increase in the number of people looking for work as well as those in retirement seeking a congenial place to live. Much of the available work is seasonal, though this might change with the new emerging patterns of tourism, and many people have to go on State Benefit in winter. There is also, as in many resort towns, the problem of looking after and providing for all those permanently in the benefits system.

The problem of unemployment has been endemic in the South West and great efforts have been made to bring other types of employment, besides tourism, into the area. In the mid-1960s the introduction of new technology brought new jobs into the region and by the end of the century much of the

95 *The harbour at Brixham. It is the absence of a public beach and town promenade that has helped Brixham maintain its original character.*

work was in the electronics field. Torquay has some light industry in that field but, with the restrictions of the landscape, there was little room for expansion and it was in Paignton that land was found for the building of factories. Firms were encouraged by starter packages that ensured rents were low until the business got off the ground, whereupon the correct rate would then apply.

Nortel Networks optoelectronics plant was a pivotal part of Torbay's re-structuring plan in the 1990s, at the same time attracting other investors to the area including some from North America. It was a tremendous blow to the local economy when, through outside economic pressure, the staff of 5,000 was reduced to an uncertain 1,000 and an even more uncertain future. And, unlike other areas, Torbay has none of the new call centres that have proved so useful in mopping up pockets of unemployment.

In order to provide housing and employment, there is an ongoing and urgent search for land, and issues that have become, for very good reasons, fashionable, have affected this search. Environmental groups, such as Friends of the Earth, and conservationists have become a very active and knowledge-able lobby group able to exercise control over proposed land developments. The search for suitable land highlights the scarcity of brownfield sites and the increasing need to use open country, that is, greenfield sites. (The problem is compounded by the known presence of 'hot spots' or Radon Gas.) The problem South West Water has encountered is a case in point. They had the mammoth task of responding to EC regulations and have created a complete and modern sewage treatment system. Since 1969, £25 million has been spent updating the sewers from the 19th century and adding others as the population grew. At the same time they have dealt with the raw sewage on Torbay's beaches and brought them up to EU standards: as a reward Oddicombe, Meadfoot and Breakwater beaches can advertise the prestigious Blue Flag and so can Paignton's Preston Beach. The work is planned to finish in 2003 but South West Water is finding it difficult to locate sites for the remaining sewage treatment and screening plants. Well-informed local lobby groups are not entirely convinced by assurances, that, with advanced technology, the plants will be odour free and hidden from sight. One proposed site, over which there was much disagreement, had an additional objection. There were real fears over buried US army wartime ammunition.

Despite environmental concerns, land for development has been found and on the outskirts of Torbay's towns are the retail parks that are found on the approach roads to towns and cities up and down the country. But this is a development at odds with another major problem that has grown steadily over the last 40 years – road congestion. Torbay's basic infrastructure is not very strong – has indeed been blamed for discouraging would-be investors – and there are constant attempts to improve the road system. It is a problem shared with the rest of the country as modern life demands increasing mobility in all aspects of the daily routine but, of course, in Torbay the roads have to be shared with all its visitors.

By the end of the century there was new government legislation that covered matters important to Torbay. The environment and wildlife were worldwide issues that generated a lot of publicity and people were interested in seeing the results of local initiatives: it was all part of the new world of tourism. Back in 1969, a far-sighted Torbay Council had bought Berry Head headland to preserve the open area. It is now Berry Head National Nature Reserve, administered by Torbay Coast and Countryside Trust, with free entry to see many rare species of plants and the chance to watch the famous Guillemot (Brixham Penguins) colony, close up on a TV screen. Torbay's vigilant care of the coastline, supported by the watchful National Trust, protecting the coast near Brixham and also between Salcombe Hill and Branscombe, prevents any coastal building development. This has become part of the South-West Coast Path, 613 miles, the longest footpath in Britain. With the public awareness of the importance of forestalling health problems there are plans to launch a Baywalks Initiative organised by the Trust, the Countryside Agency and the British Heart Foundation, and also in the pipeline are plans for Torbay's own coastal cycle network that will eventually link up with the National Cycle Network. The Council's 1995-2011 Plan ensures the survival of the English Riviera tradition that was originally based, in part, on the range of exotic plants that could be cultivated close by the sea – they flourish to this day. And so, too, do the New Zealand 'Cabbage Trees', the Cordylines from Australia, the Mediterranean Fan Palms and the Date Palms from the Canaries. The plan, also, recognises the importance of trees in the landscape and promises to protect significant trees during any construction work and, at the same time, preserve any corridors of wildlife on the site.

The Devon and Cornwall Police have the considerable responsibility of protecting the longest coastline in the country. The remote beaches make them ideal venues for IRA or other terrorist groups with plans to bring in arms and explosives. Indeed, in 1985, the *Palm Court Hotel* in Torquay found it had been unwittingly entertaining members of the IRA when, after their departure, a bomb was discovered primed to go off a week later. Continuing a tradition from the 17th century, Torbay is still home to drug smuggling and Anstey's Cove and Brixham are well known to the police. It is the biggest centre in the South West for heroin distribution from Liverpool and the West Midlands. Bulk loads of nine or ten tons of cannabis were also regularly smuggled onto the beaches of the South West but the profit margin on cannabis at £1,200 a kilo and the fact that people grow their own has lessened its importance. It is heroin at £50,000 a kilo that the police are after and they have had success against local distributors. As with all south-coast resorts Torbay is an unwilling host to the drug culture, especially in the summer months: the easy availability of all kinds of drugs is a magnet and an unwelcome problem for the police.

Over the years nationwide publicity of Torquay has been generated by 'Fawlty Towers', which has become one of the all-time greats of television. Its inspiration came from one such hotel in Torquay. It was known that John Cleese and the Monty Python team (from another TV classic of the 1970s) had stayed at the *Gleneagles Hotel* in Torquay for three weeks, while filming in Paignton in 1970. In 2002 Beatrice Sinclair, allegedly the real-life Sybil Fawlty, broke the silence of 30 years to complain that Cleese had 'held my family up to ridicule'. This was challenged by Rosemary Harrison who, as a student, worked the summer season at the *Gleneagles Hotel*. She said her experiences mirrored those of one of the characters in the series. This was Polly, an art student, working at the hotel, as portrayed by Connie Booth, Cleese's former wife and co-writer. John Cleese in an interview in the *Herald Express* said:

> My recollection is somewhat different from Mrs Sinclair's. I do remember all the other Pythons left but Connie Booth and I were lazy. We stayed on and didn't realise we were accumulating material. I take the point that he was a war hero but as a hotelier he was astonishingly rude.

A letter was published in *The Daily Telegraph* with another memory:

> We were very much looking forward to dancing on their small dance floor. Guests had complained about it being sticky. Nothing was done, so one day the guests cleaned the floor themselves while Mr Sinclair was out. They were caught and the band cancelled.

What is interesting is how similar the hotel is to many others at that time. Mrs Sinclair had bought the property as a private house and turned it into a family hotel business. Her husband, a former Commander in the Royal Navy who had been torpedoed three times during the war, reluctantly left the Navy to help her. But it was Mrs Sinclair who was the driving force behind the business, although, unlike Sybil, she allowed her husband to keep the books and the accounts as well as run the bar. Curiously, they did have a foreign waiter at that time, though no one like the bewildered and charming Spanish waiter, Manuel.

Another curiosity occurred but with far less publicity. In fact, it was quite a mystery and was not solved for three years. It started in 1989 when church leaders and parishioners at St John the Apostle in Torquay proposed selling two paintings by Sir Edward Burne-Jones to pay for renovation work that was to cost £300,000. The church had commissioned the Pre-Raphaelite paintings for £400 in the 1890s and the paintings, depicting a Jew and a Gentile being led to the Nativity by angels, were widely regarded by the critics as being among Burne-Jones's finest works. An unholy row broke out and the plan became known as Torbay's equivalent of the 'Mappa Mundi', opposed by Anglican authorities who claimed that national heritage treasures from the church could not be sold. An ecclesiastical court sat in judgment in Exeter and agreed that the church's need for renovation was foremost in importance. The sale went ahead at Sotheby's in London, in November 1989, and made an astonishing £1.3 million, far exceeding the original modest hope. The proceeds were spent on repairing the mosaics and stained glass windows, badly damaged by water leaking through the roof. Copies of the paintings were commissioned and put in place whilst the churchwardens spent over two years wondering whom their saviour was. Then, one March day in 1992, composer Andrew Lloyd-Webber walked into St John's church to see for himself where the works of art, that he now owned, had hung for 100 years.

During this period much of the political life of Torbay was in the hands of the colourful Rupert Allason – *alias* espionage writer Nigel West. He won the seat for the Tories in 1987 and was to represent the constituency for the next 10 years until the Liberal Democrats took over. Rupert Allason was the son of a former lieutenant-colonel and Conservative MP. Educated at Downside, the University of Grenoble and a college in Oxford, he became a Lloyds name at 23. He failed to win a parliamentary seat in 1979 and started researching and writing the espionage books that were to be enjoyed by a public fascinated by what was going on in the Cold War.

Torbay has indeed been caught up in the spirit of our times and whilst retaining much of its historic attraction has responded to the expectations of the 21st century. People have long memories, which tend to be sentimental, and there is still a perception of Torbay, and Torquay in particular, as it was in the immediate aftermath of the war, together with its associated values. It is a view the modern world has little time for. The inevitable changes demanded by natural town development have to accommodate opportunities regardless of where they have come from. So, it has been discovered that nightclubs can move into an area, where no other business would survive, and not only make a success of the venture but, under the scrutiny of checks and balances, maintain the property to a high degree. A famous chain of pubs can finance the restoration of a listed building with good quality work making an attractive success of it. A good example of this is just opposite the new Fleet Walk Precinct. It is a very old Torquay building which draws the eye, partly because the façade is well preserved but also because of the inscription, 'enlarged by public subscription a memorial for the Queen's Jubilee in 1887' on the front. And it is a pizza bar. The one does not detract from the other. As time passes different perspectives come into play and it is interesting that, with the lapse of 40 years, new critical judgements are made of the much criticised buildings of the 1960s: a younger generation, reflecting opinion in the rest of the country, is now interested in and appreciative of the innovative work.

As predicted, Torbay with a steadily increasing population has emerged as one large residential district and overtaken Plymouth in size. Yet each of the three towns has maintained its own template, despite having to adapt to the changes in the society around it. Torquay, always regarded as grand, has endured the most major structural changes (and criticism) and now regards itself as a sophisticated continental-type resort. Paignton has steadily built on its reputation as a family resort concentrating on amenities that appeal to that target market. Brixham has been able to retain the quirky mix of a hard working fishing port, labouring under the yoke of EC directives, while holding on to its reputation for the picturesque.

The South West has been able to keep much of its traditional character, compared with other regions in the country. This is due, in part, to the fact that, although there has been a big increase in the population, there has been very little overseas immigration. The pattern for immigrants has been to settle into an existing community where there have been opportunities to make money as well as receive support from established family and friends: there is no such community in the Torbay area. Exeter airport concentrates on regional services and the lack of easy air connection with the Indian subcontinent, for example, has discouraged exploration from the West Midlands. There is awareness, too, that the area has severe employment problems. Asylum seekers are also not attracted to the area, presumably because it is seen as too far from the centre of things.

A retired headmistress made an odd comment, describing Torbay as the end of the line. Yet, looking at its geographical place on the map this does make sense because of the distance from the major cities and big urban areas. Torbay is still, for the people who live there, a quiet seaside place and a traditional part of Britain with a familiar round of events. And last year it seized the opportunity to join in a national event, even though it was bypassed for a visit. The Queen opened the Golden Jubilee celebrations in the county town, Exeter, but still there were bumper crowds, many of them young people, a spectacular fireworks display on Preston Green and 'No Vacancy' signs up all over Torbay. The Last Resort is still in business.

APPENDICES

APPENDIX I
Members of Parliament who have Represented Torquay 1832-1990

Members for South Devon
Lord John Russell (Whig), 1832-5
John Crocker Bulteel (Whig), 1832-5
Sir John Yarde Buller (Conservative), 1835-58
Montagu Edmund Parker (Conservative), 1835-49
Sir Ralph Lopes (Conservative), 1849-54
Sir Lawrence Palk (Conservative), 1854-68
Samuel Trehawke Kekewich (Conservative) 1858-68

Members for East Devon
Sir Edward Courtenay (Conservative), 1868-70
Sir Lawrence Palk (Conservative), 1868-80
Sir John Henry Kennaway (Conservative), 1870-85
Lt Col William Hood Walrond (Conservative), 1880-85

Members for Torquay
Lewis MacIver (Liberal), 1885-86
Richard Mallock (Conservative), 1886-95
Commander Arthur Phillpotts (Conservative), 1895-1900
Francis Layland Barratt (Liberal), 1900-10
Colonel Charles Rosdew Burn (Unionist), 1910-23
Captain Piers Gilchrist Thompson (Liberal), 1923-24
Charles Williams (Conservative), 1924-55
Frederic Bennett (Conservative), 1955-74

Members for Torbay
Sir Frederic Bennett (Conservative), 1974-87
Rupert Allason (Conservative) 1987-1997
Adrian Sanders (Liberal Democrat) 1997-to date

Note: Before 1832 there were two members for the county of Devonshire. By the Reform Act of 1832, the county was made into two divisions – North and South – each returning two members. By the Reform Act of 1867, the county was now divided into three divisons: North, South, and East, each returning two members. The Redistribtion of Seats Act, 1885, created eight divisions, each of which returned a single member. The Torquay Division, set up by this Act, included within its boundaries the Sessional Division of Paignton and the Municipal Borough of Dartmouth.

APPENDIX II
The Palk, Cary, Mallock and Singer Families

Sir Robert Palk, 1717-98. 1st baronet. MP for Ashburton, 1767-8; and 1774 87. Knighted 1772
Sir Lawrence Palk, 1766-1813. 2nd baronet. MP for Ashburton, 1787-96; MP for Devonshire, 1802-12
Sir Lawrence Vaughan Palk, 1793-1860. 3rd baronet. MP for Asburton until 1831
Sir Lawrence Palk, 1818-83. 4th baronet. Raised to the peerage as Baron Haldon of Haldon, Devon, in 1880. MP for South Devon, 1854 68; MP for East Devon, 1868-80
Lawrence Hesketh Palk, 1846-1903. 5th baronet and 2nd baron. Bankrupt in 1891
Lawrence William Palk, 1869-1933. 6th baronet and 3rd baron. Bankrupt in 1903

Lawrence Bloomfield Palk, 1896-1938. 7th baronet and 4th baron. Died unmarried

Edward Arthur Palk, 1854-1939. 5th baron. Fourth son of the 1st Lord Haldon. No heir. Haldon peerage now extinct.

Wilmot Lawrence Palk, 1876-1945. Heir presumptive to the baronetcy, but not to the peerage. Great grandson to the second baronet and second cousin to Edward Arthur Palk. No heir. Palk baronetcy extinct.

The Cary Family of Torre Abbey, 1662-1930

Sir George Cary (I) died 1678. Sir George Stowell of Bovey Tracey, Devon, sold the Torre Abbey estate to Sir George Cary in 1662

Edward Cary, 1650-1718

George Cary (II), 1674-1758

George Cary (III), 1731-1805. Nephew of the former

George Cary (IV), 1769-1828. His son

Henry George Cary, 1800-1840. A distant relative of the former

Robert Shedden Sulyarde Cary, 1828-1898. His son

Colonel Lucius Falkland Brancaleone Cary, 1839-1916. Younger brother of the former. Col. Cary's only surviving son, Henry, died of enteric fever at Standerton, South Africa, in 1901, during the Boer War. Col. Cary did not take up residence at Torre Abbey until 1907, as it was occupied by Robert Cary's widow

Launcelot Sulyarde Robert Cary, 1890-1916. Colonel Lucius Cary's second cousin. Killed in the battle of the Somme on 25 July 1916 only three weeks after Colonel Cary's death in battle

Captain Lionel Henry St Croix Coxon (later Cary), 1859-1929. A relative by marriage to the Carys, the only son of Col. Lucius Cary's eldest sister. Millicent

Commander Henry Lionel Meyrick Cary, 1885-1959, son of the former. who sold Torre Abbey in 1930 to Torquay Corporation for £40,000. but retained other parts of the estate

George Augustus Lancelot Skerret Cary (1920)

Henry John Cary (1951-)

The Mallock Family of Cockington Court, 1654-1932

In 1654 the Cary family sold the manor of Cockington to Roger Mallock, a merchant and goldsmith, Mayor of Exeter. Roger Mallock died in 1658 and Rawlyn, his son, was the first of the Mallocks to make Cockington Court his home

Rawlyn (I)

Rawlyn (II) only son, died unmarried in 1699

Rawlyn (III) a cousin of the former, died childless in 1749

Rawlyn (IV) died childless in 1779

Revd Samuel Mallock, 1728-1786, a distant kinsman of the former

Revd Roger Mallock, 1772-1846

Charles Herbert Mallock, 1802-1873

Charles Herbert Mallock, 1840-1875

Richard Mallock, 1843-1900. Younger brother of the former. MP for Torquay, 1886-1895

Major Charles Herbert Mallock, DSO, 1878-1917. Killed in a gas attack at Ypres, Nov 1917

Richard Herbert Mallock, 1907. Took up residence in 1929 but sold the whole Cockington estate in 1932 to Torquay Corporation for £50,000

The Singer Family of Oldway Mansion

Isaac Merritt Singer, 1811-1875. Married in 1863 his mistress, Isabella Eugenie Boyer, 1842-1904, the divorced wife of a Mr Summerville.

Isabella Eugenie Boyer, 1842-1904. After Isaac Singer's death she married Victor Reubsaet, Duke of Composelice, died 1887; and Paul Sohege in the early 1890s. Isaac and Isabella had six children born in wedlock:

Adam Mortimer Singer, 1863-1929. Born in Yonkers, New York. Educated at King Edward VI Grammar School, Totnes, and Downing College, Cartridge. Naturalised British subject 1900. KBE 1920. Married (1) Mary Maund Oxley of Yorkshire in 1888; and (2) Aline Madeleine Pilavoine of

Biarritz in 1913. No children from either marriage.

Winnaretta Eugenie Singer, 1865-1943. Born in Yonkers, New York. Privately educated. Married (1) Prince Louis Scey Montbeliard in 1887 (marriage annulled 1892); and (2) Prince Edmond de Polignac, 1834 1901, in 1893.

Washington Grant Merritt Singer, 1866-1934. Born crossing the Atlantic on the *Great Eastern*, Brunel's iron ship. Married (1) Blanche Emmeline Hale of Paignton in 1887; and (2) Ellen Mary Allen, widow of A.A. Longsdon, in 1915. No children from either marriage. Adopted Guy Land and eventually Grant Longsdon. Grant was Ellen's child by her first husband and born in 1915, the year Longsdon died. Washington Singer married the widow soon after.

Paris Eugene Singer, 1867-1932. Born in Paris. Educated for a short period at Cambridge. Married (1) Lily Graham of Western Australia in 1887; (2) and again in the 1920s. His only daughter, born to Lily Graham and named Winnaretta, married Lieutenant Commander (later Sir) Reginald Leeds in 1926. Lady Leeds lived at Little Oldway until her death 1980. (Paris Singer also had two children by Isadora Duncan, Deirdre, born 1905, and Patrick, born 1908. Both were drowned in the Seine in 1913.

Isabelle Blanche Singer, 1869-1896. Born in Paris. Privately educated. Married the Duke Jean Elie Decazes in 1888. Two children. The son became the Marquis (later the fourth Duke) Decazes and the daughter the irrepressible Daisy Fellowes (the Hon Mrs Reginald Fellowes), 1890-1962

Franklin Morse Singer, 1870-1939. Born in Paris. Married an American girl in 1891.

APPENDIX III
Torquay and Paignton: Population Growth

	Tormohun[1]	Torquay[2]	Paignton
1801	838		1,575
1811	1,350		
1821	1,925		
1831	3,582		1,960
1841	5,982		
1851	11,474		2,746
1861	16,419		3,090
1871	21,419		3,590
1881	24,767		4,613
1891			6,783
1901	33,625		89385
1911	38,772		11,241
1921	39,432		14,443
1931		46,165	18,414
1951		53,216	25,369
2001		64,600	45,500

Sources: the decennial censuses. There was no census for 1941
[1] Tormohun was later included under the rubric Torquay. The figures given for Tormohun in early censuses refer to Torre and Torquay.
[2] Separate figures for St Marychurch were included in earlier censuses. The boundaries of the town been enlarged over time to take in St Marychurch, Babbacombe, Cockington and Chelston (1928), and the coastal strip from St Marychurch to the Shaldon boundary (1935). The figures listed are not really comparable since the delimited Torquay area changed size, as stated.

APPENDIX IV
Population of Torbay and Adjacent Towns

	1801	1851	1901	1931
Brixham	3,671	5,936	8,092	8,145
Dartmouth	2,398	3,147	3,702	69708
Newton Abbot[1]				15,010
Paignton	1,575	2,746	8,385	189414
Tormohun[2]	838	11,474	24,473	
Torquay			46,165	
Totnes	2,503	3,828	3,116	4,526

Sources: Decennial census figures.
[1] The town had about 4,000 inhabitants in 1850.It was situated in the parish of Wolborough and was formed from the amalgamation of Newton Bushel and Newton Abbot. After the South Devon Railway reached Newton in 1846 the town became a focus for railways and its population grew rapidly. The Newton Urban district was created 1894 1901.
[2] Now included in Torquay.

BIBLIOGRAPHY

(All books published in London unless otherwise stated)

Acland, Anne, *A Devon Family*, 1981

Allom, Thomas, *Devonshire Illustrated*, 1829

Anderson, Janice, and Swinglehurst, Edmund, *The Victorian and Edwardian Seaside*, 1978

Andrews, Robert, *The Rough Guide to Devon and Cornwall*, 2001

The Architect, 27 June 1874 [The Arena at The Wigwam]

Bainbridge, Cyril, *Pavilions on the Sea: A History of the Seaside Pleasure Pier*, 1986

Bannatyne, Emily Gertrude, *Report on the Palk Manuscripts in the Possession of Mrs Bannatyne, of Halton, Devon*, Historical Manuscripts Commission, No 74, 1922

Baring Gould, Sabine, *A Book of the West*, 2 vols, 1899; *Devonshire: Characters and Strange Events*, 1907; *Devon*, 1907

Bateman, John, *The Great Landowners of Great Britain and Ireland*, revised edition, 1883

Becker, Bernard, *Holiday Haunts*, 1884

Beckett, J.W., *The Aristocracy In England 1660-1914*, 1986

Blair, Fredericka, *Isadora: Portrait of the Artist as a Woman*, New York, 1986

Blewitt, Octavian, *The Panorama of Torquay*, 2nd edition, 1832

Boggis, Revd. R.J., Edmund, *History of St John's, Torquay*, Torquay, 1930

Born, Anne, *The Torbay Towns*, Chichester, 1989

Boussel, Patrice, *Histoire des Vacances*, Paris, 1961

Bowlby, John, *Charles Darwin*, 1990

Brandon, Ruth, *Singer and the Sewing Machine: A Capitalist Romance*, 1977

Brockett, *The Devon Union List*, Exeter, 1977

Brunner, Elizabeth, *Holiday Making and the Holiday Trades*, Oxford, 1945

Bulloch, J.M., 'Peers who have married Players', *Notes and Queries*, clxix, 1935

Burke, Sir Bernard, *A Visitation of the Seats and Arms of the Noblemen of Great Britain and Ireland*, 2 vols., 1855

Burke, John, *A Genealogical and Heraldic History of the Commoners of Great Britain and Ireland*, 4 vols., 1834-38 [and other editions]

Burn, W.L., *The Age of Equipoise: A Study of the Mid Victorian Era*, 1964

Burnett, John, *A Social History of Housing*, 1978

Cannadine, David, *Lords and Landlords: The Aristocracy and the Towns, 1774-1967*, Leicester, 1980; *The Decline and Fall of the British Aristocracy*, Princeton, 1990; 'Aristocratic indebtedness in the nineteenth century: the case re-opened', *Economic History Review*, 2nd series, xxx, 1977

Cannadine, David, and Reeder, David (eds.), *Exploring the Urban Past: Essays in Urban History by H.J. Dyos*, 1982

Carey, G.S., *The Balnea: or, an Imperial Description of all the Popular Watering places in England*, 3rd edition, 1801

Carr, Raymond, *English Fox Hunting: A History*, revised edition, 1986

'The Cary Family', *The Torquay Directory*, 2 February 1910

Chandos, John, *English Public Schools 1800-1864*, 1984

Checkland, S.G., *The Rise of Industrial Society in England 1815-1885*, 1964

Cherry, Bridget, and Pevsner, Nikolaus, *The Buildings of England: Devon*, 1989

Chitty, Susan, *The Beast and the Monk: A Life of Charles Kingsley*, 1974

Christie, Agatha, *An Autobiography*, 1977

Clapp, Brian W., *The University of Exeter: A History*, Exeter,1982

Clunn, Harold P., *Famous South Coast Resorts Past and Present*, 1929

Cockrem's Tourist Guide to Torquay and its Neighbourhood, Torquay, 1856

Cokayne, George Edward, *Complete Peerage ...* 8 vols., 1887-98

Colloms, Brenda, *Charles Kingsley: The Lion of Eversley*, 1975

Connon, Bryan, *Beverley Nichols: A Life*, 1991

Cooke, George Alexander, *A Topographical and Statistical Description of the County of Devon*, 3rd edition, 1825

Cocks, J.V. Somers, *Devon Topographical Prints, 1660-1870*, 1977

Curtis, Charles E., *Estate Management: A Practical Hand Book For Landlords, Agents, and Pupils*, 3rd edition, 1889

Debrett, John, *Peerage*, 1802 [and other editions, including his *Baronetage*, 1808]

De Cossart, Michael, *The Food of Love: Princesse de Polignac (1865-1943) and Her Salon*, 1978

Denes, Gabor, *The Story of the Imperial*, Torquay, 1982

Dod, Robert P., *The Peerage, Baronetage and Knightage of Great Britain and Ireland*, 1859 [and various editions]

Duncan, Isadora, *My Life*, 1928

Dyos, H.J., *Victorian Suburb: A Study of the Growth of Camberwell*, 1961

Eastley, Charles M., *The Singer Saga*, Braunton, Devon, nd.

Ellis, Arthur C., *An Historical Survey of Torquay*, Torquay, 1930

Ewans, M.C., *The Haytor Granite Tramway and Stover Canal*, Newton Abbot, 1964

Finnegan, Frances, *Poverty and Prostitution: A Study of Victorian Prostitutes in York*, Cambridge, 1979

Foulston, John, *The Public Buildings erected in the West of England as designed by John Foulston*, 1838

Frondeville, Guy de, *Les Visiteurs de la Mer*, Paris, 1956

Gosse, Edmund, *Father and Son: A Study of Two Temperaments*, 1907

Granville, A.B., *The Spas of England and Principal Sea Bathing Places*, 3 vols., 1840

Guide to the Watering Places of South Devon, Teignmouth, 1840

Haggard, H. Rider, *Rural England*, 2 vols., 1902

Haldon House Sale Catalogue, 1894

Healey, Edna, *Lady Unknown: The Life of Angela Burdett-Coutts*, 1978

Hern, Anthony, *The Seaside Holiday: The History of the English Seaside Resort*, 1967

Hembry, Phyllis, *The English Spa 1560-1815: A Social History*, 1990

Horn, Pamela, *The Rise and Fall of the Victorian Servant*, Gloucester, 1975

Hoskins, W.G., and Finberg, H.P.R., *Devonshire Studies*, 1952

Hoskins, W.G., *Devon*, Newton Abbot, 1954; *Devon and Its People*, Newton Abbot, 1959; *Two Thousand Years in Exeter*, 1960

Howell, Sarah, *The Seaside*, 1974

Jefferies, Richard, *Hodge and His Masters*, 2 vols., 1880

Johnston, Alva, *The Incredible Mizners*, 1953

Kelly's *Directory of Devon*, 1856 [and various editions]

Kingsley, Charles, *Glaucus, or the Wonders of the Shore*, Cambridge, 1855

Lambert, R.S., *When Justice Faltered*, 1935; *The Cobbett of the West*, 1939

Lindley, Kenneth, *Seaside Architecture*, 1973

Mallock, W.H., *Memoirs of Life and Literature*, 1920

Mingay, G.E., ed., *The Victorian Countryside*, 2 vols., 1981

Mullen, Richard, *Anthony Trollope*, 1990

Murray's *Handbook for Devon and Cornwall*, 1850 [and various editions]

Mackenzie, Eileen, *The Findlater Sisters*, 1964

Nichols, Beverley, *Father Figure*, 1972; *The Unforgiving Minute*, 1978

O'Casey, Eileen, *Sean*, 1971

O'Hara, *The South Devon Hunt*, Porthtowanan, Cornwall, nd.

Pakenham, Simona, *60 Miles from England: The English at Dieppe 1814-1914*, 1967

Palk, Lawrence Hesketh, *The Evils of Party Government*, 1886

Palk, Lawrence William, 3rd Baron Haldon, *'Tharna', A Foreword Concerning the Wonderful Discovery*, 1921

Palk, Hon. Mary Evelyn, *Donna Agnes: Stories of the Neapolitan Underworld*, 1932

Patterson, C.H., *The History of Paignton*, nd.

Pevsner, Nikolaus, *The Buildings of England: South Devon*, 1952

Penwill, F. Ralph, *Paignton in Six Reins: The History of Local Government in Paignton*, Paignton, 1953

Pike, John, *Torquay, Torbay: A Bibliographical Guide*, Torbay, 1973; *Brixham, Torbay: A Bibliographical Guide*, Torbay, 1974; *Paignton, Torbay: A Bibliographical Guide*, Torbay, 1974

Polignac, Princesse Edmonde de, 'Memoirs', *Horizon*, vol. xii, no. 68, 1945

Powell, Violet, *The Life of a Provincial Lady: A Study of E.M. Delafield and Her Works*, 1988

Polignac, Hedwige, Princesse Francois de, *Les Polignac*, Paris, 1960

Presland, John, *Torquay: The Charm and History of its Neighbourhood*, 1920

The 'Queen' Newspaper Book of Travel: A Guide to Home and Foreign Resorts, 1903 [and other editions]

Rae George, *The Country Banker: His Clients, Cares, and Work*, 1885

Richardson, Sir Arthur, *Regional Architecture in the West of England*, 1924

Russell, Percy, *Dartmouth: A History of the Port and the Town*, 1950; *A History of Torquay and the Famous Anchorage of Torbay*, Torquay, 1960; *The Good Town of Totnes*, Exeter, 1964

Sager, Peter, *The West Country*, 1999

Searle, Muriel, *Spas and Watering Places*, Tunbridge Wells, 1977

Seaside Watering Places, 1895 [and other editions]

Shields, Urry, *Tourism and Society*, 1999

Spring, David, *The English Landed Estate in the Nineteenth Century: Its Administration*, Baltimore, 1963

Stanes, Robin, *A History of Devon*, Chichester, 1986

Stone, Lawrence, and Stone, Jeanne, *An Open Elite? England 1540-1880*, Oxford, 1984

Sutherland, Douglas, *The Landowners*, 1968

Thompson, F.M.L., *English Landed Society in the Nineteenth Century*, 1963; *The Rise of Respectable Society: A Social History of Victorian Britain, 1830-1900*, 1989

Thwaite, Ann, *Edmund Gosse: A Literary Landscape 1849-1928*, 1984

Underhill, Arthur, *Our Silver Streak: or the Yachtsman's Guide from Harwich to Scilly*, [1892]

Vancouver, Charles, *General View of the Agriculture of Devon*, 1794

Wagner, Anthony, *English Genealogy*, Chichester, 3rd edition, 1983

Walford, R., *The County Families of the United Kingdom: The Titled and Untitled Aristocracy, A Dictionary of the Upper Ten Thousand*, 1860

Walton, John K., *The Blackpool Landlady: A Social History*, Manchester, 1978; *The English Seaside Resort: A Social History 1750-1914*, Leicester, 1983

Walton, John K., and Walvin, James, eds., *Leisure in Britain 1780-1939*, Manchester, 1983

Walvin, James, *Beside the Seaside: A Social History of the Popular Seaside Holiday*, 1978

White, J.T., *The History of Torquay*, Torquay, 1878

White, William, *History Gazetteer and Directory of the County of Devonshire*, Sheffield, 1850 (and other editions)

Wilson, John, 'Italy in England', *Country Life*, 25 December 1958

Worth, R.N., *Tourist's Guide to South Devon*, 3rd edn., 1883 (and other editions); *A History of Devonshire*, 1886

Young, Michael, *The Elmhirsts of Dartington*, 1982

INDEX

Numbers in **bold** refer to illustration page numbers

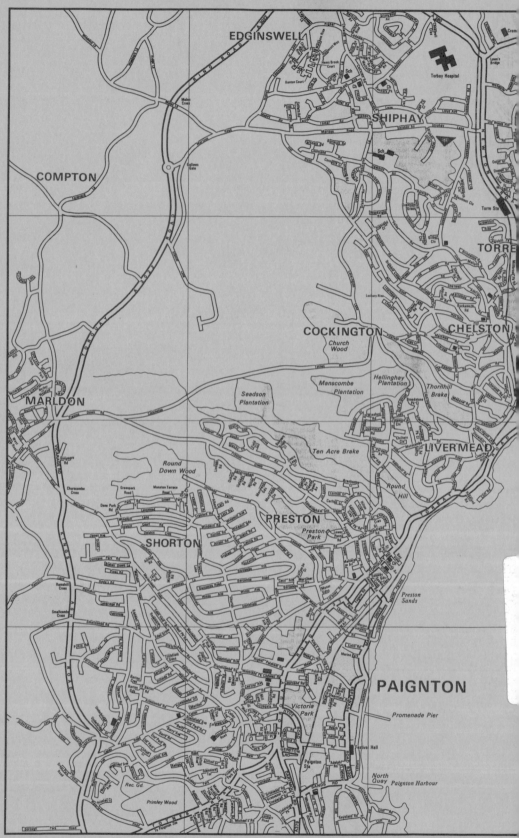

Street map of the Torbay area, 1987. (© Tele-page Directories Ltd)